CHINESE MYTHOLOGY
A TO Z

Jeremy Roberts

Facts On File, Inc.

Chinese Mythology A to Z

Facts On File, Inc.
132 West 31st Street
New York NY 10001

Library of Congress Cataloging-in-Publication Data
Roberts, Jeremy, 1956–
Chinese mythology A to Z: a young reader's companion / by Jeremy Roberts.—1st ed.
p. cm.—(Mythology A–Z)
Includes bibliographical references and index.
ISBN 0-8160-4870-3 (hardcover: alk. paper)
1. Mythology, Chinese. I. Title. II. Series.
BL1825.R575 2004
299.5′1′03—dc22   2004005341

Facts On File books are available at special discounts when purchased in bulk quantities for businesses, associations, institutions, or sales promotions. Please call our Special Sales Department in New York at (212) 967-8800 or (800) 322-8755.

You can find Facts On File on the World Wide Web at http://www.factsonfile.com

Text design by Joan M. Toro
Cover design by Cathy Rincon
Map by Jeremy Eagle

Printed in the United States of America

VB Hermitage 10 9 8 7 6 5 4 3 2 1

This book is printed on acid-free paper.

CONTENTS

ACKNOWLEDGMENTS

I wish to thank my wife, Debra Scacciaferro, for her help in researching and preparing this book.

Also I would like to thank Dorothy Cummings; my editor, Jeff Soloway; Lauren Goldberg; and everyone else at Facts On File who helped prepare this volume.

INTRODUCTION

China covers nearly 4 billion square miles in Asia, roughly 14 percent of the world's landmass. It has grasslands and deserts, a long coastline, and some of the highest mountains in the world. Its rich river valleys have hosted civilizations for thousands and thousands of years. When Rome was still young, China's ancestors were wrestling with the problems of governing an empire as populous and diverse as any ever known. When Europe was struggling to recover from the Dark Ages, China was outfitting merchant vessels to sail across the oceans.

So it is not surprising that China has a long history, rich with events and achievements. This long history has produced a tapestry of interwoven myths, religious stories, legends, and folk beliefs, which have all changed over time. Even today, as the stories are told to a new generation, the tellers transform them in the very process of preserving them—one more reminder that myths and mythmaking are a vital part of the human experience.

FIRST CIVILIZATIONS

One of humankind's oldest ancestors, *Homo erectus,* was discovered in China during the early part of the 20th century. Named "Peking man" in honor of the city near where the remains were found, this forerunner of present-day *Homo sapiens sapiens* roamed China between 400,000 and 200,000 years ago. (Peking is an old way of saying Beijing, the capital city of China.)

Peking man's offspring eventually turned from hunting to farming as a way of life. The Neolithic Age—sometimes called the end of the Stone Age—started in China perhaps 5,000 years ago. Archaeological sites along the YELLOW RIVER (Huang Ho in Chinese) show that the early Chinese in this area had thriving industries of pottery, cloth making, and farming. Symbols have been found on the remains of their pottery that archaeologists believe indicated different clans or connected families.

THE SHANG

The word *dynasty* refers to the ruler of a country and his or her successors, generally chosen from his or her descendants. Archaeologists and historians break up much of China's history according to these different families of rulers. In the case of the SHANG, the word is also used by archaeologists and historians to describe the civilizations of the same period. (In this broader usage, *Shang* includes the Shang mentioned in early Chinese writings, once thought to be entirely legendary or mythic. The ruling family's actual name was Tzu.)

The exact myths and religious beliefs of the Shang, along with other Paleolithic human ancestors in China, are lost in the dark mists of time, but archaeologists have gathered much information about a period known as the Shang dynasty, which began around 1550 B.C. or earlier. Since it seems likely that the Shang evolved directly from earlier local inhabitants, their beliefs may illustrate much older ideas.

The Shang kings had power not only as rulers but also because they had a personal, religious connection to the deities that could control the outcome of the harvest and all natural life. In the Shang culture, the direct ancestors of the kings and their families, especially the founder Ta I, were believed to intercede with nature or the deities who controlled it and thus to affect the present. These ancestors were revered and honored. The people regularly made sacrifices to them, as well as to different spirits of mountains and rivers.

The highest god in the Shang pantheon was Di (or Ti in the older style of writing Chinese names in the Roman letters used in the West), who was seen as an overall deity with great powers. He was separate from the ancestor gods and did not have his own cult, or group of worshipers devoted to him. Besides the offerings of grain, wine, and animals made to ancestors and other figures, the religious sacrifices apparently included humans, today generally thought to be prisoners from outside the kingdom. Their bodies have been found in many excavations.

DIVINATION

One of the most interesting features of Shang times was the use of special bones to ask questions about the future, a process called DIVINATION, or fortune-telling. Questions were inscribed on the bones, called ORACLE BONES, then heated with a bronze poker. The cracks that appeared provided answers to the questions, which were then recorded on the bones. The related rituals included sacrifices and have provided much information about Shang times. Scholars say that the rituals changed over time; eventually, the kings used them simply to prove that their decisions had been correct. But the impulse itself to divine or see the future—and therefore to control it—remained a powerful one. Divination was not only practiced by the Shang or by the leaders of Chinese culture. By no later than the eighth century B.C. the stalks of yarrow plants (also called milfoil) were being used to read the future. The system was set down in the I CHING, or *Book of Changes*. Newer systems of thought did not displace fortune-telling but instead gave new explanations and, in some cases, different methods. Magnetic needles seem to have been introduced into FENG SHUI (a form of divination that uses geography to determine good and bad energies that affect future events around the 11th century. Along with standardized manuals, they altered the science but retained its basic core and purpose.

ANCESTOR WORSHIP

The people of the early Shang culture, like all who followed them in China, revered their ancestors, the generations of family members who preceded them. Ancestors were considered able to talk to the all-important god, and, in some cases, they seem to have been treated much as we would treat a god today.

The importance of ancestors in Asian thought can be confusing to those raised in different traditions. There are two general schools of thought common not only in ancient China but also in other Asian cultures. Both begin with the idea that the living and dead continue to be very important to each other. The spiritual realm of the dead is similar to that of the living. The Shang people believed the land of the dead was real and physically close, perhaps on the mountains on the horizon or the islands off in the mist at sea. Someone who is a king in this life, for example, will be a king when dead.

Family ancestors are remembered at a family altar in the home. The names are recorded on tablets that represent and, in some cases, may be inhabited by the person. Sacrifices are regularly made to help feed the deceased. In return, the spirits of the dead can help the living by interceding with the powers in the spirit world who affect the here and now.

Another strand of ancestor worship honors the ancestors of CLANS and important founders of a community. While these ancestral figures started as real people, over time their features would become generalized. These ancestors would generally stretch back much further—perhaps 40 generations rather than five or six. In this tradition, ancestors were honored in special halls, which played their own important role in villages and cities as centers for feasts and even services like schools.

Connected with the richest and most powerful families of the present—who were the only people who could afford to maintain the halls—these ancestors were seen as powerful and influential in the other world. In some cases, these figures would be honored by many outside the family line, in much the same way as a Westerner might remember and honor an important political or military leader of the past. The figures might then be revered as local gods in the informal FOLK RELIGION. As time passed, some might gain popularity in other areas as well. Occasionally this process happened on its own, as word of a deity's particular powers spread. Other times, an emperor or regional governor might use the god to win friends and influence others. Honoring the local god would be good politics, since it would please those who were part of his or her cult or lineage.

CONFUCIANISM AND TAOISM

In the centuries following the Shang, different clans and states struggled for domination over the Chinese world. All of the rulers faced one problem in common: how to govern a large area with diverse needs and traditions. While the inhabitants shared a common overall culture, local differences and power struggles continually threatened to pull kingdoms apart. The Chinese developed elaborate bureaucracies and legal systems to keep their territories together.

At the same time, philosophical systems arose and played a part in this process. Chinese thought over the centuries has been strongly influenced by CONFUCIANISM and TAOISM. Both philosophical traditions remain important today, even outside Asia.

CONFUCIUS (551–479 B.C.) is one of the most important philosopher-teachers in the history of the world. His teachings, known as Confucianism, provided a system for moral government. Confucian practices include veneration of ancestors and of the past in general. Confucianism emphasizes the importance of learning and also gives consideration to caring for others.

Confucius did not have much to say directly about myth as myth. However, by citing important legendary figures as examples of proper conduct, Confucius indirectly encouraged mythology. He also made a great use of texts believed to be historic; these books of prose and poems included much mythic material.

Unlike Confucianism, Taoism directly encouraged, created, and altered Chinese myths and lore. Taoism is often said to have been founded by a single teacher who lived around the time of Confucius, LAO-TZU, who is credited with writing the TAO-TE-CHING (usually translated as "the Way" or "the Way of Power"), a classic Taoist text. But Taoism is actually a broad collection of ideas and beliefs involving as much religion as philosophy. Scholars are not exactly sure who Lao was or when he lived. A few have even suggested that he was not a real person.

Nearly as important to Taoism was ZHUANGZI (Chuang-tzu), whose work as it survives is much longer than Lao's and covers wider ground. Zhuangzi, for example, spoke of the IMMORTALS, beings who have reached perfection and therefore can exist forever. While some believe that Zhuangzi was speaking in metaphors, his followers considered the idea literal.

Taoist beliefs are rich in myth and what we would call magic, such as ALCHEMY. Some scholars divide the philosophy of Taoism, which sees the world as a constant flow and expression of something that cannot be named, from the mythical and magical aspects. But these facets were always closely connected in China, where Taoism was thoroughly intertwined with the culture. Taoist beliefs about alchemy and the nature of the universe are not separated in texts or practice, no matter the period. According to Taoist belief, the constant flow of energy and interconnected forces could be tapped and used by someone who understood the universe—a Taoist master. Likewise, the human form was considered just an illusion, so there had to be a way to change it—and thus SHAPE SHIFTING from human to DRAGON.

BUDDHISM

BUDDHISM arrived in China roughly around the time Jesus Christ preached in ancient Palestine. In A.D. 166, the Chinese emperor Wendi (Wen-ti) built a shrine in his palace to honor BUDDHA ("the Enlightened One"), showing that the religion had assumed an important place in the kingdom. At the same time, the emperor also honored a Taoist deity, demonstrating how even then the different traditions were intertwining.

Buddhism originated in India during the fifth and sixth centuries B.C. Founded by Siddhartha Gautama, the religion recognized that to be human is to suffer. Buddhists believe that humans are reborn in many different forms in order to learn different lessons. To escape suffering, one must renounce desires and follow the EIGHTFOLD PATH of righteousness. These eight facets or parts call for a Buddhist to understand Buddhism, think, speak, act, work, strive, develop awareness, and concentrate in the right manner. Only by doing this may a soul reach ENLIGHTENMENT, or NIRVANA. Enlightenment is defined in many different ways. We might think of it as an escape from the endless cycle of rebirth, an unending state of bliss and peace.

By the time Buddhism reached China, there were many different forms, or sects. Each emphasized different teachings from and about Buddha. Gradually these sects came to have different attitudes about the nature of the universe and the methods of attaining enlightenment.

In terms of mythology, the most important forms of Buddhism are those of the MAHAYANA, or "Greater Vessel" or "Greater Vehicles" sects. One of the central teachings they share is the idea that all creatures contain the innate Buddha. If a person can touch that innate character, he or she can gain enlightenment. But it is difficult, if not impossible, for most people to do so without help.

Adherents of Mahayana Buddhism believe that the historical Buddha was only one manifestation or incarnation of the everlasting Buddha or life force. According to Mahayana Buddhism, there have been many Buddhas, and there is always one Buddha in the world. These powerful beings have different aspects (characteristics) that emphasize certain qualities of the everlasting Buddha.

There are also a number of BODHISATTVAS, or Buddhas-to-be, who can help people achieve enlightenment. A number of Buddhist gods and other beings may be called on as well. Together, these holy beings form an array of mythological figures. Their nature is complex, but most are able to present themselves in human or near-human forms.

MINISTRIES OF GODS

Buddhism had a great deal of influence on Chinese society and mythology. For example, important to the religion is the idea that after death a person must work off the sins committed during his or her lifetime. This meant that there had to be a place for this to happen—a hell. While the ideas about hell changed over time and differed from sect to sect, this concept remained important.

A 19th-century artist's view of many popular Chinese gods (The Dragon, Image, and Demon, *1886)*

Taoism seems not to have had a hell until Buddhism arrived in China. The exact structure of hell may have been different and may have differed from telling to telling, but the basic idea was similar. Taoism changed on its own as well. New figures were added to the pantheon, or collection of gods. In telling their stories, Taoist priests, writers, and others shaped them to reflect their own or current beliefs. Old stories and old heroes took on different characteristics.

The complex bureaucracies of the empire's government may have inspired the idea that there were departments of deities in charge of different phenomena, such as the ministry of thunder, LEI BU. This department had 24 ministers, including its president, LEI ZU, "the Ancestor of

Thunder." Ancient mythic figures mixed with historical people in the MINISTRIES OF GODS. The ancient god became something of an office for another deity to hold. For example, Lei Zu was identified with a minister known as WEN ZHONG said to have worked for the ZHOU DYNASTY. This mythic ministry was not limited to Taoist or legendary figures. Other members included three Buddhist storm devils, or demons.

At different times, EMPERORS would celebrate local ancestral figures or gods as a political gesture to win favor with people in a certain area. In a sense, the local god was "promoted" by being placed into the celestial ministry or identified with another god. Once famous, a god might be prayed to with a request. If the god delivered, her or his fame would grow. As a show of special favor, an emperor might promote a god to a higher place in the ministry or overall pantheon. This was possible because the emperor, through his ancestors, had an important position in the world of the gods himself.

DIVISIONS IN MYTH

The overlaying of many generations of beliefs makes for a rich tapestry of myth, but it can appear daunting and confusing for outsiders, even those who study myth. It may be helpful to divide Chinese myth artificially into the following sections:

- distant prehistoric, a time of ancient spirits and beliefs largely lost to us but surviving in later periods in remnants, such as shamanism (see SHAMAN) and ANIMISM.
- prehistoric and early historic, from before the Shang dynasty (ca. 1550 B.C.) to about the second century A.D. This span of more than 1,000 years included the golden age of Chinese myth and history, with sword-wielding emperors and the supernatural forces that assisted them. Taoist figures, including DRAGONS and sages who could control the wind, belong to this category, as do many humans who were either real or thought to be real. The earliest part of this period is usually the time that anthropologists study for hints about early civilizations and comparative mythologists study for clues about what it means to be human.
- Buddhist figures and religious beliefs. Though heavily influenced by other Chinese beliefs, the core of Buddhist mythology originated outside of China, mostly in India.
- later Taoism, which flourished as the empire grew more sophisticated. In this period, the large ministries of gods were popular. Earlier gods were adapted and changed, mostly through a natural process as their stories were retold.

These artificial categories simplify a very complicated picture. As China itself continued to evolve, different systems of thought evolved and influenced each other. Reacting to Buddhism, Confucianism began to emphasize the unchanging nature of the universal power beneath the surface. Taoist practitioners adopted the techniques of Buddhist monks and made their own versions of Buddhist saints and concepts. And people continued to honor local gods considered important for the harvest and other facets of life.

Ancient myths and legends have continued to evolve to the present day. For instance, every time a parent tells a bedtime tale about the HARE on the MOON, the silk horse and the MULBERRY tree, or the WEAVER GIRL AND HEAVENLY OX, he or she is passing an ancient answer to the question of what it means to be human. Mythology is not a thing of the past; the gods walk with us even today, their shapes constantly changing.

USING THIS BOOK

This book contains entries on the major figures in Chinese mythology, in alphabetical order. It also includes information about some of the most popular legends and folktales that readers may encounter as they begin to learn about China. Finally, it explains a few important terms relating either to China or to the study of myths, to help the reader in his or her studies.

In many of the entries, phrases such as *in Buddhist myth* or *in Taoist myth* are used. This is intended only to point out important features of the myth and its origin. For most of history, there was no distinction between many of these terms, including Taoist and Chinese. And Taoist priests saw fit to borrow (and modify) Buddhist figures, and vice versa.

Cross-references to other entries are written in SMALL CAPITAL letters. Some topics with entries in this book are known by more than one name (see below). Alternate names are given in parentheses after the entry headword in full capital letters.

A NOTE ON NAMES

One of the first things a student of Chinese mythology discovers is that the same god often has several different names. There are several reasons for this.

First of all, many differences arise simply because the Chinese and English (or other) languages are different. They use different kinds of symbols and pronunciations. Translating between the two has presented scholars with many interesting problems over the years.

Most often, scholars want to write the names of Chinese gods in English the way they sound in Chinese. The idea is a good one—except that pronunciations may differ from region to region, and even when the pronunciation is the same, each listener may have a different way of writing the same sound in English.

For much of the 20th century, most scholars used the Wade-Giles Romanization system (popularized by the publication of Herbert Allen Giles's dictionary of Chinese in 1912) to write Chinese words in English. This system has some quirks, but it follows fairly consistent rules. Gradually many came to use this style, and it remains popular. Many of the common myth names became familiar in English in that style.

In 1979 China adopted a new system called the pinyin system to standardize representation of Chinese language in Roman letters. The system makes it easier to read (and type) Chinese in English. To reproduce the sound of the Chinese words, pinyin uses letter combinations more familiar to English speakers. So, for example, the soft sound of *c* is written as *c* in pinyin rather than the *ts'* in Wade-Giles. Dashes that once showed the relationship between syllables or concepts were removed, and many of the Wade-Giles accent marks were taken away.

On the whole, the new system has many improvements. Some sounds that had given writers trouble before—like soft or unaspirated consonants—were standardized. A soft *p*, for example, was now written as a *b*. This better reflected the sound as spoken in Chinese, at least in the area around Beijing, the capital of modern China. But this change has caused confusion as names that were once familiar can now be written differently. For example, the god usually rendered as Yü Ti in the Wade-Giles system is rendered as Yu Di in pinyin.

One way around the different systems has been to translate the names of gods completely into English rather than just reproducing the sound of the Chinese names. Yu Di was considered the purest of the pure and therefore identified with jade, a precious stone that symbolized purity. Thus, the god was "the Jade Emperor" to the Chinese scribes who wrote his tales. This name in English appears often in translations dating back at least to the end of the 19th century.

Another common reason for variation is the fact that the Chinese themselves often used different names to describe the same deity. Names that described his or her attributes might be substituted—sometimes causing the god to be confused with another. The god Yu Di also had another name, even more commonly used by Chinese speakers: Yu Huang. Yu Huang can be translated in several ways. Both words in the name mean "god," so Yu Huang might be thought of as "The God of Gods" or the highest god. He might also be described as the "Pure August Emperor on High." But that name and the name Yu Huang and the name Yu Di all refer to the same god.

Finally, the practice of identifying real people with many of the gods in later Chinese history (see MINISTRIES OF GODS) causes even more confusion for modern readers. The god can be called by both his title and the name of the person holding the "office" of the god. Americans do the same with political officeholders, such as the president.

Meanwhile, Buddhists saw the living as reincarnations of past heroes, holy men, and bodhisattvas. So Yu Huang might be called a reincarnation or version of Indra and thus referred to as Indra in certain stories.

I have tried in this book to include the most common names used for the gods, with both the new and the old systems and important variations whenever possible. As a main entry, we have followed Facts On

File style and used the pinyin spelling, except in cases where English style and clarity demand that the older, more familiar version be used. For instance, the word used to describe the important philosophy and religion developed in ancient China is spelled as Dao in pinyin and Tao in the older Wade-Giles. Taoism long ago entered the English language, and so we have used that here.

PINYIN AND WADE-GILES, COMPARED

Here are a few common terms and letters that may help ease some confusion in the different transliterations of names.

Di in pinyin equals *Ti* (used for "god") in Wade-Giles

Dao (used for "the Way" in Taoism) in pinyin equals *Tao* in Wade-Giles

c (a soft sound, as in *centimeter*) in pinyin equals *ts'* in Wade-Giles

ch (as in church) in pinyin equals *ch'* in Wade-Giles

g in pinyin equals *k* in Wade-Giles

j in pinyin equals *ch* in Wade-Giles

k in pinyin equals *k'* in Wade-Giles (a hard *k*)

t in pinyin equals *t'* in Wade-Giles (a hard *t*)

xi in pinyin equals *hs* in Wade-Giles

z in pinyin equals *ts* in Wade-Giles

zh in pinyin equals *ch* in Wade-Giles

Letters with accents or apostrophes after them, such as *t'*, are meant to be pronounced with the hard sound so that *t'* sounds like the sound at the beginning of *top*.

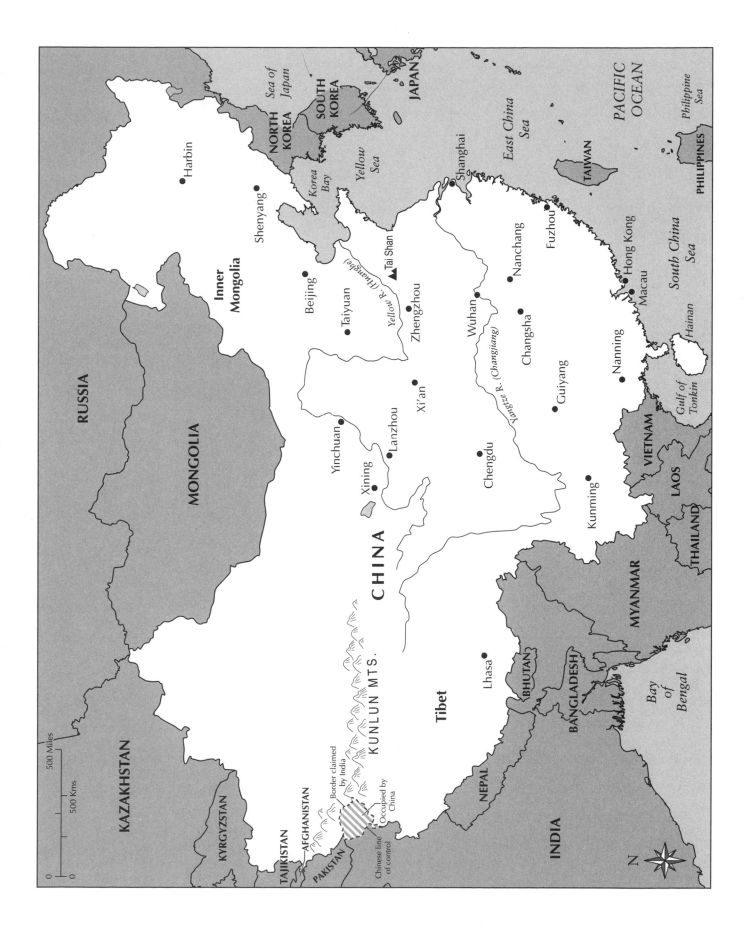

RUSSIA

KAZAKHSTAN

KYRGYZSTAN

TAJIKISTAN

AFGHANISTAN

PAKISTAN

MONGOLIA

Inner Mongolia

Harbin

Shenyang

NORTH KOREA

SOUTH KOREA

Sea of Japan

JAPAN

Korea Bay

Yellow Sea

Beijing

Taiyuan

Yellow R. (Huanghe)

▲ Tai Shan

Zhengzhou

Shanghai

Yinchuan

Xining

Lanzhou

Xi'an

CHINA

KUNLUN MTS.

Border claimed by India

Occupied by China

Chinese line of control

Tibet

Lhasa

NEPAL

INDIA

Chengdu

Wuhan

Yangtze R. (Changjiang)

Changsha

Guiyang

Nanchang

Fuzhou

Kunming

Nanning

Hong Kong

Macau

BANGLADESH

BHUTAN

MYANMAR

LAOS

THAILAND

VIETNAM

East China Sea

TAIWAN

PACIFIC OCEAN

Philippine Sea

PHILIPPINES

South China Sea

Hainan

Gulf of Tonkin

Bay of Bengal

N

500 Miles

500 Kms

0

0

xv

A

ACHU The Chinese name for Aksobhya, one of the FIVE GREAT BUDDHAS OF WISDOM. Achu is known as "the Imperturbable." He never gets angry or upset, no matter what happens.

In Buddhist mythology, Achu is associated with east, the direction of the sunrise. In TIBET he is called Mi-bskyod-pa and Mi-khrugs-pa.

AGRICULTURE The business of growing crops. Much ancient Chinese mythology and many ritual practices revolve around agriculture, starting with legends about the mythical emperor SHEN NONG, who was said to live in 2840 B.C. and to have taught Chinese people how to farm the land.

For centuries, most families in China lived in farming villages, using very simple tools. Plows were made with a piece of bent wood, its tip sharpened to a point, pulled by OXEN, donkeys, or the farmer. Bamboo waterwheels were built to irrigate the fields by diverting water from nearby streams. Grains, such as wheat and MILLET, were important in the North; RICE was important in the South. Families would usually have a PIG and maybe chickens.

Besides Shen Nong, the gods most often associated with agriculture in Chinese myth include LAI CHO, LIU MENG JIANG-ZHUN, MANG SHEN, BA ZHA, BAI ZHONG, SHUI FANG, SHUI YONG, and Si Se. There were also innumerable gods associated with local soils and farming plots.

Agriculture was important in ancient China, and each spring the emperor offered special sacrifices to ensure a good growing season. (The Dragon, Image, and Demon, *1886*)

AFTERLIFE Chinese beliefs about what happened to the soul after death varied greatly from time period to time period and were strongly influenced by different religious beliefs as well as by myths. In general, during the late prehistoric and early historic periods, the Chinese seem to have seen the afterlife as very similar to the earthly life they lived. EMPERORS would remain emperors, and would be buried with the tokens and tools they would need to reign in the next life. This basic idea continued even as beliefs grew more complex.

BUDDHISM brought the concept of a hell or underworld where all souls must work off their sins before being reentered into life as a reincarnated being (see REBIRTH AND REINCARNATION). Depending on the sect, hell consisted of from eight to 128 or more different courts where a person was judged on his or her life. Each court had different divisions and punishments.

The Taoists took this idea and modified it so that the afterlife had 10 courts. Depending on his or her sins, a person might skip the courts completely before being reborn. This afterlife applied only to those who were not IMMORTALS. Perfect beings shed their skin and ascended to one of the three Taoist HEAVENS.

The Chinese hells are not like the Western, Christian hell. In the Chinese traditions, souls entering hell are purged of their sins and then continue on. See QIN GUANG WANG and FENG DU DADI, among others, for gods connected with the Taoist afterlife.

ALCHEMY   The pseudoscience of turning one element into another, such as CINNABAR into gold. Alchemy was an important part of TAOISM. Adherents believed in the existence of an ELIXIR OF ETERNAL LIFE, a potion thought to extend one's life or make one an IMMORTAL, if only one could find it.

AMIDA   See OMITU FO.

AMITABHA   See OMITU FO.

AMOGHASIDDHI   One of the FIVE GREAT BUDDHAS OF WISDOM. He is the BUDDHA of the North and represents the historical Buddha's entrance into NIRVANA.

ĀNANDA   One of the historical BUDDHA'S DISCIPLES. He is known in Tibet as Kun-dgah-bo. According to Buddhist tradition, Ānanda was a cousin of the historical Buddha and was born on the same day. Tradition holds that he remembered all the words that Buddha preached and recited the SUTRAS, or teachings, at councils. Gentle and humble, Ānanda founded an order of nuns and taught them the principles of BUDDHISM. In TIBET, he is known as Kun-dgah-bo, "the First to Have Heard Buddha."

ANAVATAPTA   See LONG WANG.

ANCESTORS AND ANCESTOR CULTS
Most ancient Chinese believed that there was a very strong connection between the living and the dead. They saw humans as having a temporary body and a permanent soul; although a body would die, the soul would continue to live. Family ties continued long after death and helped both the living and the dead.

The living had an obligation to honor the dead, making offerings to them so that they could be "fed" in the AFTERLIFE. The home would include a small altar for this purpose. Wooden tablets or pieces of paper with the names of the dead were kept at the altar. As each new generation died, the list would be updated to reflect only the names of the most recent five or six generations. The living regularly offered prayers and small gifts of food, keeping the ancestral spirits happy.

In exchange, these spirits would look out for the living. They might bring the living good fortune and help them prosper financially or in other ways. It was also possible for the dead to offer advice to the living, usually with the help of a local priest who was skilled in reading signs from the spirit world. The priest might follow Taoist practices or use more general ritual or fortune-telling techniques considered part of a FOLK RELIGION. Ancestors were honored along the family's father's line.

Ancestors can be broken into two groups: the recent dead and those who existed in the very distant past. Ancestor worship in China can be split the same way. For most families, the immediate ancestors were the only ones honored; after the fifth or sixth generation, the names of the dead were lost from the list and often simply forgotten. However, in some cases—usually those involving very wealthy or important families—the ancestors could be honored centuries after they died at special halls built in their honor. These halls, which could be large and magnificent buildings, honored the most prominent families and their founding generations in a local town. Tablets representing those who had died were kept in the hall; these were treated as the representatives of the ancestral spirits. Some of the larger halls played an important role in the community's social life, and they were used for marriages and other important ceremonies. Historians note that the cost of the halls was extremely high. They usually depended on estates or gifts left by the original ancestors for funding. Thus only the most powerful families could celebrate their ancestors this way.

Scholars sometimes call worship of one's distant ancestors a "lineage CULT," since the word *lineage* refers to ancestors and descendants (the "line" one is born to). This is to separate it from a "domestic cult," the honoring of more recent ancestors. The word *cult* has no negative meaning in this context.

ANCESTRAL HEALING   The term used for a medical practice that tried to cure an illness by appeasing the spirits of ancestors (see MEDICINE).

ANIMALS OF THE FOUR DIRECTIONS Creatures connected with the different directions in Chinese mythology. The animal's color also symbolized the direction.

The GREEN DRAGON was the power of the east. The RED BIRD (or scarlet bird) was connected with the south. The WHITE TIGER was linked to the west, and the DARK WARRIOR to the north. The Dark Warrior was a mythological beast combining the characteristics of a turtle and snake. Artists depict it as a snake wrapped around a TORTOISE. There is also a fifth direction, "sky" or "center," in some mythological systems. The YELLOW DRAGON is connected with this direction.

The animals are often seen in art from the HAN DYNASTY period.

ANIMISM   The idea that inanimate objects, such as rocks and trees, and forces of nature, such as hail and fire, have a spirit. This spirit causes nature to do things for the same emotional reasons that motivate human beings. Animism was a popular idea in many ancient cultures.

In Chinese mythology, natural forces are sometimes personified as gods and sometimes shown as being under the gods' control. For example, in the story of the great battle between the gods CHIYOU and Huang Di (the YELLOW EMPEROR), three forces of nature—wind, rain, and drought—act as if they were living creatures who took opposite sides in the battle.

Animism was incorporated into BUDDHISM and TAOISM, two great religions of China that teach that all things are part of the sacred universe and animated by a spiritual force.

AO BING (AO PING)   The third son of Ao Kuang, the Dragon King of the Eastern Sea. Ao Bing was drawn into a series of confrontations with the violent warrior hero NAZHA, also known as the Third Prince. After Nazha killed one of Ao Kuang's messengers, Ao Bing went to demand an apology from Nazha. Nazha ended up killing Ao Bing and plucked out his tendons to make a belt that he wore on special occasions. When the Dragon King of the Eastern Sea found out about his son's death, he attacked Nazha in revenge. But Nazha trampled the Dragon King and tortured him, although he finally spared his life.

AO CH'IN   One of the dragon kings. Others include Ao Jun and Ao Kuang. See LONG WANG.

ARCHERY   Archery was important in warfare and hunting for the early Chinese. In mythology, archery plays a large role in the story of YI, the divine archer who shot down nine of the 10 SUNS of the god of the eastern sky.

ARHAT   See LUOHAN.

ASIAN MYTHOLOGY   Those who study the myths of China and other parts of Asia often notice a great number of similarities as they go from country to country. Scholars point out that this has to do with the connected history and prehistory of these places. Often a story or myth originated in one place, then traveled without much change to another. This might have happened when one group of people conquered or invaded another, bringing their myths. It could also have happened during trade or through the efforts of people spreading religion. As the dominant power in Asia for centuries, China spread its culture and its myths throughout the area.

Many Chinese myths have parallels in Japan. This is especially true of legends and myths connected with BUDDHISM. In many cases, these stories actually originated in India, where Buddhism started, before coming to China and Japan. Besides Japan and India, parallels to Chinese myths and legends can be found in the myths of Korea, a land China dominated for centuries.

ASOKA   According to Buddhist legend, a lay follower of BUDDHA. He is said to have reigned in India from about 234 to 198 B.C.; inscriptions supporting this have been found. Chinese Buddhists say Asoka killed his nearest relatives so he could become a ruler in India but then converted to BUDDHISM. His regret for his sin was greatly admired. Chinese Buddhist legend claims Asoka could raise pagodas from rocks.

ASTROLOGER A person who studies heavenly bodies for use in fortune-telling. In China, astrologers had a highly evolved system for studying the movements of the STARS and planets. Its practical value was that it provided seasonal forecasts and was used as a yearly CALENDAR. But the ancient Chinese also believed that the movement of the stars and planets could influence a person's life and determine the outcome of individual and social events. Many people in ancient China turned to astrologers for help in telling the future and discovering the right time to start a project or journey, according to favorable or unfavorable alignment of the stars and planets.

Events such as an earthquake or a gentle rain were believed to be a punishment or a blessing according to the behavior, good or bad, of the villagers. The appearance of comets and eclipses of the SUN and MOON were considered evil omens. Changes in the appearance of planets were said to have individual meanings. For instance, if the planet Mercury looked white, it portended a drought; if yellow, it meant that the crops would wither on the stalk. But if the planet looked red, it meant that soldiers would come.

During the 13th century, the Chinese government began printing an official yearly calendar that offered advice in interpreting the meaning of astrological events throughout the year. YIN AND YANG, the FIVE ELEMENTS, the EIGHT DIAGRAMS, the CYCLE OF SIXTY, and the Chinese signs of the zodiac (a star chart made up of 28 constellations) were all part of Chinese astrology and the ideas that explained it.

AUGUST ONE A title applied to GODS and mythological rulers.

AZURE A term used to describe the sections of Taoist HEAVEN.

B

BA The goddess of drought in Chinese myth. She appears in several tales as an ally of Huang Di, the YELLOW EMPEROR, to dry up a great storm that his enemy CHIYOU brought against Huang Di's army.

BA (PA) A state of ancient China in the Szechwan region of south central China. It was an independent state until conquered by the QIN shortly before 316 B.C. In the second century B.C., it became part of SHU (see LORD OF THE GRANARY).

BA GUA (PA KUA) The eight trigrams (EIGHT DIAGRAMS) that are the basis for DIVINATION in the *I Ching*. They were said to be invented by FUXI.

BAI HU See WHITE TIGER OF THE WEST.

BAI ZHONG (PAI CHUNG) The first seed planter, one of several Chinese agricultural gods (see AGRICULTURE). He was associated with the job of sowing seeds into freshly turned soil. A sacrifice was offered to this god, asking him to watch over the seeds so that they wouldn't be scattered or eaten before they could take root.

BALDNESS Artworks that include Buddhist monks, saints, and other deities in myth and legend often portray them with shaved or bald heads. This is one way for the artist to symbolize that the person or god has reached peace, or NIRVANA, through BUDDHISM. The clean-shaven head is also associated with the wisdom that comes with age.

Buddhist monks shave their heads to symbolize their devotion and humility.

BALLAD OF THE HIDDEN DRAGON A famous legend in Chinese myth that tells the story of Liu Zhiyuan. He has to overcome many challenges in strange lands before he finally returns to become the emperor in A.D. 947. The tale is also a love story, since Liu Zhiyuan was separated from the woman he loved for many years.

The tale is found in literature as a *zhukong*, a style combining alternating prose and verse sections. Scholars believe that the ballad was first sung in the 11th century and that the words were finally written down in the 12th century.

BAMBOO An important plant in Chinese culture and myth. There are many different species, some as big as 40 feet high and three feet in diameter. Bamboo was considered a symbol of longevity and also was said to have many healing properties.

One folktale about bamboo tells of a sick woman who longed for a healing soup made from bamboo shoots. But it was winter, and her son couldn't find any. He cried so much for his poor mother that his tears warmed the ground like a spring rain. Bamboo shoots grew, and he brought them home to his mother.

BAOSHENG FO The Chinese name for Ratnasambhava, one of the FIVE GREAT BUDDHAS OF WISDOM. Baosheng Fo is considered the BUDDHA of ascetic life, representing that phase in the historical Buddha's life. He is also identified with the direction of south. In TIBET, his name is Rin-chen-Hbyung.

BAT Symbols of happiness and longevity in common Chinese belief.

There are many different names given to bats, including *t'ien shu* ("a heavenly rat"), and *fei shu* ("a flying rat"). Certain medicines in ancient times contained the blood, gall, or wings of bats.

Artists often portrayed FUXING, one of the SAN XING, or three Chinese gods of good fortune in Chinese myth, as a bat. Another popular motif was a drawing of five flying bats to symbolize the Five Blessings: long life, wealth, health, a virtuous life, and a natural death. This motif is still used today on the gold-embossed, red-paper envelopes given to children at New Year feasts.

BA XIAN (PA HSIEN)

The Ba Xian, or the Eight IMMORTALS, are a group of eight legendary beings or immortal sages that Taoist teachers often used as role models to teach people how to live in balance and harmony with the world.

The Eight Immortals include six men (LI TIEGUAI, ZHONGLI QUAN, CAO GUOJIU, HAN XIANG, LU DONGBIN, and ZHANG GUOLAO) and two women (LAN CAIHE and HE XIANGU). Li Tieguai is depicted as a beggar leaning on one iron crutch and carrying a MEDICINE gourd around his neck; he is the patron of pharmacists. Zhongli Quan is the messenger of heaven. Cao Guojiu learned about the limits of the powers of the nobility, and he has become their patron. Han Ziang plays the flute. Lu Dongbin is the patron of scholars and the guardian of ink makers. Zhang Guolao is a magician who has the power to bring children into the world, and he is a patron of married couples. Lan Caihe is the patron of the poor, sometimes depicted as a boy, but most times as a woman. He Xiangu is a young woman who has the powers of flight and is the protector of unmarried women.

The Eight Immortals are not gods. They are ordinary men and women who renounced corruption, greed, and wealth in order to study nature's secrets and live according to the principles of TAOISM. In return, the gods rewarded them with immortality, or the power to live forever, which, according to the tales, they received from eating the PEACHES of Immortality. They lived in the mythical islands of PENG LAI, Fangchang, and Yingzhou in the East China Sea, and they were often depicted as wandering the Earth to do good deeds or to find new converts to the Tao.

Their individual stories are filled with magic and comical situations, such as the Ba Xian's fondness for wine (which is why they are sometimes called "the Eight Drunken Immortals"). They often traveled together and used magic to cross the sea: Each one threw down an object on the water that turned into a sea monster to ferry him or her across.

Probably intended as a device to teach Taoist principles, the exact date of their grouping is a matter of debate, with some scholars suggesting the Sung dynasty (960–1280) and others the Yuan (1280–1368). Individually some of the figures have been traced back or connected to other myths in early Chinese history. Their stories were widely recorded in the 15th century, and the Ba Xian became extremely popular figures, as popular as any movie hero today. They turn up on pottery, porcelain plates, embroidery, rugs, paintings, bronze and porcelain sculpture, and carved ivory reliefs.

BA ZHA (BA CHA, PA CHA)

A spirit protector against locusts, grasshoppers, and CICADAS in Chinese myth. Called "Great King Ba Zha," he is one of many mythic deities connected with AGRICULTURE.

According to the myths, his upper body is human, but he has a bird's beak, claws, and wings. His lower body is often in the shape of a bell. Ba Zha was said to be able to catch harmful insects with a magic liquid. Sometimes he carries a mallet, a sword, or a banner used to summon locusts and imprison them.

A Mongolian legend tells of Ba Zha Yeh, who lived in a wild valley filled with wolves, scorpions, locusts, and other dangerous creatures. But Ba Zha Yeh was never harmed or bothered by them.

Annual ceremonies were held in ancient China to ask for Ba Zha's protection. Wandering musicians were paid by villagers to erect a tent at the entrance of the village or town's main street and beat their drums and chant the proper prayers for half a day. Children and adults would crowd around and take home a charm to place over their front doors.

Some scholars believe the god may be the same spirit as LIU MENG JIANG ZHUN, who is also a protector against locusts.

BEAR

A symbol of bravery and strength in Chinese myth and lore. Some ancient Chinese kept a carved bear charm or a picture of a bear to prevent robbers from breaking into their homes.

China has several varieties of bears. The most famous is the panda. Its white-and-black body and black ears, legs, and tail once decorated the court robes of some high officials. There are also brown and black bears in China, similar to those in Europe and North America.

A legend tells of an emperor receiving ideas on how to run his government from a bear who visited his bedroom at night.

BEAST OF THE WHITE MARSH In Taoist myth, a deity said to know the languages of all birds, animals, and humans. Huang Di, the YELLOW EMPEROR, met him while on a tour of his kingdom.

The Beast of the White Marsh knows about all of the REINCARNATIONS, or new births, that a soul could make. He told the Yellow Emperor about each one. The total came to 11,520.

BEGGING BOWL Wooden bowls carried by Buddhist priests to use when asking for money or food. BUDDHA was said to have a stone begging bowl that had many miraculous powers.

BEI DOU (PEI TOU) The spirits of the Northern Dipper (an Asian term for Big Dipper) in Chinese mythology. They are said to keep track of everything a person does in her or his lifetime.

A group of stars in this constellation is called the Three Stars. They represent happiness, rewards (or, in some versions, payments or wealth), and long life.

BENG MENG (PENG MENG) A character from the myth of the divine archer YI. Beng Meng was a human student of the divine archer; he became so jealous of Yi's superior abilities that he ended up killing Yi with a club.

BENSHI HESHANG See OMITU FO.

BHAISAJYAGURU See YAOSHI FO.

BIAN QIAO (PIEN CH'IAO) A "king" of MEDICINE in Chinese legend and early history. Bian was said to have lived in Lu, a kingdom of ancient China. In A.D. 521, he is said to have cured Zhao Jianzi, who had been in a coma for five days. Though rewarded handsomely, his success led to his assassination by jealous court rivals.

According to legend, Bian was given a special medicine to be taken with the morning mist by a genie named Chang Sangjun. He also learned how to see through the wall of the body to the organs and bones beneath.

BIXIA SHENGMU See SHENG MU.

BLOCK See TAO WU.

BLUE DRAGON See QING LONG.

BODHISATTVA According to Buddhist belief, bodhisattvas, or Buddhas-to-be, are devout Buddhists who have achieved ENLIGHTENMENT but have delayed entering NIRVANA to help others. Exact beliefs about the powers of bodhisattvas vary from sect to sect, but, in general, they are considered to have great powers and to be important models for the faithful to follow. Bodhisattvas are almost exclusively venerated by sects in the MAHAYANA branch of BUDDHISM. The sects in the THERAVADA branch venerate MILO FO.

Some bodhisattvas are historical figures, though their stories have been embroidered with legend. Others seem to have been based on or confused with older gods, either from India or China.

Important bodhisattvas in Chinese Buddhism include Milo Fo, GUANYIN (also known as Avaloki-teśvara or Kannon), and XUKONGZANG (Akasagarbha).

BODHIDHARMA (DAMODASHI) The Chinese name for Damodashi, a historical figure important in the development of BUDDHISM. According to Buddhist tradition and legend, the monk Bodhidharma introduced meditation to China in the sixth century; today he is mainly revered by the CHAN, or ZEN, sects of Buddhism, which use meditation as important techniques in seeking ENLIGHTENMENT.

Born in India, Bodhidharma and his brother Daxisekong traveled to China in the first half of the sixth century. His birthday is celebrated on the fifth day of the 10th month.

According to one set of legends, Bodhidharma lived in the Chuzu'an Buddhist monastery in Henan province after arriving in China and visiting King Liang Wudi in 527. There he meditated for nine years. His concentration was so great that his arms and legs were forever paralyzed; he died in 535. Another legend credits him with discovering TEA when he was still in India.

Figures of Damodashi are considered good luck, especially in Japan, where Damodashi is known as Daruma.

BODHI TREE According to Buddhist legend, the historical BUDDHA sat underneath a sacred Bodhi tree (sometimes called a "Bo tree") when he gained ENLIGHTENMENT. It is also sometimes called the "tree of wisdom."

BOOK OF CHANGES See *I CHING*.

BRIDGE GODS Spirits said to rule over the souls that have drowned in the nearby stream or river. In ancient China, funerals paused before crossing the bridge so that the god could be properly worshiped.

BROOM Folk belief in ancient China held that evil spirits were afraid of brooms, so one of the customs on the last day before the New Year was to sweep the house clean of evil spirits.

The broom was also a symbol of seventh-century poet Shih Te. He was said to sweep away all his daily worries and troubles, instead concentrating on more important pursuits of wisdom and nature.

BUDDHA Buddha means "Enlightened One." The term is used in BUDDHISM to refer to a universal, enlightened soul without beginning or end; a manifestation or aspect of this soul; or the historical founder of Buddhism.

Especially in the West, the word *Buddha* is often used to refer to the man who started the religion. He was known as Shāka or Siddhartha Gautama before reaching ENLIGHTENMENT.

The historical Buddha was born in India around 560 B.C. The following story is told of how he reached enlightenment. While the historical specifics may or may not be accurate, the story summarizes what many feel is the essence of the individual search for truth that led to one of the world's greatest religions:

A wealthy prince, Siddhartha had every possible luxury growing up. Yet he became concerned that

Buddha, in a 19th-century drawing of a temple statue (The Dragon, Image, and Demon, *1886*)

he was missing something. One day, he left the palace with his servant Channa. They came across a sick man writhing in pain.

"Why does he suffer?" Siddhartha asked.

"Many do," said the servant. "It is the way of life."

Siddhartha continued on his walk. He found an old man who was suffering in great pain.

"Why?" Siddhartha asked.

"He is dying," said the servant. "That, too, is the way of life."

Siddhartha went home and thought about all the suffering he had seen. He decided he must find a solution for his people. He left the palace and went out to live with holy HERMITS. These men believed they could find great spiritual understanding by fasting and denying themselves pleasure. Siddhartha joined them. He fasted and denied himself everything. But when he nearly fainted from hunger, he realized that he could no longer think clearly.

He finally saw that this was not the way to understand suffering, let alone to solve it. He left the others. After eating to regain his strength, Siddhartha sat under a BODHI TREE and meditated. At first, he felt and thought nothing but fear and doubts. All night long he meditated. And then in the morning, as the sun lit the horizon, he found enlightenment. He understood the basic state of humankind and the world.

The core of his understanding was the FOUR NOBLE TRUTHS:

- There is much suffering in the world. For example, humans suffer from illness, old age, and death.
- Desire causes suffering. For example, we suffer when we are dying because we desire or want life.
- Suffering can be ended by ending desire.
- The way to do this is by the EIGHTFOLD PATH: right understanding, right thinking, right speaking, right acting, right occupation, right effort, right mindfulness, and right concentration.

After reaching enlightenment, Siddhartha was called Śākayumi (or Shakayumi) Buddha. Śākayumi means "Sage of Sakya," the tribe or people he belonged to, and Buddha means the "Awakened" or "Enlightened One."

Buddha established monasteries and schools to share his ideas. His talks were recorded and organized as SUTRAS, or teachings, after his death. Buddhism as a religion spread over several hundred years, first throughout India, then into China, Japan, other parts of Asia, and eventually the rest of the world.

Tradition holds that the Buddha's soul lived many lives before his birth as Siddhartha. Several traditions or legends are connected with his birth. It is said, for example, that his coming was announced by an earthquake. His wife, horse, elephant, and charioteer were all said to be born at the same time.

In MAHAYANA BUDDHISM (see BUDDHISM), the historical Buddha is seen as only one of several manifestations or instances of the universal Buddha. In the tradition in TIBET, the different manifestations are seen as aspects of different forces or powers in the universe.

BUDDHA'S DISCIPLES

According to Buddhist tradition, the historical BUDDHA had 10 great disciples, or close followers, who lived as his companions. These disciples are sometimes mentioned in very old texts, although today historians say that their representations are rare in China and elsewhere. The disciples are JIGONG LAOFO PUSA, ANANDA (called Kun-dgah-bo in TIBET), SHELI FO (Nid-rygal in Tibet), SHUBOJIA (Rabhyor in Tibet), PURNA, MULIAN, Katyayana, Aniruddha, UPALI (Nye-var-khor in Tibet), and LUOHULUO (Sgra-gchan-jin in Tibet). Each disciple has a specific characteristic, which he is considered "first" in. For example, Sheli Fo is considered first in wisdom and stands as an example to the faithful of wisdom's power.

BUDDHISM   One of the world's great religions, Buddhism is based on the teachings of Śākayumi BUDDHA, known before ENLIGHTENMENT as Siddhartha Gautama. There are now many sects, or schools of belief, but, in general, all Buddhists agree that humans must give up earthly desire and take the EIGHTFOLD PATH to truth in order to reach lasting happiness, or NIRVANA. Buddhists believe that the souls of those who have not achieved enlightenment are reincarnated, or born again, repeating the cycle until they can fully understand the nature of existence.

Buddhism began in the sixth century B.C. in India. As it developed and spread, Buddhism was influenced by both new interpretations of its core ideas and the ideas of the culture around it. Since the historical Buddha and his early followers lived in India, they spoke and wrote in Sanskrit. That language forms the basis for many Buddhist terms and names to this day.

Buddhism reached China in the first century A.D. During its development, Buddhism separated into two main branches, each of which contained a number of smaller sects. One branch known as THERAVADA, or the "Way of the Elders," attempted to stay close to the literal teachings of Buddha. In general, the sects in this branch believed that enlightenment must be earned by individual souls striving on their own.

The other branch, MAHAYANA, saw the earthly Buddha as only one manifestation of a universal soul or Buddha. Enlightenment could be achieved through the help of others who had already perfected their souls. These were BODHISATTVAS, or Buddhas-to-be.

Mahayana—or "Greater Vessel" or "Greater Vehicle"—more freely adapted and absorbed the other religious traditions that it encountered. It absorbed and included local gods and myths into its conception of the universe.

Many Americans are familiar with ZEN BUDDHISM, an important school of Buddhism that began in India and blossomed in China as Chan Buddhism. It became popular in Japan around the start of the 13th century and remains popular there and in the United States.

BUDDHIST DIVINITIES According to some sects, a Buddhist may call directly on any of a number of important legendary and mythic figures to help him or her reach ENLIGHTENMENT. Not all sects honor all the individuals in the same way, and many use different names to refer to the same deity.

The divinities can be grouped into different categories. The most important are BUDDHAS and BODHISATTVAS. Buddhas are the manifestations of the eternal Buddha. Buddhas are thought to appear at regular intervals on Earth. There are many; some sects count literally thousands.

The bodhisattvas, or Buddhas-to-be, have delayed entering NIRVANA to help others. Some bodhisattvas are historical figures, though their stories have been embroidered with legend. Others seem to have been based on or confused with older gods, either from India or China.

Other deities include PROTECTORS OF THE DHARMA (or faith) and kings of hell (see AFTERLIFE).

BUDDHIST MYTH As one of the world's great religions, BUDDHISM has affected a wide range of cultures and people. As Buddhism grew, it borrowed and assimilated legends and myths from the different cultures where it flourished. It also transported myths from different areas to new ones.

One reason Buddhism is rich in myth and legend is that it spread over a large area over centuries. As it spread, it wove new stories into its body of beliefs. In some cases, the stories were originally told by monks as examples for teaching newcomers to the faith. In others, they were old legends and myths retold in Buddhist terms, reinterpreting the story to demonstrate religious points.

Since Buddhism began in India, many of its earliest figures—both historical and mythic—were Indian. In time, however, the attributes of these figures owed as much to the areas where Buddhism spread as to India. As the religion evolved, so too did the different stories and accounts of the many figures. Myth, legend, and historical fact intertwined.

BODHIDHARMA, for example, was probably a real person from India who came to China in the early sixth century, where today he is known as Damodashi. The CHAN or ZEW sect of Buddhism reveres him for bringing Indian meditation techniques to China. Legends about him say that he meditated so hard for nine years that he could no longer use his arms or legs. Bodhidharma's legend eventually spread to Japan, where he is known as Daruma; according to popular belief, his statuettes can bring good luck to any who possess them.

Another reason Buddhism is rich in myth and legend is its wide variety of sects, or schools. While to outsiders the differences between different sects may seem slim, each tradition has a rich store of individual narratives highlighting different aspects of Buddhist belief. Legends and myths are an important part of these narratives.

BUTTERFLY A symbol of joy, summer, and love in Chinese myth and lore. The butterfly was a common decoration on clothing and paintings.

It is associated with a famous story told by Taoist philosopher ZHUANGZI, said to sum up the most important ideas of TAOISM. The philosopher dreamed that he was a butterfly, then woke. This led him to wonder: Was he a man dreaming he was a butterfly, or was he a butterfly dreaming he was a man?

BUZHOU (PU-CHOU) One of the EIGHT PILLARS or mountains, which hold up the sky in ancient Chinese myth. GONG GONG knocks into the Buzhou and creates a flood.

CAI SHEN (TS'AI SHEN, XIANG CONG, HSIANG TS'UNG) A Chinese god of wealth, identified with many legendary and historic people dating from prehistory to the 14th century.

The god, like many who confer prosperity, was very popular. He was often symbolized in art by his money tree—when shaken, it was said to deliver gold and silver. Sometimes he is accompanied by his TIGER.

Cai Shen was identified with several legendary figures, including Zhao Gongming, the name of two different Chinese heroes. Cai Shen is sometimes seen as a combination of a pair of gods—He Who Brings Riches and He Who Brings Gain.

The celestial ministry of finances is headed by Zhao Gongming. Two of his ministers, Xiao Sheng and Zao Bao, are known together as HE-HE.

Cai Shen, a Chinese god of wealth, accompanied by his tiger (The Dragon, Image, and Demon, *1886*)

CALENDARS In ancient China, time was divided into a predictable cycle. The qualities of a person and the world were thought to be connected with this cycle (see CYCLE OF SIXTY, TEN CELESTIAL STEMS, TWELVE TERRESTRIAL BRANCHES).

As part of this system, each month and year were thought to have characteristics determined by a complicated interplay of factors. These were popularly symbolized by an animal, which served as a kind of shorthand for the influences. The years were then called by these animal names. The order of the animals remains constant through the cycle of years. The animals, in order, are rat, bull (sometimes called the cow), TIGER, HARE, DRAGON, serpent, horse, sheep (or goat), monkey, rooster (or cock), DOG, and boar. Knowing a person's birth date could help a practiced ASTROLOGER determine the person's characteristics and fate.

Months were based on the new MOON and lasted 29 or 30 days, with 12 months in a year. Every few years an extra month was added to the calendar to make up for the fact that the system did not quite add up to a full orbit around the SUN. The Chinese New Year falls on the first day of the lunar month in late January or early February.

Since 1911 China has used the Gregorian calendar, the same calendar as that used in the West.

Buddhists developed a legend to explain the selection and order of animals in the calendar. It is said that during his days on EARTH, the historical BUDDHA selflessly preached to all creatures, animals as well as humankind. When he died and his body was to be cremated, all of the animals that had heard his holy words ran to do him honor. The system of years commemorated their arrival.

CALLIGRAPHY The art of writing. Calligraphy is an art on its own, with the strokes of letters having a beauty aside from the words and meanings they convey.

The Chinese language is especially suited for the art of calligraphy, because it is constructed from a set of pictograms, or symbols that directly represent a specific item. Writing a word can directly convey emotion in a way that portraying Western letters cannot.

Scholars say the earliest characters were simply tiny stick-figure drawings. For example, a simple drawing of an animal's body, with a dot for an eye, four lines for legs, and two twiglike antlers, was the character for *deer*. Over time, the characters were changed, in many cases simplified, and eventually stylized. Many were combined with other characters to create more complex ideas. For example, combining the character for *woman* with the character for *broom* created a new character for the word *wife*. The symbol for *mountain* turned on its side made *mound*.

Writing these symbols can be a complicated art. Strokes can have thick or thin lines depending on the style of calligraphy. As in a painting, the different brush strokes can be used to convey different feelings. Many in China consider calligraphy an important art form, one that emphasizes balance and beauty.

Traditional calligraphy was done with a BAMBOO brush. The hair or feather at the tip was in a tuft or knot, which allowed the calligrapher control over the line.

A style called Kaishu, the "Standard Characters," became the basic style of Chinese calligraphy at about A.D. 200 and has been used since that time. The style is credited to a man named Wang Cizhong, but, except for his name, historians have no record of him.

Kaishu is said to have one drawback: It cannot be written very quickly. Hsing-shu, or "Running Script," overcomes that limitation by combining some cursive style with the Standard Characters so that the writing can flow more quickly. It is said to be a more personal style, expressive of creativity and emotions, and it is therefore popular for personal letters and manuscripts.

Less formal script is often written in a style called Sutizi (or "Unorthodox Characters"). In mainland China, a somewhat different grouping called "Modern Simplified Characters," or Jiantizi, is used.

Earlier historic styles included the following:

- Guwen, the name given to the style of writing found on ORACLE BONES from the SHANG DYNASTY (c. 1550–1027 B.C.). The same characters were used on pottery and other items up to the Chou dynasty. The name means "Shell and Bone Characters," a reference to the tortoise shells and animal bones used by the oracles.
- Xiaozhuan, the style first used during the QIN DYNASTY (ca. 221–206 B.C.). It was developed by Li Si, a prime minister of the dynasty, to simplify the many different styles and variations used around the empire. Characters in this style are also known as the "Small Seal Characters."
- Lishu, the style that followed Hsiao-chuan. The style was surprisingly subtle and complex, with great emphasis on the control of the brush. Called "the Clerical Style," it is usually connected to the HAN DYNASTY (202 B.C.–A.D. 220). While very artistic, it is difficult to master. Today, even experts consider it hard to read.
- Caoshu, the "Grass Style." Faster than Lishu, this cursive style allowed the calligrapher's brush to flow from character to character. The style follows a set of conventions that allow strokes to be dropped and characters abbreviated. While admired for artistic reasons, the art of the design tends to make it very hard to read for someone who is not an expert.

CAN CONG (TS'AN TSUNG, HSIEN TS'AN)

In ancient Chinese mythology, the deity who taught humans how to make SILK. Can Cong is said to be the ancestor of the kings of SHU, the region of modern Szechwan. He wore green clothes, and he is sometimes referred to in myths as the god in green clothes.

His son was Po Huo, and his grandson was Yu Fu. According to the myths, people at the time did not die. When the time came for them to leave Earth, they simply vanished and became immortal. Can Cong himself was said to have vanished and become a deity while hunting on Mount Yu.

Can Cong was said to have had several thousand golden silkworms. Each new year, he gave the people one of these silkworms. The silkworms reproduced in great numbers, and the people always returned his gift afterward.

Can means "silkworm"; *cong* indicates a "group" or "cluster." The sense of the name Can Cong is someone or something that can encourage the growth of many silkworms, which are needed to make silk.

CAN NÜ (TS'AN NÜ) The goddess of silkworms in Chinese myth. Can Nü is also known as the "Lady with the Horse's Head" because of a famous story, which appears in a range of variations. Here is one version:

There was once a sad girl who missed her father. Left all alone, she told her horse that if he could go and bring her father home, she would marry him. The horse immediately bolted.

Her father found the horse, which was clearly saddened. Suspecting that something was wrong, he mounted it and rode it home. But after they arrived, the horse continued to act strangely, never eating. Whenever he saw the girl, he became quite excited. Finally, the father asked the girl what was going on. She told him. Worried and ashamed, he killed the horse with his bow and arrow, then skinned it.

While he was away, the girl kicked the horse skin. She laughed at the dead animal, telling it that it had been killed because it wanted a human for its wife. As she spoke, the horse skin rose up, grabbed her, and went off.

A neighbor saw what had happened and told her father. A few days later they found the girl and the horse skin wrapped as a cocoon on a tree. They called the tree a MULBERRY tree. Silkworms eating on the tree did much better than on any other tree, and its seeds were soon used to grow many others.

CANOPUS   See SHOUXING.

CAO GUOJIU (TS'AO KUO-CHIU)   One of the legendary BA XIAN, or Eight IMMORTALS, of TAOISM.

Most of the legends about Cao Guojiu say he was the brother of Empress Cao (or Empress Ts'ao Huo) of the SONG DYNASTY, who lived in the 11th century. He was a good man who disliked the corruption of imperial life. After his brother committed murder and tried to seduce his victim's wife, Cao Guojiu disappeared into the mountains to find a monk who could teach him Taoism.

When he arrived at a river, he found he had no money to pay a boatman. Rather rudely, Cao Guojiu demanded that the boatman row him across anyway.

Cao Guojiu, one of the Ba Xian, or Eight Immortals in Taoist and popular Chinese myth (The Dragon, Image, and Demon, *1886*)

He pulled out a golden tablet—in some versions, golden medallion—to prove his high rank entitled him to special treatment.

But when the boatman pointed out how badly he was behaving, Cao Guojiu was ashamed. He apologized and threw the token of his rank into the river. The boatman turned out to be LU DONGBIN, another of Eight Immortals. He agreed to take Cao Guojiu on as his disciple and help him gain immortality.

Artists portray Cao Guojiu in official robes. In his statues, he wears an elaborate court headdress and holds either a golden tablet or a pair of brass chimes struck with brass rods during temple ceremonies and in theatrical performances.

The nobility and theatrical performers considered Cao Guojiu to be their patron.

CAT   There are many superstitions about cats in Chinese folklore. A cat was believed to ward off evil spirits, because of its ability to see in the dark. Since they like to eat rats, cats were also considered protectors of silkworms (which were thought to be killed by rats). Some people thought just hanging a picture of a cat on the wall could prevent evil spirits or rats from entering the house.

But cats were also sometimes considered bad omens. A stray cat was believed to bring bad luck in financial matters.

CELESTIAL MINISTRIES   See MINISTRIES OF GODS.

CHAN BUDDHISM   See ZEN BUDDHISM.

CHANCHU (CH'AN-CH'U)   The striped toad that ZHANG E was changed into as she floated to the Moon.

CHANG E   See ZHANG E.

CHANG FEI   See ZHANG FEI.

CH'ANG-HSI   See CHANGXI.

CHANG HSIEN   See ZHANG XIAN.

CHANG KUNG-I   See ZHANG GONGYI.

CHANG LIANG   A historical person (d. 189 or 187 B.C.) honored as a model hero by Taoists. In life, Chang Liang helped the HAN DYNASTY during their battles with the Qin. Later Taoists considered him an IMMORTAL.

CHANG-MEI   See JIGONG LAOFO PUSA.

CHANG O   See ZHANG E.

CHANG TAO-LING   See ZHANG DAOLING.

CHANGXI (CHANGYI,   CH'ANG-HSI)   In ancient Chinese myth, the wife of TAIYANG DIJUN and mother of the 12 moons. She is also considered a goddess of the MOON.

According to some tales, she regularly bathes her children in a sacred lake in the west of China (see ZHANG E).

CHANGYI   See CHANGXI.

CHAOS   The term used to describe the primal universe before the creation of the EARTH and HEAVENS in Chinese CREATION MYTHS.

In a third-century version of the story, chaos is described as a hen's EGG. When the egg hatched, after 18,000 years out came a being named PANGU. The parts of the egg separated, and the heavy elements—YIN—formed the Earth and the light elements—YANG—formed the sky. For the next 18,000 years, Earth and sky began to move apart at a distance of 10 feet each day. Pangu grew at the same rate so that his body always filled the space between the Earth and the sky.

One of the legendary figures known as the BA XIAN, or Eight IMMORTALS, ZHONGLI QUAN, was said to be the incarnation of chaos.

CHAO SAN-NIANG   See ZHAO SAN-NIANG.

CHARIOT   An open cart with large wheels pulled by a team of horses. Chariots were used in ancient China. In myth and legend, many were large enough to fit three men across.

In many of the Chinese myths, gods, EMPERORS, and famous heroes drive elaborately carved or painted chariots. The mythic YELLOW EMPEROR, Huang Di, was said to ride in a chariot drawn by six DRAGONS whenever he visited the sacred mountain to make his sacrifices to the gods of heaven.

CHARMS   Many ancient Chinese believed that displaying amulets, charms, and talismans brought good fortune or prevented attacks from spirits that could bring bad luck or prevent success. Charms were made out of many things. The written word was thought to be very powerful, and the proper word or combination of words was a strong talisman.

The following are some popular charms and the legends connected with them:

- Mirrors were worn by brides to protect them from evil spirits. Looking into an old brass mirror was supposed to heal anyone who had become hysterical after seeing a spirit or demon.
- Strips of paper printed with religious sayings or lucky words, such as *happiness* and *fortune*, were pasted over doors and on walls; they were even pinned to clothing.
- PEACH wood was a symbol of long life and immortality. It was often made into amulets. Children sometimes wore necklaces of carved peach pits.
- Brass or copper coins were strung on an iron rod in the shape of a sword and hung in rooms or at the head of beds where someone had died violently to keep spirits or demons from taking their next victim. And coins supposedly helped the sick recover faster.
- Little metal padlocks were made for children to bind them to the community and their parents and to ensure a long life. The Hundred-Family Lock was a custom in which a father collected coins from 100 different friends and relatives, then had them melted down to make a lock and a necklace for his child. Zodiac necklaces with the eight characters from a child's astrological horoscope or the animal from her or his year of birth were also considered to bring good luck (see ASTROLOGERS and CALENDARS).
- Children wore all kinds of charms to keep them from being snatched by spirits or demons. A lock of an infant's hair twisted around hair from a dog would protect it from the heavenly dog, which was said to steal children. An earring might be attached to a baby boy's ear to make a spirit think he was female and not worth taking, since boys were considered more valuable by the ancient Chinese.
- Part of the New Year celebrations included decorating with new charms to encourage 12 more months of good fortune.

CHA YU (YA YÜ) A god killed by two lesser gods in Chinese mythology. He is mentioned in connection with an early SHAMAN story, making his story of great interest to mythologists seeking information about practices before the Chinese historical period.

The shamans mentioned in the story, who are preserving the body in the paradise of KUNLUN, are seen as symbols of early religious ceremonies to honor the dead.

CHA-YU A monster with a DRAGON's head and a beast's body in Chinese myth. A *cha-yu* is one of the monsters that the divine archer YI kills after 10 SUNS appear in the sky.

CHENG HUANG The City God. In Chinese mythology, the god who kept China's walled cities and towns safe from harmful spirits. Cheng Huang

Cheng Huang, or the City God, protected the walls of each city and town in ancient China. (The Dragon, Image, and Demon, *1886*)

was also called the god of ramparts and ditches, a reference to the way the walls were usually constructed.

Cheng Huang was the specific god of each city wall. There was also a kind of Cheng-in-chief who presided over all of these gods.

The City God commanded an army of tame demons, who could control or scare away harmful ghosts, demons, and spirits of evil ancestors. The City God was believed to be able to persuade the spiritual judges of the AFTERLIFE to speed up the time when a dead spirit was allowed to be reincarnated or born again back on Earth (see REBIRTH AND REINCARNATION).

Each individual god was usually identified with a historical or legendary person from the city. While the memories of esteemed residents were often honored in this way, it was not unheard of for a criminal or other person whose life had been less than ideal to be made City God after his death.

Many cities and towns in ancient China kept a temple to the City God. Believers would come to pray in front of his statue, which was dressed in richly colored silk robes and a gold crown.

Every City God had two secretaries who helped him keep track of town affairs: Niu Tou and Ma Mian. Niu Tou had an ox's head; Ma Mian had a horse's head. There were also a variety of other aides. The City God's wife had a separate room in his temple.

CHENG SAN-KUNG   See ZHENG SANGONG.

CHENG TANG   See TANG THE CONQUEROR.

CHENG T'IEN CHÜN   See ZHU TIAN.

CHEN JEN   The second class of IMMORTALS in TAOISM. They are perfect sages or wisemen who have learned to rule themselves and therefore control nature. Chen Jen are called "heroes" and rank in the middle of the three groupings of Immortals. Chen Jen live in the second HEAVEN of the three Taoist heavens. Their powers come from their knowledge and purity.

The title is also applied to the head of the Taoist Cheng-I sect.

CHEN STAR   See STARS.

CH'I   See QI.

CH'I   See KAI.

CHIA-LAN   Buddhist deities said to keep out evil spirits at temples and monasteries. The *chia-lan* are named after a disciple of BUDDHA, Chia-lan. They have three eyes, enabling them to see all.

CHIANG RIVER   The Great River, mentioned in some Chinese myths. It is known today as the Yangtze River.

CHIANG TZU-YA   See LU SHANG.

CHIANG YUAN   See JIANG YUAN.

CHIEH   See KING CHIEH.

CHIEN DI (CHIEN TI)   The goddess who bore XI or Hsieh, the mythic founder of the SHANG DYNASTY, in a miraculous virgin birth. According to myth, she became pregnant after touching an egg of a dark or black bird. Chien Di was married to DI KU.

CHIEN-MU   Ladder tree that connects HEAVEN and EARTH in Chinese myth. It is said to be in Tu-kuang, or beyond the South Sea. The tree is often described as being at the center of the universe.

The Chien-mu goes up for 1,000 feet without branches. Once it reaches the sky, it begins to branch out.

According to one myth, it was created by Huang Di, the YELLOW EMPEROR.

CHIEN TI   See CHIEN DI.

CHIGUO   The Guardian King of the East in Chinese Buddhist myth. Chiguo played a guitar and was associated with music. His army contained a band of musicians and demon vampires. He was associated with the spring. Taoists call Chiguo Molihai. In TIBET his name is Yul-hkhor Bsrungs; in MONGOLIA, Orchi-long Tetküchi. Chiguo is the Chinese version of the Sanskrit Dhrtarāstra.

CH'IH-CHIA HSIEN   See CHI-JIA XIAN.

CH'IH CHING-TZU   See CHI JINGZI.

CH'IH SUNG-TZU   See CHI SONGZI.

CH'IH YU   See CHIYOU.

CHI-JIA XIAN (CH'IH-CHIA HSIEN) "The Barefoot IMMORTAL," a Taoist figure in late Chinese myth. According to his tale, around A.D. 1009 an emperor of the SONG DYNASTY asked the gods to grant him an heir. When the request reached heaven, Chi-jia Xian laughed—and was sent by YU DI to rule the EARTH. Chi-jia Xian was incarnated on Earth as the son of Emperor Chen Tsung (998–1023). The prince, it is said, loved to go barefoot, hence the nickname.

CHI JINGZI (CH'IH CHING-TZU)   A fire god in Taoist myth. He represents the idea of spiritual fire. According to some traditions, he brought fire to humans by discovering how it could be made from the wood of a mulberry tree. The story of the FIRE DRILLER (Sui-jen) is another version of the myth about fire.

CH'I KU-TZO   See QI GUZI.

CH'I-LIN   See QILIN.

CH'IN   See QIN.

CH'IN DYNASTY   See QIN DYNASTY.

CH'ING-CH'IU   See QINGQIU.

CH'ING DYNASTY   See QING DYNASTY.

CH'ING LUNG   See QING LONG.

CH'ING-T'U   See PURE LAND BUDDHISM.

CH'ING WA SHEN   See QING WA SHEN.

CHING WEI   See NU WA.

CHIN KUANG HSIEN   A Taoist figure in Chinese myth. The shining gold immortal is a monkey-wolf with golden hair. He is described as a *genii*, a spirit that can take human form, though that is not his natural state.

CH'IN KUANG-WANG   See QIN GUANG WANG.

CHI SONGZI (CH'IH SUNG-TZU)   A rain god in Chinese myth.

Chi Songzi was said to have appeared during a drought in the reign of legendary emperor SHEN NONG, who traditionally is said to have lived from 2838 to 2698 B.C. Chi Songzi ended the drought by sprinkling the earth with water from the branch of a tree.

Chi Songzi is often said to keep company with the RAIN MASTER, a mythological deity who figures in several tales.

CHIU-LI-HU HSIEN   See JIU LI HU XIAN.

CHIU-YI   See ZANGWU.

CH'IYU   See CHIYOU.

CHIYOU (CH'IH YU, CH'IYU)   A god of war, of rain, and of weapons and metalworking in ancient Chinese mythology. Chiyou is said to have invented metal weapons, such as shields and metal-tipped lances and axes.

In one version of the myth, Chiyou was said to have worked metal in the mountains after Huang Di (also known as the YELLOW EMPEROR) opened them.

Other accounts say that Chiyou fought the Yellow Emperor but lost and was killed by him or his forces. In this version, after Chiyou's army was ultimately defeated, his body ran across the battlefield before it collapsed. Huang Di threw the shackles that Chiyou had made into a field, where they turned into maple trees.

Yu Shih, the RAIN MASTER, is said to be ruled by Chiyou, as was FENG PO, a wind god.

Chiyou is a word for reptile, and in some works of art Chiyou has the feet of a tortoise and the head of a snake. In other works, he appears as a bull-like man with hooves and horns. Some writers say he and his 72 brothers had heads made of bronze with iron eyebrows. The family ate rock for nourishment.

CHONG AND LI (CH'UNG AND LI)
According to very ancient Chinese mythology, two brothers who separated the sky and EARTH. Chong pressed up against HEAVEN as Li pressed downward.

Later accounts have Chong as the god of the South controlling heaven, with his brother Li, the god of fire, controlling Earth during a time of disorder. The two brothers were said to have restored order but also to have broken the link between heaven and Earth. Until that time, deities could come to Earth and mingle with humans.

CHOU   See ZHOU.

CHOU DYNASTY   See ZHOU DYNASTY.

CHOU HUA (CH'OU HUA)   A mythical marsh mentioned in some early Chinese tales; it is said to be in the south.

CHRISTIANITY   Missionaries from a branch of Christianity centered in Persia came to China during the early TANG DYNASTY (618–906), and Syrian Christians are mentioned in edicts from A.D. 683. Various Westerners visited China during the European medieval ages, and in their wake came Catholic missionaries seeking converts. The Christian population was eventually large enough for two bishops to be named in the country, one at Beijing and the other at Zaitun. These missions ended in 1369 after the Chinese expelled the last Beijing bishop, and it was not until 1583 that a new mission, this one led by Jesuits, arrived in China. Over the next 100 years, the Jesuits gained some popularity in the country. But decisions by Roman Catholic leaders that members of the church could not follow native Chinese rituals caused the Chinese emperor to expel them.

Russian Orthodox missions began in 1689; Protestant missions began shortly after the beginning of the 19th century. The influence of Christianity increased somewhat as European trade increased, but reaction to European imperialism stoked feelings against the religion. During the Boxer Rebellion (1900–1901), hundreds of Protestant missionaries and thousands of Chinese converts were killed.

Later in the 20th century, the Communist government at first discouraged and then persecuted Christians, creating an official church that all believers were supposed to join. About 6 percent of China's 1.26 billion people were estimated to be Christian in 2000.

With its relatively minor influence on Chinese culture, Christianity did not add much to China's store of mythology. However, Chinese Christians did identify some figures from existing traditions with Christian figures. For example, the goddess DOU MU (also identified as the North Star), was seen by some Christians as an incarnation of Mary, the virgin mother of Jesus.

CHRONICLE OF TSO   A classic text and source of information about early Chinese myth and history. Scholars say it was written around the fifth or fourth century B.C. It claims to document the period from around 722 B.C. to 481 B.C.

CHU (CH'U)   A state in southern China during the ZHOU DYNASTY. It was conquered by the JIN DYNASTY and became part of the Chinese empire in 233 B.C. TAOISM has traditionally been said to have been associated with the early culture of Chu.

CHUANG-TZU   See ZHUANGZI.

CHUAN HO   See GAO YANG.

CHUAN HSU   See GAO YANG.

CHU CHÜAN SHEN   See ZHU JUAN SHEN.

CH'Ü HSIEH YÜAN   See CHU XIE YUAN.

CHU JUNG   See ZHU RONG.

CHU LING   See JU LING.

CHU LUNG   See ZHU LONG.

CH'UNG AND LI   See CHONG AND LI.

CHUNG-LI CH'UAN   See ZHONGLI QUAN.

CHU PA-CHIEH   See ZHU BAJIE.

CHU T'IEN   See ZHU TIAN.

CHU TZU CHEN   See ZHUZI ZHEN.

CHU XIE YUAN (CH'U HSIE YUAN)   The ministry of exorcism in Chinese myth, responsible for removing demons from buildings and other places (see MINISTRIES OF GODS). Among its resident members are Yang, Shih, Chou, Sung, Ning, Li, and Ho, who are each called Great Heavenly Prince (Da Tian jun).

Exorcisms were very important in Taoist and FOLK RELIGION. Important activities, such as the construction of a new building, could not begin until evil spirits were cleared from the site. Likewise, MEDICINE was believed at one point to be a matter of determining which demons were haunting a body. This was done by contacting the proper deity in charge.

CHU YUNG   See ZHU RONG.

CICADA   In Chinese myth and folklore, the cicada is a symbol of resurrection and eternal youth.

Cicadas are a common insect in China. Depending on the species, they spend years underground in the larva stage. Then they tunnel their way out in the pupa stage, split open their shells, and emerge into the world. This process suggests several human parallels, including the process of becoming an IMMORTAL in Taoist belief (see TAOISM).

Pieces of jade, carved in the shape of a cicada, were often placed in the mouth of a corpse before it was buried in ancient China.

CIHUA (TZ'U-HUA)   Short tales and ballads from the 15th century that include stories from Chinese popular legend. Among these stories are a number of GHOST tales.

CINNABAR   Mercuric sulfide. The material was important in TAOISM because of the belief that it could be changed to gold through ALCHEMY. The formula required summoning special spirits through ritual and sacrifices. Cups made of this gold would lengthen life and allow the drinker to view the Taoist IMMORTALS.

Pure cinnabar was much sought after by Taoist alchemists. Among those who looked for it was Ko Hung, who lived in the fourth century. Ko Hung wrote extensively about MEDICINE as well as alchemy,

since a pure body was a necessary part of the science. He is said to have been on a journey to Vietnam to collect cinnabar when he died near Canton, China.

CINNABAR SCARLET   See DANZU.

CLAN   A group of families or households who are related to each other through one common ancestor (see ANCESTORS AND ANCESTOR CULTS).

CLASSIC OF CHANGE   See I CHING.

CLASSIC OF HISTORY   See SHUJING.

CLASSIC OF MOUNTAINS AND SEAS   A collection of Chinese myths dating from the third century B.C. to the first century A.D. often used as a source by scholars studying myths.

CLASSIC OF POETRY   See SHIJING.

COINS   Besides being used as money, Chinese coins were sometimes worn as amulets and ornaments. Most Chinese coins were round, with a square cut out in the center, so they could be strung together on string, sticks, or thin iron rods. Coins with characters or words stamped on the reverse side were believed to bring good luck when strung together to make the characters form a saying or rhyme. Coins were often strung on red string and hung around the neck of a statue of the CHENG HUANG (City God) for good luck. Some children would wear a necklace of as many coins as their age, and parents would add a new coin on each birthday to protect them from danger. Coins were also hung over shop doors to attract wealth, tossed into the bed of a daughter on her wedding night to ensure that she would have children, and melted down and made into the shape of a small sword to ward off evil spirits (see CHARMS).

COLORS   Colors had specific symbolic meanings in Chinese folk belief. Red symbolized joy and virtue. It was used on special holiday and festive occasions, such as the New Year. Yellow was considered the national color, and at one point it was worn only by the emperor and his sons and descendants.

White was the color of grieving for the dead. Black was a sign of evil and not worn.

Colors also indicated the rank of a person in ancient Chinese government or society, and this is sometimes reflected in mythical tales. Purple clothing indicated an educated person. The nine ranks of government officials each wore a different color ball of stone or glass on the top of their caps. Each dynasty had its own colors. Colors were also associated with the different directions—green (or blue) was east, white west, black north, and red, south.

In BUDDHISM, gods were shown in white garments, goblins were red, and devils black. Yellow was the color of Buddhist priests and the cloths used for burying the dead.

In Chinese theater, or pageants, red makeup was used to portray deities, black makeup to portray a simple but honest man, and white for a villain.

CONFUCIUS (KONG FUZI, K'UNG FU-TZU)

The most important philosopher and teacher (551–479 B.C.) in early China and among the most influential people to have ever lived. Confucius's teachings, called CONFUCIANISM, remain embedded in Chinese and Asian cultures, and his genius is recognized around the world more than 2,500 years after his death.

Details of his birth and life are scarce and in dispute. Born in 551 in the state of Lu (now the Shantung province of China), Confucius probably came from a noble but not well-off family. Some hold that Confucius was descended from the SHANG, the ancient family that ruled China. In any event, he seems to have been orphaned at an early age and had a poor childhood. However, he taught himself well, and eventually he got a job in government. Scholars are not exactly sure what this job was. One tradition holds that he was the minister of crime in Lu, but there is considerable doubt about this.

Whatever his position, Confucius began to teach others, and at some point he came to see that his duty was to restore traditional values to Chinese society. Confucius held up an idealized past as his model, emphasizing harmony and order and valuing ancestors and tradition. The best source of his teachings is the *Analects* (Lunyu), a collection of sayings and conversations recorded by his followers, not by Confucius

Confucius, shown here in the garb of a Chinese high official (The Dragon, Image, and Demon, *1886*)

himself. In the *Analects*, Confucius often refers to a perfect man by making examples, but he does not set out a comprehensive philosophy. One of the most important qualities a person can have, he says, is *ren* (or *jen* in the old style of rendering Chinese into English), but he does not specifically define this quality. Translators have called it "benevolence," "goodness," and even "love."

Confucius taught a number of young men who went on to hold important government positions in Lu. When he was nearing 60, he traveled to other Chinese states. There he tried to convince other leaders of the importance of following his teachings, which emphasized moral leadership based on ancient ideas and traditions. Scholars say, however, that he returned home disappointed and felt that he had failed in his mission. He may also have considered himself something of a failure because he had not obtained a high-ranking post in Lu.

Confucius died in 479 B.C. Some of those who had been taught by him spread his teachings, developing different parts of his philosophy, and writing down his ideas. Scholars say that while his school of thought was important, it was only one of many at first. By A.D. 59, Confucian thought was so important as a model for behavior that the emperor of the HAN DYNASTY declared that sacrifices should be made to Confucius. Ironically, this great honor clashed with Confucius's own teachings. He had held that one should only make offerings to one's own ancestors as immortal beings (see ANCESTORS AND ANCESTOR CULTS). A cult of scholars and others offered sacrifices to him, and he was viewed as a deity, ranking near or at the top of the Chinese pantheon.

Confucius became the subject of various legends after his death. Many had to do with his supposed ties to noble families; these were possibly invented to make him seem more important and therefore worthy of honor. At times, he is used in stories as a general example of a great teacher.

The name Confucius comes from Western pronunciations of his Chinese name, K'ung Fu-tzu, which means "Venerable, or Great Master, K'ung."

CONFUCIANISM An important philosophy, or system of ideas about people's proper role in society and what they must do to live their lives properly. Confucianism developed from the teachings of CONFUCIUS, a teacher and government official who lived from 551–479 B.C. In ancient China, Confucianism was important for the rulers of government and those who worked for them. Its basic ideas filtered all through society, and even today its principles remain important for many.

The "way" of Confucius honors the past. Individuals must live a moral life by being humane and good to others. They must be virtuous and honest. Loyalty to one's family and ruler is critical. Basic education should include study from classic texts, which are read for their examples of behavior as well as entertainment. Everyone in society must know her or his place—father, scholar, wife, ruler, subject—and must try to maintain it.

Confucius himself recommended that students learn the *Book of Odes of* SHIH CHING, which contains poems from the early ZHOU DYNASTY. His students gathered some of his teachings in the *Analects*. Much later, followers added more complex books that focus on metaphysics, or the study of the nature of things. The *Four Books*, a special grouping of works that formed the basis of Confucianism for many years, includes the *Analects, Ta hsüeh* (Great learning), *Chung Yung* (also written as *Chung-yung* [The Great mean]), and *Meng-tzu* or the Book of Mencius (a work by early Confucian teacher Master Meng or Mencius, for whom it is named).

Historians often look at two different periods when studying Confucianism. The first begins with Confucius's life, when he taught in Lu, a state in ancient China. It includes the early development and spread of his ideas in the centuries that followed. This first period ends roughly in the fifth century A.D., when BUDDHISM begins to dominate China.

The second period begins with a revival of Confucian thought in the 11th century, generally called "Neo-Confucianism," or the new Confucianism. (Some date its beginning earlier.) While the school can be seen as a reaction to the influence of Buddhism, writings from this period are clearly influenced by Buddhist thought.

TAOISM is sometimes viewed as being an opposite of Confucianism. One reason is that Taoism sees the "Way" as something that cannot be fully known but must be followed, rather than something that can be studied and learned. Confucianism, on the other hand, emphasizes strict scholarship and is very scientific in its approach. But Confucianism also emphasizes the importance of tradition and of honoring ancestors (see ANCESTORS AND ANCESTOR CULTS), ideas that are not contradictory to Taoism. In everyday life, most people found that the two philosophies easily coexisted.

Confucianism's impact on Chinese society is hard to overestimate. For hundreds of years, its main texts were mandatory reading for anyone considered educated in society. Its emphasis on ancient tradition, education, and reverence toward elders continues to be important to all Chinese. Its influence is felt far beyond China's borders.

COSMIC EGG The egg that hatched PANGU at the dawn of creation, according to one CREATION MYTH. Occasionally in Chinese myth, gods or figures who are the result of unions between humans and deities.

COSMOLOGY
A theory of the universe; a kind of map of the way everything works.

In very ancient China, the universe was thought to consist of a square EARTH, bounded on each side by the ocean. The sky was round or arched above. There was nothing beyond. The AFTERLIFE was a place similar to the normal earth, sometimes said to exist in the mountains. Humans had both a soul and a body; after the body died, the soul lived on. If properly honored, the souls of ancestors could watch over and help the living, usually by interceding with the powers or gods who controlled nature (see ANCESTORS AND ANCESTOR CULTS). In essence, human life provided the basic model for the way the universe worked and continued to do so as society evolved and became more complicated.

BUDDHISM brought the idea of a hell or purgatory where sins had to be worked off before a soul was reborn in the world. TAOISM adopted this idea, changing it slightly but retaining the basic concepts. The complexity of the government may have suggested another later invention, the MINISTRIES OF GODS. In this view, natural forces and such things as disease were overseen and potentially controlled by large bureaus of deities. The positions in these celestial ministries could be filled by appointments, just as the government was.

On a more philosophical level, Chinese from very ancient times saw the universe and everything in it as an expression of YIN AND YANG, the basic opposing forces. All nature displayed these two opposing but complimentary forces: male-female, day-night, and so on. Additional dynamic forces shaped activities to a specific cycle. Such ideas remained at the core of Taoist thought from the very ancient times up through the historical periods.

COUNTRY OF WOMEN
A mythological land said to exist in the North, surrounded by water. Only women lived there. Any male child born would die within three years.

CRANE
A symbol of longevity in Chinese folklore and myth. Cranes were believed to be able to fly

The crane often symbolized longevity in Asian art.

souls to HEAVEN, and funeral processions often placed a statue of a crane in flight on top of the coffin. Artists often draw a pair of cranes standing under a pine tree as a symbol of long life and old age.

In Chinese myth and legends, people were sometimes changed into cranes. The Taoist mythic figure, Ting Ling-wei, for example, was said to have turned himself into a crane after spending 1,000 years in the mountains studying TAOISM. He then flew away to heaven as an IMMORTAL.

CREATION MYTHS
Stories about the beginning of the world. The stories may have been passed down verbally for many generations before being written. Scholars study them for clues about the people and society that created them. As a society changes and grows, it adds to and alters its creation myths. Different variations may arise as the story is told in different places. Sometimes these differences are put together in a way that makes the story even more complicated. Scholars sometimes study stories for signs of this stitching together and other changes. Creation myths also give scholars many clues about the people who lived at the time the stories were popular.

The earliest account of a Chinese creation myth dates from the fourth century B.C. and is included in a work entitled "Questions of heaven," which is in question-and-answer format. The accounts say that the first, or primal, mist appeared from a blank state. This creative force is made up of pairs of opposing forces, or YIN AND YANG. From the interaction of the forces, the world begins to take shape. The HEAVENS are held up by EIGHT PILLARS in the EARTH. The Sun, MOON, and STARS move in an ordered way. NUMBERS are used in a way that suggests that they have special significance. The number eight carries a sense of harmony, whereas two suggests the interplay of yin and yang.

Creation myths recorded during the HAN DYNASTY, around 139 B.C., show the influence of TAOISM. In this version, two gods divided the CHAOS into yin and yang and the hard and soft.

The last and fullest account of the creation myth in early Chinese literature comes from a third-century text by Hsu Cheng called *Historical Records of the Three Sovereign Divinities and the Five Gods*. The work itself has been lost, but portions remain as fragments in other works.

In this version, the universe before creation is a kind of COSMIC EGG of chaos. PANGU was born from the middle of this egg. Gradually the birth material separated into two parts, heavy and light, or yin and yang. Yin became the earth, yang the heavens. Each day the distance between them grew by 10 feet. Pangu grew as well, filling the space. At the end of 18,000 years, Pangu had fully grown.

As Pangu reached the end of his day, his body began to change. Each part of the world was made from him. His left eye transformed into the Sun. The Moon was made from his right. People were made when the wind touched the tiny bugs on his skin.

Another creation myth involves the goddess NÜ GUA. According to this myth, she made humans from yellow earth, as a ceramic artist might make statues. These first humans were fine yellow creatures, who became rich aristocrats and leaders of society. Unfortunately, she did not have quite enough strength to finish the job. So rather than making all human beings by hand, she took her cord and dragged it through a muddy furrow or ditch. This created the common people.

Another later creation myth comes from the writing of ZHUANGZI. He tells how Hu, the emperor of the Northern Sea, and Shu, the emperor of the Southern Sea, would sometimes meet halfway between their kingdoms in the land of Hun-tun (the "Center," but the name also means "chaos"). Hun-tun lacked the seven orifices for seeing, hearing, eating, and breathing. To repay his kindness, Shu and Hu decided to bore the necessary holes in Hun-tun, one a day. But on the seventh day, Hun-tun died. At that moment, the world came into being.

The combined names of the two emperors, Shu-hu, means "lightning," and some scholars have suggested that the author implied that the heavens demolished chaos so that the world would emerge.

CROW The crow appears in many Chinese myths. According to one myth, a crow carries the SUN to the top of a tree each morning to start the day. In some ancient art, a red or golden crow with three feet symbolized the Sun. The bird also appeared in folktales as a shining example of a creature who cares for its parents in old age.

Depending on their COLOR, crows were considered good or evil omens in ancient China. The most common Chinese black-and-white-necked crows were often said to bring bad luck. Sometimes called white-winged ravens, these crows had a harsh cry. If you heard their caw while going to court, it meant your case would not be successful. If it was heard between 7 and 11 A.M., it meant rain and wind

Several myths and superstitions are attached to the common crow.

would begin. On the other hand, a caw from the south between 3 and 7 A.M. meant someone would receive presents.

CULT A group of devoted believers who share a set of beliefs and rituals related to worship or religion. The word is often used to describe the veneration of specific deities or clan ancestors (see ANCESTORS AND ANCESTRAL CULTS). The word is not meant to have a negative sense when used in connection with this practice or with mythology in general.

CYCLE OF SIXTY A system used in ancient China to divine the nature of events. It is said to govern all that happens in the universe. It uses the TEN CELESTIAL STEMS, the TWELVE TERRESTRIAL BRANCHES, and the FIVE ELEMENTS.

According to legend, the system was first used in the 27th century B.C., though scholars doubt that assertion. The DIVINATION system could be used to tell the future.

CYCLE OF YEARS See CALENDAR.

D

DABIANCAITIAN NU In Buddhist myth, associated with Vairocana, the Buddha Supreme and Eternal being, the first of the five Dhyani-Buddhas. (See BUDDHISM.) Chinese Buddhists claim that Vairocana created a system of philosophy and meditation used by some to achieve ENLIGHTENMENT, and taught it to the Hindu sage Vajrasattva, who was said to live in an Iron Tower in Southern India. Vajrasattva's disciples then brought the knowledge to China. SEE PALUSHENA

Dabiancaitian Nu is also the Chinese version of Sarasvati, the Buddhist Goddess of Music and Poetry. Some Buddhist sects in China considered her a patron of these arts or symbols of them. Dabiancaitian Nu is said to have had 15 or 16 sons (the versions vary), each a patron of a different craft. Dabiancaitian Nu is one of the very few WOMEN honored as deities in Buddhist mythology.

DACI DABEI See OMITU FO.

DALAI LAMA The head of Dge-lugs-pa, the "Yellow Hat" sect of BUDDHISM in TIBET. Until 1959 the Dalai LAMA was also the head of the Tibetan government.

To devoted followers, the Dalai Lama is the reincarnation of the BODHISATTVA Avalokiteśvara (called GUANYIN in Chinese). At his death, the bodhisattva is reincarnated; his followers must then search and find the young boy who is the BUDDHA-to-be's new earthly form.

DAM-CHAN A Tibetan name for the FIVE GREAT KINGS.

DAMODASHI See BODHIDHARMA.

DANZHU (TAN CHU) In Chinese myth, the ne'er-do-well oldest son of YAO. Danzhu is also known as "CINNABAR Crimson" or "Cinnabar Scarlet." Concerned that he would not rule wisely, Yao sent him to a distant land called "Cinnabar Gulf" to govern. It was there that he got his name.

Some versions of the myth have Yao killing his son.

Ordinarily, the oldest son took over as EMPEROR in Chinese DYNASTIES. But several myths feature an oldest son who is not up to the job and thus does not inherit the kingdom.

DAODEJING See TAO-TE CHING.

DAOISM See TAOISM.

DARK LADY A goddess in late TAOISM who taught Huang Di (the YELLOW EMPEROR) the art of war. Darkness in Taoism usually signified mysterious and magical powers.

DARK WARRIOR The Dark Warrior was a mythological animal, shown in art as a TORTOISE with a snake wrapped around it. The animal is one of the ANIMALS OF THE FOUR DIRECTIONS. It is associated with the north and with winter. Its element was water, and its COLOR was black.

DAYU See YU.

DEATH The ancient Chinese believed that life after death was very similar to life on EARTH. Elaborate rituals served as a way of preparing dead relatives for the AFTERLIFE, but they also connected the living to the dead.

Taoist priests performed a series of rites over several weeks following a person's death. The most important was to remove the *SHEN* Shin, a demon responsible for bringing the soul back to the home where it had lived, but a potentially evil force.

During a funeral, relatives would scatter on the streets round paper slips called "road money," which could be used to buy the goodwill of DEMONS and wandering ghosts so that they would not hurt the deceased on the way to the grave or to HEAVEN.

In ancient times, EMPERORS would have massive armies of small statues made, representing the forces they would command in the afterlife. Deceased wealthy people would be buried with an entire set of household and personal items, including money and jewelry. In later practices, pictures of household possessions would be burned in the belief that the smoke would reach the deceased in heaven and turn into a spiritual version of the earthly goods.

The dead were buried in a coffin near enough to the family's house so that the family could carry out the annual graveside ancestral rituals of offering sacrifices of food, money, and prayers in mid-April. The rituals included laying out meats, vegetables, and drink for the returning soul. Sticks of incense, firecrackers, and gold and silver paper (which were burned on the site) were also meant to help the spirit with food and money during the coming year. Afterward a family would attach long slips of red and white paper to the corners of the grave to show that they had done their duty (see ANCESTORS AND ANCESTOR CULTS).

DEPARTMENT OF GODS See MINISTRIES OF GODS.

DEMON A wide range of demons appear in Chinese myth and folklore. Perhaps the most common are GUI, bodiless souls that are like ghosts.

When someone dies, the *gui*, or lesser soul, is believed to separate from the *hun*, or superior soul. If the *gui* is not treated to the proper rituals and prayers, it can become a ghost or a demon.

Some demons were servants of the gods, including the ruler of the underworld and its judges, which employed demons to carry out their hellish punishments. Demons were also said to cause various medical ailments.

Some of the demons who play an important role in Chinese myths include CHIYOU and GONG GONG. Demons' erratic actions sometimes were used to explain the existence of geographical oddities. For example, a monstrous demon with nine heads, was said to have created large swamps by throwing up after devouring nine mountains.

DHARMA In BUDDHISM, dharma represents truth and BUDDHA's teachings. It is a reality beyond the changing world and represents the order that guides the universe and should guide an individual's life.

Legends and tales can be used to illustrate parts of dharma, placing the truth in words or pictures that are easy for all to understand. A teacher might use a story about the Ba Xian, for example, to demonstrate an important quality for a person to have.

DHARMAPĀLAS See PROTECTORS OF THE DHARMA.

DI (TI) A word in Chinese that signifies GOD or divinity. It was added to the emperor's name.

DI GUAN (TI KUAN) The "Official of EARTH and Forgiver of Sins"; one of a trio of Taoist and popular gods called the SAN GUAN DADI. The gods represent the three essences of the universe. They forgive sin and bring happiness. The others are TIEN GUAN (HEAVEN) and SHUI GUAN (water).

DI KU (TI K'U) The god of music in ancient Chinese mythology. Di Ku is said to have invented six percussion instruments (drums, chimes, and bells) and wind instruments with the help of YOU CHUI, an ancient craftsman. He then taught people to play them.

Di Ku had two consorts who, according to Chinese myth, bore sons by virgin birth. One was JIANG YUAN, who bore HOU JI, mythic founder of the ZHOU DYNASTY, after walking in the god's footsteps. The other was CHIEN DI, who bore XIE, the mythic founder of the SHANG DYNASTY, after handling an EGG Di Ku had sent.

During the HAN DYNASTY, Di Ku was said to have been a son of the YELLOW EMPEROR, Huang Di. In some traditions, Di Ku is identified as GAO XIN.

DIMU See DIYA.

DINGGUANG FO The best known of the "thousand past BUDDHAS," or QIAN FO in China.

Dingguang Fo is the Chinese name for the past Buddha called Dápankara in the ancient Indian language and elsewhere. Dingguang Fo is known as Mar-memsdad in TIBET and Chula Choqiaqchi in Mongolia.

Buddhist beliefs about Dingguang Fo vary according to sect. In some, he is considered the 24th Buddha, just prior to the historical Buddha; others say that he is the 52nd. His original name means "Creator of Light."

A number of caves in China contain ancient depictions of Dingguang Fo, demonstrating that devotion to him has a long history.

DIRECTIONS OF THE COMPASS In Buddhist myth, the four directions of the Earth are guarded by the FOUR GUARDIAN KINGS (called by some heavenly kings or gods). The gods are *deva*, or heavenly kings that predate BUDDHISM and were passed along from India (see CYCLE OF SIXTY and FIVE DIRECTIONS).

DIVINATION Methods of seeing the future. These can take the form of receiving messages from the ancestors or the gods, reading signs, or some other sort of fortune-telling. Divination methods in ancient China included reading ORACLE BONES, interpreting yarrow stalks according to the I CHING, and reading the cycles of time with horoscopes.

It should not be thought that all people believed in divination or luck, or even that those who used divination always followed its dictates. In one famous story, King WU consulted the fortune-tellers before he was about to attack the SHANG. The priest shook his head and predicted bad luck.

Wu threw the stalks and oracle bones (in this case tortoise shells) aside: "What do they know about luck?" he declared.

Wu won the war.

DIVINE FARMER See SHEN NONG.

DIVINE ARCHER See YI.

DIYA (DIMU) One of the two mythical servants of WEN ZHANG, the Chinese god of literature. Diya means "Earth Mute." She helps Wen Zhang mark his examination papers. She serves with TIAN LONG, whose name means "Heaven Deaf." The two servants could be relied on to keep the examination questions a secret.

In a different myth, Diya and Tian Long are mentioned as the mother and father of all the other creatures and human beings on EARTH. Diya is sometimes called Dimu, which means "Earth Mother."

DIZANG (DIZANG WANG, DIZANG WENG, TI-TS'ANG WANG) According to Buddhist myth, Dizang is the BODHISATTVA who keeps the faithful from hell's tortures and who brings them to Pure Earth HEAVEN. Because of his actions, Dizang is considered one of the bodhisattvas of compassion. He was also considered the first lord or king of hell by many Chinese Buddhists and others, taking the place YANLOU WANG holds for other Buddhists (see TEN KINGS OF HELL).

According to a Chinese SUTRA, or sacred Buddhist text, regarding Dizang called the Dizang Sutra, the bodhisattva was born as a girl to a high-caste family in India. Unfortunately, her mother did not lead a pious or moral life, and she was condemned to hell. The girl learned of her mother's tortures and was so appalled that she swore to save all from hell. She was made a bodhisattva by BUDDHA. Dizang journeyed to hell, lessening punishments and arguing against the kings of hell on behalf of souls, to decrease their penances.

Though the myth details her birth as a girl, as a bodhisattva, Dizang is always shown as male. Dizang is a Chinese version of the Buddhist figure known as Kshitigarbha in India and elsewhere.

DOG One of the symbolic animals of the Chinese CALENDAR and a frequent figure in folktales and popular myth. The dog was admired for its quality of loyalty to its master. Some ancient Chinese believed that a stray dog who came onto their property was a sign of future prosperity. But it could also be seen as a pest and scavenger.

One common myth and folk belief held that a "heavenly dog," usually identified with a star god, roamed the world in search of children to eat. Tokens were hung to keep him away (see YI).

Many Chinese EMPERORS and empresses kept dogs as pets. These palace dogs were treated as if they were royal children. By contrast, in parts of southern China, dogs were eaten for food. In MONGOLIA and

Many in ancient China believed that the Heavenly Dog could steal children if they were not properly protected.

Manchuria, dogs were bred for their skins, much like minks are in Western countries.

DONG WANG GONG (TUNG WANG KUNG)
The god of the IMMORTALS in Chinese mythology. He is said to keep a book of all Immortals, who, according to Taoist belief, have achieved purity and live forever. Dong Wang Gong is said to live in KUNLUN in a beautiful palace and to be married to XI WANG MU, the Queen Mother of the West.

DONGYUE DADI (DONG-YO DA-DI, T'AI SHAN)
The god who lives in TAI SHAN, the sacred eastern mountain.

As the head of the HEAVENLY MINISTRY OF FIVE PEAKS, Dongyue Dadi was believed to be ultimately responsible for all human activities. (See MIN-ISTRIES OF GODS). He and his staff of lesser gods and immortals supervised birth, death, and everything important in between. At some points in history, he was worshipped as the second most powerful celestial god after the Jade Emperor, Yu Huang. Artists often portray Dongyue Dadi sitting on a throne, wearing the richly embroidered robes of an emperor.

There are numerous stories connected with the god. One said he was the grandson of YU HUANG, the mythological Jade Emperor.

Dongyue Dadi's daughter, SHENG MU, was said to be in charge of the welfare of women and children and was very popular in her own right.

Dongyue Dadi was identified with three different historical figures, Yuan Changlong (Yüan Ch'ang-lung), Marshal Tang Zhen (Marshal T'ang Ch'en),

The God of the Eastern Peak, a powerful figure in Chinese mythology (The Dragon, Image, and Demon, 1886)

and Huang Feihu (Huang Fei-hu), all of whom served early EMPERORs. Other names for the mountain god include Tang yueh Ta-Ti, Dong-yo da-di, the Great Emperor of the Eastern Peak, and Lord of Mount Tai (T'ai Shan Fu-chün).

There are numerous stories connected with the god. One said he was the grandson of the Yu Huang; another declared that the souls of all creatures, including humans, left the mountain at birth and returned at death. Taoist priests built a stairway of 7,000 steps up to the summit of Dongyue Dadi, erecting shrines, temples, and a huge monastery at its peak, which draws thousands of pilgrims and tourists even today.

DOOR GODS (MEN SHEN)

In popular Chinese myth, spiritual guards called *men shen* who kept DEMONS and GHOSTS out of the home. Their ancient origins are supposed to be warrior spirits who prevented doomed spirits from escaping hell.

The most common figures of door guards are life-size pictures of ferocious-looking warriors, one white, one black, dressed in full battle gear. The figures were sometimes hung on doors. A second style, featuring civilian door guards holding wooden staves, was also hung on doors to ward off spirits, especially on New Year's Eve.

According to one legend, the white-faced door god is named Qin and the black-faced one Yuo in honor of two generals who volunteered to guard the doors of the emperor Taizong of the TANG DYNASTY (A.D. 618–906). The emperor was unable to sleep, because a pack of demons and spirits were causing a ruckus outside the bedroom. The next day, a grateful emperor thanked the guards for quieting the mischievous spirits. Concerned, though, that the men had had no sleep, he asked a painter to draw their pictures. The demons were unable to tell the difference.

DOU MU (T'IEN MU, TAO MU, TOU MU)

"Mother of the Great Wagon." A Chinese goddess who is said to keep the book that records the life and death of each person on EARTH. Also known as the Human Sovereign, T'ien Mu, Tao Mu, and Bushel Mother, North Star, she is the goddess of the North Star in Chinese mythology. She is shared by several traditions. According to Taoist belief, Dou Mu shone with light when she reached understanding of the

Yuo and Qin, the two generals who guard doors in Chinese myth (The Dragon, Image, and Demon, *1886*)

celestial mysteries. According to Buddhists, she is the Goddess of Light. Some Christians claimed that she was Mary, the virgin mother of Jesus. She is shown in art on a LOTUS throne wearing a Buddhist crown. She also appears with three eyes and 18 arms. She holds the books of life and death, controlling the days of humans.

DOU SHEN (TOU SHEN)

Celestial ministry of smallpox in Chinese myth. Dou Shen is also the name of the head of the MINISTRY OF GODS in charge of the disease. Gods in this ministry were thought to keep smallpox, a serious disease for which there was no cure, at bay (see MEDICINE).

DRAGON

Known by many names in Chinese mythology: Lung Meng, Long Wang, Na-achia, and NAGA. The dragon is a symbol of strength, goodness, and the spirit of change.

Dragons changed quite a bit in Chinese mythology through the centuries. At first, all were helpful and beloved water gods. In later centuries, there were two kinds of dragons, the old friendly dragons and a new breed of terrifying winged serpents of the mountains. The negative view of dragons, it is said by scholars, followed the influence of BUDDHISM, in which they were identified with harmful powers and spirits.

In ancient Chinese myth dating to the prehistoric period, dragons were presented as serpents with a horse's head, two horns, and a pearl in the center of the forehead. The earliest dragons had no wings but could fly by magic. They brought rain to the crops, blew their misty breath across the marshes, lived at the bottoms of large lakes and seas, and kept the rivers flowing to the villages and cities. The gods and IMMORTALS rode on dragons' backs across the seas from the sacred islands where they lived or flew on their backs to visit the HEAVENS. The legendary EMPERORS were said to travel in fancy CHARIOTS pulled by dragons. The mythical emperor YU, founder of the XIA DYNASTY, was supposed to have been born as a winged dragon. Emperors after him claimed to be descendants of the dragon.

It was a high honor for a person to be given an honorary dragon name. People complimented excellent scholars by saying that they used their

Dragons come in many sizes and shapes in Chinese myths. This beast is a "chiao" type—very serpentlike.

pen like a dragon's tail—which meant they had superior abilities.

The dragon is associated with the east, the direction of sunrise and, in general, positive actions. Some ancient Chinese held dragon processions or festivals, welcoming the dragons and their life-giving rains back each spring. People also painted dragons with four claws on the doors of temples and on the walls surrounding villages and towns to invite the rains and to keep these places safe from harm. Dragons were embroidered on the robes of certain powerful officials and military heroes. The Chinese emperors had their own pattern, dragons with five claws on each leg. It became a crime for anyone but the emperor to wear an image of a dragon with five claws. These imperial dragons were painted on the royal palaces, embroidered on the royal family's robes, and used to decorate the royal plates, porcelain vases, and other household items. When painting pictures of dragons, it was said to be important not to paint the dragon's eyes or else the painting would come to life and shake itself off the wall, which would then crumble into dust.

Another belief seen in some early myths was the dragon's power to change its size and shape—it could be as tiny as a silkworm or as huge as the entire sky (see SHAPE SHIFTING). It could also become invisible whenever it chose, a handy quality in war.

According to folk belief, once a year, the dragons flew to the heavens to make their annual reports to the supreme gods of heaven. Apparently, they were so big and clumsy that no other gods wanted to visit heaven when the dragons were there.

The Shuo Wen (Simple and compound characters explained) dictionary of A.D. 200 catalogues three species of mythical dragons: The most powerful is the *long*, which dominated the sky. The hornless *li* species lived in the ocean. The scaly *chiao* species was more like a serpent and lived in the mountains and marshes.

The portrayal of dragons turned more negative as Buddhism spread through China. The Indian *naga*, or dragon, was most often associated with evil or destruction. In these stories, *nagas* were terrifying, spiteful dragons of the mountains. They guarded fantastic treasures, fought with the *garuda*, or vulture, which in China became associated with LEI GONG, the god of thunder, and raided the villages.

Buddhists made a distinction between the evil mountain dragons, which made trouble for the people, and water dragons, which were considered beneficial. They also brought the myths of eight dragon kings of India. Nanda (called Nan-t'o by the Chinese) was the chief of the eight Naga-raga, or dragon kings. With four heads (one wearing a serpent crown) and six arms (with two hands holding a serpent and two hands holding a bow for shooting arrows), Nanda was a fierce enemy.

Still these dragon kings were more reasonable creatures than the mountain *nagas*. They ruled their own underwater kingdoms and lived in palaces built in caves under the sea, where they were often visited by deities and immortals.

As time went on, myths about dragons became more and more complicated. Later writers counted 10 different kinds. Each had its own specialized task. The celestial dragon, *t'ien-lung*, protected the gods and their heavenly palaces. The earth dragon, *ti-lung*, ruled over the streams and rivers. The spiritual dragon, *shen-lung*, had the power to determine how much rain and wind to bring and was worshipped regularly on the first and 15th day of each month.

There was a special dragon for each of the Four Seas of China: Ao Kuang controlled the Eastern Sea and was the greatest of the dragon kings, Ao Chin ruled the Southern Sea, Ao Chun controlled the Northern Sea, and Ao Jun controlled the Western Sea.

In one popular myth, Ao Kuang has an unlucky encounter with the great hunter NAZHA, the mischievous "Third Prince," who was charged with the task of ridding the world of demons and evil serpents. Nazha had a quick temper, which led him to kill Ao Kuang's son, AO BING. Nazha plucked out the dragon's tendons and wove them into a trophy belt, which he wore on special occasions. Ao Kuang demanded that Nazha apologize, but the proud warrior would not. Instead he fought the dragon king, trampled his body, stripped off his clothing, and skinned him alive. Overwhelmed with pain, the dragon king begged for mercy, and Nazha spared his life on one condition: that Ao Kuang turn himself into a little blue snake, which Nazha could take home in his sleeve as a prize. Even though he was defeated, Ao Kuang was widely worshipped in China.

Other dragons were worshipped in different ways. The Pu lao sea dragon was carved on the tops of gongs and bells, which were said to resemble the dragon's loud cry when attacked by its enemy, the whale. The symbol for the water-loving Chi Wen dragon was often painted on the roofs of houses to protect against fires.

Among different stories of Buddhist dragons is the myth of the Golden Dragon King, who was the nephew of an empress. The dragon was forced to run away when the Mongol troops conquered the region. He disguised himself as a Buddhist monk but decided to drown himself in a stream to avoid capture. His body was buried at the foot of the Gold Dragon mountain. One hundred years later, according to his own prophecy, he came to the rescue of Hung Wu, founder of the Ming dynasty, by hurling a swarm of bees at the Mongols and helping defeat their army.

Another Buddhist story concerns the birth of the White Dragon, Bai Long, or "White Thundercloud." According to the tale, the dragon's mother was a human who lived during the fourth century A.D. She was raped by an elderly man on a stormy night and was kicked out of her home by her upset parents. She wandered for a year, begging for her supper before giving birth to the dragon. She was literally frightened to death by the sight of the monster she had given birth to.

Full of grief, the White Dragon unleashed a violent hurricane over the land, then flew up to the summit of the hill and vanished. The neighbors buried the White Dragon's mother at the foot of the hill, later known as Dragon's Peak. Legends say the White Dragon visited his mother's tomb each year on his birthday, the 18th day of the third month of the year. The spot became a favorite place for religious pilgrims. A temple erected on a summit in Hunan is the site for an annual Buddhist festival held on the White Dragon's birthday. A popular legend says the White Dragon appears as a thunderstorm each year for 10 days before the festival.

DRAGON DRIVER   A poetical phrase for gods or deities, sometimes used in ancient Chinese poetry or tales. Since DRAGONS were heavenly beasts of great power, they were naturally the choice a heavenly being might make to pull her or his CHARIOT.

DRAGON GATE   According to the myths of YU, as he worked to control the floods, he opened a path in the mountains. This was called Dragon Gate. It was said that carp who jumped through this gate (or over the dam) became DRAGONS.

DROUGHT   In a nation depending on AGRICULTURE to survive, lack of rain can be fatal. Drought in ancient China was sometimes seen as the result of sins committed by the sovereign or king. A mythic story told after the TANG DYNASTY said that one such period lasted seven years. Finally, DIVINATION declared that the only thing that would end the drought was human sacrifice.

The emperor declared that he would sacrifice himself for his people, since that was his duty. He prepared a fire and purified himself, then laid down on the logs. Just as the fire started, the gods sent a downpour of rain, ending the drought.

DROUGHT FURY   The daughter of YING LONG, the Responding Dragon, who helped Huang Di, the YELLOW EMPEROR, in his battle against CHIYOU. She was able to stop or control the rain. She is also called Nü Ba, "Daughter of Heaven."

DUKE OF ZHOU (DUKE OF CHOU, CHOU T'AI-KUNG)   The Duke of Zhou was WU's brother and adviser, helping as Wu overthrew the SHANG ruler. He also acted as a powerful advocate for his brother's son.

DUOWEN (VAIŚRAVANA)   The Chinese name for Vaiśravana, the GUARDIAN KING of the North in Buddhist mythology. Duowen is the leader of the Guardian Kings, who defend the faithful from the four sides of the EARTH. His exceptional powers allowed him to hear all that happened in the universe. Because he is black, he is sometimes called the black king or warrior. (Some artworks, however, show him with pink skin.) Duowen has dominion over winter.

Scholars trace Duowen to the Indian god Kuvera, who was the patron of wealth and treasure in ancient Indian mythology. The god is also seen as a Buddhist version of Molishou, a Taoist deity with similar features. His Tibetan names are Rnam thos-kyi Bu and Rnam Thos-sras. In Mongolia he is known as Bisman Tengri.

DU YU (TU YÜ, TU YU, WANG)   A mythic king of SHU, the region now known as Szechwan.

The myths relate how one day Du Yu came down from HEAVEN. While he was in a city called Jiang-yuan, a girl named Li stepped from a well. He married her, then declared himself king of Shu, or Emperor Wang.

After Du Yu had been ruling for 100 years, Pie Ling, a man in another Chinese kingdom, died. His corpse magically appeared in Shu. Du Yu made him his prime minister. While Pie Ling was trying to control flooding on Jade Mountain, Du Yu had an affair with Pie Ling's wife. Du Yu was so ashamed that he gave up his throne to Pie Ling and left the empire. Pie Ling ruled as Emperor Kai-ming.

According to the popular myth, Du Yu was changed into a bird called the Zigui (*tzu-kuei*) in Chinese. (The bird is usually called a "cuckoo" in English translations, because of the pun between *cuckoo* and *cuckold*, a term for adultery.)

DYNASTIES   Scholars divide China's history into several periods, normally referred to as dynasties. The dynasties were the families or sets of rulers who governed China during that period.

The rulers of the earliest periods are legendary or mythical; no evidence has yet been found to link them to real people. Anthropologists and archaeologists have done considerable work to uncover information about these periods, and it is possible that the historical record will one day extend to this period.

The Chinese dynasties are generally given as:

Legendary/Mythological Periods   Early mythical emperors include SHEN NONG, YAN DI, Huang Di (the YELLOW EMPEROR), SHAO HAO, GAO YANG, and DI KU. (This period is sometimes described as lasting from 2953 to 2357 B.C. The dates are recorded in later annals.)

The Three Kings of the GOLDEN AGE are YAO, SHUN, and YU. (This period is sometimes described as lasting from 2347 to 2205 B.C. The dates are not historical, but they are recorded in later annals.)

Yu is said to have started the XIA DYNASTY, also called the Hsia, Yu, and Jie.

Historical Periods

SHANG, or Yin, dynasty: c. 1766–1050 B.C.

Western CHOU, or ZHOU, dynasty: 1045–771 B.C.

Eastern CHOU, or Zhou, dynasty: 770–221 B.C.

Chun Qui (Period of the SPRING AND AUTUMN Annals): 770–476 B.C.

Period of the WARRING STATES: 475–221 B.C.

QIN, or Ch'in (Shih Huang-ti): 221–206 B.C.

Western HAN: 202 B.C.–A.D. 9

Xin or Hsin dynasty (also known as the Interregnum): A.D. 9–23

Eastern HAN: A.D. 25–220

The period from the end of the Han dynasty to the beginning of the Sui dynasties was a period of great change and turmoil. During this time, China split into many different kingdoms. Historians use several names to describe the many different governments during the roughly two centuries of this period; the main names are the Wei, Jin, and Northern and Southern dynasties. The Wei dynasty—also known as San Kuo or Shu Han—extends from A.D. 221 to 265, and the Jin or Chin dynasty A.D. 265–420. Afterwards, the conflicts between the different states in the northern and southern portions of the country brought about a variety of different rulers and kingdoms. The Sui clan reestablished order and reunited the country under Yang Chien (541–604), who is called WEN ZHONG.

These dynasties followed:

Sui dynasty: 581–618

TANG (or T'ang) dynasty: 618–906

Five dynasties: 907–960

Northern Song dynasty: 960–1126

Southern Song dynasty: 1126–1279

Yuan dynasty (also called the Mongol Dynasty): 1279–1368

Ming dynasty: 1368–1644

QING dynasty (also called the Manchu dynasty): 1644–1912

EARTH The ancient Chinese saw the Earth as square, with the four sides bounded by mountains.

According to early Chinese myth, the mythic emperor YÜ ordered that the Earth be measured. The accounts give different measures about how far it might be. One from the second century B.C. declares the distance between the east and west pole as 233,500 LI (about a third of a mile) and 75 paces, with the same measurement north to south.

EARTH GOD One of the lowest ranking of the Chinese gods; considered a local deity who protected small towns and villages. The god was also said to control the wealth and fortune of the common people.

In ancient times, every small village kept a statue or likeness of the Earth God on the altar of its local temple. Artists portray him as a kindly old man with a snowy white beard, sitting on a throne and holding a crooked wooden staff in one hand and a pot of gold in the other.

People would pray to the Earth God for help with things that affected their lives or their work. At times, they would bring the god's likeness from its altar to the site of a disaster or problem so that the Earth God could "see" and thus understand what needed to be done.

EASTERN PEAK GOD See DONGYUE DADI.

EGG Occasionally in Chinese myth, gods or figures who are the result of unions between humans and deities are hatched from an egg. The egg that hatched PANGU at the dawn of creation was the COSMIC EGG (see CREATION MYTHS).

EIGHT BUDDHIST EMBLEMS A series of emblems or designs often found in Buddhist decorations. They are the wheel (also known as the chakra), conch shell, umbrella, canopy, LOTUS, vase, paired FISH, and endless MYSTIC KNOT. Each emblem can be seen as a symbol for an important idea or a feature of BUDDHISM. For example, the lotus FLOWER is often seen as a symbol of ENLIGHTENMENT, and the wheel symbolizes the cycle of birth and rebirth (see REBIRTH AND REINCARNATION). The designs can be highly stylized when used as decorations.

EIGHT DIAGRAMS (EIGHT TRIGRAMS) A system of DIVINATION used in reading yarrow stalks (see I CHING.)

EIGHTFOLD PATH The things in Buddhism that a person must do to win release from the cycle of rebirth and find NIRVANA (see REBIRTH AND REINCARNATION). The eight steps on the path are expressed in many different ways, but one way of thinking of them is as follows:

1. Have the right understanding. To do this, a person must know the FOUR NOBLE TRUTHS.
2. Resolve or think properly. To do this, a person must not be fooled by the illusions of self.
3. Speak properly. To do this, a person must not lie or be frivolous about the truth.
4. Act properly. To do this, a person must not hurt living things, including other people, and must relieve suffering.
5. Have the right work. A person's job must be in keeping with Buddhist teaching—it cannot, for example, violate other steps on the Eightfold Path.
6. Make the right effort. To do this, a person must strive for ENLIGHTENMENT, despite obstacles.

7. Keep the right mindfulness. To do this, a person must know the dangers of distracting thoughts and physical states and avoid them.
8. Have the right concentration in meditation. To do this, a person must abandon pleasure as well as pain. The devout Buddhist must be alert to the truth, which is beyond mere joyful meditation.

EIGHT IMMORTALS   See BA XIAN.

EIGHT PILLARS   In ancient Chinese myth, the sky was said to be held up by eight pillars or mountains. GONG GONG destroyed one (BUZHOU), touching off a flood.

ELEMENTS   See FIVE ELEMENTS.

ELEPHANT   In Chinese legends and mythology, the elephant symbolizes strength, wisdom, and prudence.

The road that led to the tombs of the Ming EMPERORS, near the cities of Beijing and Nanking, was lined with giant stone statues, including standing and sitting elephants. Many childless women of this dynastic period (1368–1644) believed that if they wedged a stone on the back of one of these elephant statues, they would give birth to a baby boy.

The elephant is considered a sacred animal in BUDDHISM. Myths describe the BUDDHA entering the right side of his immaculate mother Maya in the form of a white elephant at his conception. Artists have portrayed Buddha riding on the back of an elephant.

ELIXIR OF ETERNAL LIFE   The ancient Chinese, especially followers of TAOISM, believed that a variety of elements could be made into potions that would allow someone to become immortal or to live to a very old age. These elements included the metals of CINNABAR and gold, stones of JADE and powdered mother-of-pearl, the waters of certain legendary streams and fountains, and the commonly found herb ginseng, as well as a species of fungus called "Plant of Long Life." Some of the formulas were less powerful, yielding not immortality but a long life, past the age of 100.

One legend about the MOON says a HARE was employed there by the gods to mix the right combination of drugs to create the elixir of life. (Ancient Chinese believed that they could see a rabbit on the Moon, formed by the craters and shadows.)

EMPEROR   Chinese society was ruled by a king or emperor, who ran the country with the help of a court of officials and bureaucrats. The emperors were considered to rule with a mandate from HEAVEN and generally traced their ancestors back to early gods.

The power of the emperor varied during the different historical periods, but in general emperors had the power of life and death over many of their people. In the prehistory period, this might have meant that a high-ranking official would literally go to the grave with the emperor. Later emperors were usually buried with many statues representing the officials, troops, and helpers they would need to command in the AFTERLIFE.

A number of prehistoric or legendary emperors appear in Chinese myth, including Emperor YAO and the FIVE EMPERORS.

EMPEROR WANG   See DU YU.

EMPEROR YAO   See YAO.

EMPRESS OF HEAVEN   See QUEEN OF HEAVEN.

EMPRESS WU   Empress Wu, or Wu Zhao (Wu Chao) (c. 627–705), ruled during the TANG DYNASTY. Starting as a consort (one of the lesser wives) of the emperor Gaozong (Kao-tsung) (628–83), she managed to oust the empress and replace her after her death. She increased her influence after the emperor became ill. After his death, she manipulated two successors and finally took over herself in 690.

Although she achieved her position through intrigue, this was a period of more freedom and importance for Chinese women in general. It was a short-lived period, however.

ENLIGHTENMENT   In BUDDHISM, the term *enlightenment* is used to describe a special state of understanding. Achieving this understanding frees one from the chains of ordinary existence. Since enlightenment can only truly be understood by those who have obtained it, it is usually spoken of in

metaphors. It is sometimes called "reaching NIR-VANA," the blessed state of understanding.

BODHISATTVAS are those who have achieved enlightenment but have delayed their final entrance into Nirvana so that they may help human beings.

ERLANG (EHR-LANG) Chinese guardian god who sets the hounds of HEAVEN on any evil spirits. He is related by his mother to the Jade Emperor, YU HUANG.

EXORCIST An exorcist is someone who chases DEMONS away, from either a human or a place. Exorcists have a long history in China, stretching far back into prehistoric times. Much Taoist MEDICINE involved exorcism, since disease was thought to be caused by demons. According to later Chinese mythology, exorcisms were under the control of the celestial ministry of exorcism, CHU XIE YUAN (see MINISTRIES OF GODS).

F

FANG CHANG   See PENG LAI.

FANG-FENG   A god in ancient Chinese myth. Fang-feng had the misfortune to come late to the very first assembly of gods called by YU. He was put to death.

FANG HSUN   See YAO.

FAN WANG   In Buddhist myth, said to be the father of all living things. He is not the highest god, however; that role is reserved for BUDDHA.

Fan Wang was said to have hatched the universe from a cosmic egg much as a hen sets on an egg.

FARMER GOD   See SHEN NONG.

FA SHI *(FA SHIH)*   A folk priest or magician (see FOLK RELIGION; TAOIST FOLK BELIEFS).

FEI LIAN (FEI LIEN)   A god of wind in Chinese myth. He is sometimes seen as a DRAGON and sometimes as a bird that has the tail of a snake.

He helps CHIYOU in a great battle against his enemy Huang Di, the YELLOW EMPEROR (see FENG BO).

FENG BO (FENG PO)   A god of the wind and the constellation Chi in Chinese myth. Feng Bo has several identities. He is said to be a DRAGON named FEI LIAN or a creature of the same name with a bird's head and the tail of a snake. He is also called Chi Po, the STAR god.

There is a Chinese belief that the wind blows when the MOON leaves Chi's constellation associated with the constellation of Sagittarius, which may be connected to the myth.

Feng Bo is commanded by CHIYOU, a war god, in some myths. He was portrayed in different ways by artists, perhaps most often as an old man carrying a sack of cold wind, which he would point in the direction he wanted it to blow. In North and Central China, artists showed him riding a TIGER. But in some depictions he holds a pair of fans to produce gentle breezes.

FENG DU DADI (FENG TU TA TI)   A god of the underworld in Taoist mythology. He interviews all souls entering the AFTERLIFE and files reports to the Jade Emperor, YU HUANG, and the god of the eastern peak, DONGYUE DADI.

Feng Du Dadi was identified with a rebel named Chu Bawang during the JIN DYNASTY.

FENG HUANG   The Chinese PHOENIX.

FENG MENG (FENG MEN)   A great archer in Chinese myth, who learned the skill from YI. However, he is said to have grown jealous of Yi's greater mastery of ARCHERY. He made a bat from a piece of PEACH wood and killed Yi. It is said that from that point on DEMONS were scared of peach wood, which is why the wood was used in TAOISM for EXORCISMS.

FENG PO PO   A female wind god in Chinese myth. She is an old woman who rides a TIGER through the sky.

FENG SHUI (FENG-SHUI)   Literally, "wind-water"; the basic forces active in the EARTH that can help humans.

Feng shui is a Chinese folk belief that specifies ways of organizing buildings to take advantage of wind-water forces according to geographic location. Positive and negative forces interact in sometimes complex ways.

Feng shui supplies a blueprint for where everything from outhouses to palaces should be built. Locating parts of a house in certain directions are considered bad luck; for example, it is thought that putting a door in the northeast corner of a house allows evil spirits to enter.

Part of feng shui's importance in ancient China came from the belief that the Earth, like people, is a living being. In this view, it has veins and arteries just like the human body. Positive energy—QI—passes through these veins in the earth. While the course of the energy is winding, it is possible to tap into it by locating oneself very precisely on the earth. On the other hand, SHA, or the evil nature, moves through the earth as well. *Sha* seems to prefer humanmade paths, such as ditches or roads, and tends to move in straight lines, but only a trained practioner can properly "read" the geography to determine how the energy flows.

The practioners of feng shui were called Feng-shui hsien-sheng—Wind-water gentlemen. Feng shui is a type of geomancy, which combines geography with DIVINATION, or fortune-telling.

FENG TU TA TI See FENG DU DADI.

FIRECRACKER A canister of gun powder rolled up in paper (usually red BAMBOO paper in ancient China) that explodes when lit. Firecrackers were used to scare away evil spirits in all kinds of religious ceremonies, on holidays (such as the New Year), at funerals, and as a farewell when a popular person or visiting government official left a town. Fireworks have been used in China since the seventh century.

FIRE DRILLER (SUI REN, SUI-JEN) According to very early Chinese myth, a supernatural being called by mythologists the Fire Driller (or Sui Ren or Sui-jen) brought the knowledge of fire to humans. The importance of fire and its connection to food is celebrated in his basic myth:

The Fire Driller came from a faraway land, a paradise where there was no such thing as day or night and no seasons to divide the year. A tree called Sui-wood grew in that land. The branches of the tree could be rubbed together easily to make fire.

The Fire Driller traveled from the land to China. A wise man, he gave food to all creatures who needed it. One day he came to a tree and saw a bird that looked like an OWL. The bird began pecking at the tree, and suddenly flames shot from it.

The Fire Driller realized that fire could be started from the branches, just as in the paradise he had come from. So he took a twig and drilled it into another branch, starting a fire.

The technique described in the myth for starting fire is an ancient one but is still taught in some wilderness classes. Friction from a smaller stick can cause shavings, sawdust, or similar material in a large branch, generally held on the ground, to smolder. The procedure makes it appear as if one stick is being drilled into the other.

The Fire Driller brought fire to humans in Chinese myth. (The Dragon, Image, and Demon, *1886*)

FIRE GODS   There were a large number of gods associated with fire in China, with most communities having a local fire deity. Celebrations honoring the fire god lasted for several days each year in the eighth month of the Chinese CALENDAR. The streets were hung with lanterns and lamps in the god's honor, and prayers were offered in hopes of preventing fires.

SHEN NONG was at times called the "Fire God" or "Fire Emperor," perhaps because his imperial sign was said to be the symbol for fire. He is sometimes confused with YAN DI, the Flame Emperor, another early mythological figure.

In later Chinese myth, HUO BU, the Chinese name for the ministry of fire (see MINISTRIES OF GODS) was run by the god LUO XUAN, the "Stellar Sovereign of Fire Virtue." He had five assistants, who were identified with early Chinese ministers of the ZHOU DYNASTY or earlier periods.

Artists portray him in various ways, sometimes as an animal with a human face, except for a third eye located in the center of his forehead, accompanied by two DRAGONS. Others show him with a human body, a fierce, red face, and a third eye. He or his attendants are often shown holding a variety of fire-connected symbols, including a pair of birds, a round fire wheel or fireball with sparks shooting out of it, a fiery serpent, a fan with a fiery plume at the top, and a writing implement and pad to take note of the places he intended to burn down.

FISH   A token of wealth and abundance in Chinese myth and lore, as well as a symbol for harmony, reproduction, and marital happiness.

The ancient Chinese carved stone, wood, and PEACH pits in the shape of a fish to use as CHARMS of good fortune. Temple courtyards often contained pools or ponds filled with carp or goldfish to signify abundance and harmony. The carp was considered a symbol of perseverance and skill in the martial arts.

FIVE   Many NUMBERS in ancient China gained special importance because of how they related to ideas of how the universe was organized. The number five was extremely important, because it was the number common to many things—there were thought to be five senses, five planets (all that were visible at the time), FIVE DIRECTIONS, and FIVE ELE-MENTS, or agencies, underlying the universe. This led to other groupings thought to be significant or in some way related to the others, such as the five emperors who together demonstrated all of the qualities of a perfect ruler.

Through this process, the number itself took on special significance, as did many others.

FIVE AGENCIES   See FIVE ELEMENTS.

FIVE DIRECTIONS   Besides north, south, east, and west, ancient Chinese myth and literature often speak of "center" as a fifth direction. (Occasionally, this is given as "sky" or even "up" in translations.)

FIVE ELEMENTS (WU HSING, WU XING) According to ancient Chinese COSMOLOGY, the forces that animate the EARTH. Like YIN AND YANG, they are live energies that interrelate in recurring patterns. The five are earth, wood, metal, fire, and water. They activate other groups of five, such as the five COLORS. The system was important in Taoist philosophy and was commonly accepted for much of Chinese history.

The Chinese term *wu hsing* is sometimes translated as "five agencies" to better convey the idea that these elements are seen as forces rather than as static chemical states. They are also called the five phases or processes. According to the earliest inclusion in the classic Chinese SHUJING (*Classic of History*), these phases work in the following way: Water produces (or nurtures) wood but destroys (or extinguishes) fire; fire produces (or renews) earth but destroys (or melts) metal; metal produces (or helps retain) water but destroys (or helps chop down) wood; wood produces fire but destroys earth; and earth produces metal but destroys (or soaks up) water.

FIVE GREAT BUDDHAS OF WISDOM The English term for the five conquerors revered as manifestations of the BUDDHA spirit. Some see them as symbolizing the five great moments in the historical Buddha's life; others believe that they represent the five Buddhas who preceded the historical Buddha on Earth. Each is associated with an earthly direction—north, south, east, and west, along with the fifth direction of "center." They can also be seen as symbolizing the different steps one must take before

ENLIGHTENMENT, such as awakening to the spirit and pursuing the ascetic life, or life of self-denial.

FIVE GREAT KINGS In Tibetan and Mongolian legend, a group of five brothers who became divine spirits after death. Brave warriors, they protected society and granted wishes after death.

Pe-har was the leader of the brothers. He watched over Buddhist monasteries as he prowled the mountains and countryside on his red TIGER. (In some depictions, he rides a white LION.) Choi-chung rode an ELEPHANT and was the special protector of fortune-tellers and their predictions. Dra-lha protected soldiers. The other two were Klu-dbang and Taha-'og-chos.

The five great kings are known as Sku-inga and Dam-chan in TIBET. In Mongolia they are called the Tabun Qaghar.

FIVE PEAKS Five sacred mountains, considered holy in Chinese myth from prehistoric times. WU YUE, the heavenly ministry of the Five Peaks, was said to hold power over all humans (see MINISTRIES OF GODS).

There were four originally: Heng Shan Bei in the North (in Shanxi Province), Heng Shan Nan in the South (in Hunan Province), Tai Shan in the East (in Shandong Province), and Hua Shan (in Shanxi) in the West. A fifth mountain was then added for the direction of "center," Song Shan (in Henan).

During the TANG DYNASTY, Ho Shan (in Anhui) was substituted for Heng Shan (Hunan) in the South. Afterward, Ho Shan was sometimes called Heng Shan.

The peaks were connected with numerous myths as well as religious and government ceremonies. According to Taoist writers, when the creator of the EARTH, PANGU, died, his head became Tai Shan in the East, his feet became Hua Shan in the West, his right arm and left arm became the northern and southern Heng Shan, and his stomach became the Song Shan mountain in the center of China.

Taoist priests built shrines and temples at the summit of these mountains and along the often precarious mountain paths to the top. The sacred mountain of the West has a temple at its flat-topped summit. Pilgrims (and in more recent history, tourists) must climb the 7,000 steps of "the Stairway to Heaven," lined with shrines and temples, to reach the summit of the holiest peak, Tai Shan.

Huang Di, the mythic YELLOW EMPEROR, was said to make sacrifices at the summit of Tai Shan, after driving there in a CHARIOT harnessed to six DRAGONS. That set the pattern for real EMPERORS of later historical periods who made ceremonial journeys, inspecting their realm, reinforcing the boundaries of their territory, and performing religious rituals to honor the divine mountains and their spirits.

FLAME EMPEROR See YAN DI.

FLOOD There are three main flood stories or motifs in ancient Chinese myth. The most famous stories involve YU, who rebuilt the EARTH after his father, GUN, failed in his attempt to stop a flood. A second set reveals how NÜ GUA repaired the HEAVENS and stopped a great flood. There is also the story of GONG GONG, who caused a flood with his blundering.

FLOWER Flowers are a common motif in Chinese art and depictions of myth. The goddess of flowers was called Hua Xian and is shown accompanied by servants carrying baskets of flowers. One of the BA XIAN, the Eight IMMORTALS, Lan Caihe, is also pictured holding a basket of flowers.

The Festival of Flowers, held in certain parts of China during early spring, was a ceremony performed by women and children who prepared red paper flowers or a variety of colored SILK flowers to hang on the branches of flowering shrubs in order to ensure a fruitful harvest.

According to one ancient Chinese belief, every woman on EARTH was represented in HEAVEN by a tree or flower.

FLOWERS OF THE FOUR SEASONS See FOUR FLOWERS.

FLY WHISKS In Buddhist art, priests often carry a fly whisk in their hands. It was both a symbol of the priest's religious function and a practical tool to wave away flies, which Buddhist priests were not allowed to kill. The whisk was also considered a symbol of gentle leadership, derived from the Chinese belief that a herd of deer was guided by the movement of an OX's tail. (The bristles of the whisk were usually made of the tail of an ox or yak.)

FO   A Chinese word used to describe BUDDHA. The sense is of the Buddha spirit, not the historical Buddha.

FOLK RELIGION   When studying myth and legend, scholars often make a distinction between the beliefs and practices of ordinary people and the highly organized religions followed by leaders or the elite. These distinctions can lead to interesting and important insights about different beliefs.

In studying Chinese myths, scholars sometimes use the term *folk religion* to separate ancient beliefs practiced in local areas from the "state" traditions, such as BUDDHISM and TAOISM. However, the line between them is not very neat and should not be seen as anything more than a useful guide.

In ancient China, people maintained a close relationship with the spirits of their ancestors (see ANCESTORS AND ANCESTOR CULTS). This was done in a variety of ways, including offering them sacrifices and asking for their help and advice. There were also different CULTS and sects that honored or worshipped local gods. Some of these gods were very old spirits, perhaps in the form of animals, that were seen as useful to the community. Other gods were not quite as ancient; often they were the spirits of people who had lived in the area and played an important role in the community while alive. As time passed, the image of the local god depended less on historical fact and more on the legends with which the god came to be connected. A temple might be built for the god, with elaborate customs for worshipping and soliciting aid. Certain deities who might be seen as helping the community in significant ways—bringing a good harvest, for example—would receive more attention, with more elaborate ceremonies and temples. Priests who could talk with spirits to gain their favor presided over ceremonies to help the faithful communicate with them.

It was not considered a contradiction to honor a local deity any more than it was considered a contradiction to honor one's ancestors as well as the emperor. Thus one could be a Buddhist and still go to a temple to ask a local spirit for rain. Different practices mixed together, and, in many cases, the organized religion borrowed rituals and ideas from the local or folk religions.

For example, what scholars call the folk religion of the spirits (*shen chia*) included a wide range of practices and deities similar to those in Taoism and undoubtedly was influenced by it. In the same way, Taoism was inspired by and sometimes grew from these basic folk beliefs. The ritual practices of a *fa shi*, or folk priest, were often called "little rites" by Taoist priests, who practiced the "great rites" or rituals.

FOOLISH OLD MAN   See YUGONG.

FOUNDING MYTHS   Myths that explain how a nation, culture, CLAN, or group of leaders came to be. Such myths may combine elements of history with legend and differ from CREATION MYTHS, which seek to explain the beginning of the world. They usually emphasize traits or things the nation or civilization feels are important. In ancient China, each new DYNASTY, or group of leaders, had important founding myths about their origins. These myths generally shared several characteristics. They showed how the clan could trace its ancestors back to deities. They usually justified the overthrow of the last emperor by demonstrating that he was unjust and unworthy. They showed that the first ruler of the line was a hero. Although they contained mythical aspects, they were usually presented as historical fact.

For some different founding myths, see XIE, HOU JI, KING ZHOU OF THE SHANG, KING HAI, KONG JIA, LORD OF THE GRANARY, TANG THE CONQUEROR, WEN, WU, XIA DYNASTY, and XIE.

FOUR BOOKS   A special grouping of works that formed the study of CONFUCIANISM for many years. They include the *Analects, Ta hsüeh* (Great learning), *Chung Yung* (also written as Chung-yung, ["The Great mean"]), and *Meng-tzu* (or "Book of Mencius," a work by early Confucian teacher Master Meng or Mencius). The grouping was emphasized by ZHU XI.

FOUR EMPERORS   Mythical kings in Chinese mythology said to have fought against Huang Di, the YELLOW EMPEROR.

According to the tales, Huang Di did not want to fight these rulers. But they paraded around his city walls wearing their armor. They refused to back off. Finally, he decided he had to fight or else he would lose his kingdom. The EMPERORS were quickly destroyed.

The emperors are identified as TAI HAO, god of the East; YAN DI, the Flame Emperor and, in this story, god of the South; SHAO HAO, god of the West; and GAO YANG, god of the North.

FOUR FLOWERS
A grouping of FLOWERS sometimes mentioned in Chinese myth and seen in paintings and decorative art. They are the camellia, peony, LOTUS, and chrysanthemum. Each is connected with a season—camellia with winter, peony with spring, lotus with summer, and chrysanthemum with fall. The gardenia and sometimes the Chinese PLUM tree are occasionally mentioned instead of camellia. The group is also called the flowers of the four seasons.

FOUR KINGS OF HEAVEN (DIAMOND KINGS OF HEAVEN)
Originally a Buddhist group of temple guardians, the Four Kings of Heaven, or Si Da Tian Wang, appear in Chinese mythology as powerful gods able to take on different shapes. The deities are Duo Wen, the Black Warrior, who guards the North, a place of treasure; Zen Chang, the southern spirit, who holds an umbrella and controls rain (or darkness in some tellings); Chi Guo of the East, who commands an army of musicians; and Guang Mu of the West, who controls an army of *nagas*, or serpent gods.

FOUR NOBLE TRUTHS
The most essential beliefs in BUDDHISM. Though the truths may be phrased slightly differently, they are at the heart of all Buddhist sects and schools. The truths are interrelated:

- There is much suffering in the world. For example, people suffer from illness, old age, and death.
- Desire causes suffering. This leads to the rebirth of the soul, preventing it from reaching ENLIGHTENMENT (see REBIRTH AND REINCARNATION).
- Suffering can be ended by ending desire. Thus we can reach NIRVANA by ending desire.
- Desire can be eliminated by taking the EIGHTFOLD PATH: right understanding, right thinking, right speaking, right acting, right occupation, right effort, right mindfulness, and right concentration.

FOX
Common in northern China, foxes appear in several folk stories and mythic tales. Many ancient Chinese believed that they had supernatural powers and, when writing stories about them, showed them as crafty and cunning creatures to be avoided.

Some of the folk beliefs involved SHAPE SHIFTING. Foxes were thought to live long lives and to change shape depending on their age. At 50, a fox could assume the shape of a woman; at 100, it could become the shape of a young and beautiful girl. It was also said that at 1,000 years old, foxes were admitted to HEAVEN.

DEMONS were also commonly believed to take the shape of a fox, jumping on roofs or crawling along the beams of a home to find a soul to possess.

FU
In TAOISM, special talismans or written symbols used in ritual MEDICINE. The *fu* symbolizing a certain disease would be written on a piece of paper, then burned in a special ceremony. The ashes, mixed with water, would be swallowed as part of the cure.

It is important to note that the talisman itself was not thought to cure the patient. In effect, it was a note being sent to one of the Taoist dieties in charge of different ailments and the demons that caused them. (See MEDICINE.)

Fu is also the Chinese word for "ax." In Buddhist legend and art, axes symbolize the need to clear a path to the truth.

FU HSI
See FUXI.

FUKUROKUJO
Better known in Japan as one of the Shichi Fujukin, or "Seven Gods of Luck." Fukurokujo was a legendary Chinese Taoist HERMIT said to have lived in China during the SONG DYNASTY. Though short, Fukurokujo is shown with a massive head, symbolizing his wisdom.

FU SHEN
See FUXING.

FU TREE (FU-TREE)
In some English accounts of Chinese myths, the LEANING MULBERRY TREE, from which the SUNS are hung.

FUXI (FU HSI)
An important mythological king from prehistoric China. He is credited with a wide

Fukurokujo was a Chinese Taoist hermit who was transformed into a mythic figure in Japan. (Japan, Its Architecture, Art, and Art Manufacturers, *1882*)

range of inventions, from the CALENDAR to the fishing net, from writing to the symbols used in fortunetelling (see DIVINATION).

According to Chinese myth, Fuxi, and his sister, NÜ GUA, were the only survivors of a great FLOOD that wiped out humankind. After the flood, they became the parents of all the human beings who followed. Fuxi became the first and most famous of the legendary EMPERORS of ancient China, followed by SHEN NONG and Huang Di, the YELLOW EMPEROR.

This basic myth has been told and retold in many ways. One popular tale of Fuxi's childhood combines a flood motif with a CREATION MYTH. As the myth goes, Fuxi's father was working in the fields when he heard the first rumble of thunder. He took Fuxi and his sister into the house and went to the shed for his pitchfork and an iron cage. He hung up the cage from the rafters and waited with the pitchfork to catch the terrifying thunder god, LEI GONG. A huge clap of thunder made the house shudder. Lei Gong appeared, an ax in hand.

Fuxi's father jabbed Lei Gong with his pitchfork. The god leaped into the air and landed in the iron cage. The farmer slammed and locked the door.

The next morning, the father decided to kill the thunder god and keep him pickled in a jar. But he had no spices, so he told his children to stay away from the cage and not to give Lei Gong anything to eat or drink. As soon as he left for the market, the thunder god began to cry. He begged the children to give him something to eat.

The children said no. Then he began to whine that he was thirsty. He begged for some water to drink. Remembering their father's command, the children refused. After many hours had gone by and the father still had not returned, the children took pity on the thunder god and decided to give him one drop of water. As soon as the water touched his lips, his powers returned. With a great bellow, Lei Gong burst out of the cage. The poor children cowered in the corner, but the thunder god didn't harm them. Instead, to their amazement, he thanked them over and over again. Then he pulled out a tooth from his mouth and offered it to them. If they planted it in the ground, he said, it would grow into a GOURD. They planted it, and it immediately began to grow. Then Lei Gong thundered off, bringing the rain back in full force.

By the time their father returned home, he had to slosh through water up to his knees. When he saw that the cage was empty, the children told him what happened. He began to build a boat. Soon the water was up to his waist. He tucked the children into the magic gourd, laid them in the boat, and began to row. Up, up, up the floods rose, taking the boat straight to HEAVEN. The father began banging and thumping on heaven's door, calling for the Lord of Heaven to end the rains and remove the floods. When the Lord of Heaven heard the plea and looked out his windows, he realized that the flood would soon overtake heaven itself. So he called for the water god and ordered him to remove the flood at once.

The water god did as he was commanded, and the waters magically disappeared. But it happened so fast that the father's boat crashed to EARTH. He died from the impact. The two children, who were still tucked snugly in the gourd, survived. (Some English versions translate the name Fuxi as "Hidden Victim.") When the children began to look around, they found that they were the only people who had survived the flood.

Different tales offer different versions of what happened next. One story says the brother suggested that they marry and have children to repopulate the Earth. But Nü Gua said they would have to get permission from the gods. The couple climbed a sacred mountain, and each of them built a bonfire on its summit to get the attention of the gods. The smoke from the two fires came together into a plume that rose to heaven, and the two took it as a sign from the gods that they were supposed to marry. Time passed, and Nü Gua gave birth to a ball of flesh. Fuxi hacked the ball into pieces and built a long, long ladder to heaven. When Fuxi reached the top, the wind scattered the pieces of flesh all over the Earth. Wherever a piece landed, it became a human being, and soon the world was full of people again.

In another version, Fuxi suggested that they have children, but Nü Gua was very reluctant. After Fuxi pestered her about it, Nü Gua agreed to marry him if he could catch her. She immediately ran away, but eventually Fuxi caught her. She bore him many children, who became the subjects and descendants of Emperor Fuxi.

Fuxi's main narratives date from the ZHOU DYNASTY. During the HAN DYNASTY, he was called TAI HAO. Mythologists point out that this was also the name of an earlier god, about whom not much is known, and it is possible that several stories were combined.

Fuxi's different names suggest different meanings—"sacrifice," "victim," and "hidden" especially.

These may have to do with early mythological stories once connected to the god but now lost.

FUXING (FU SHEN) A god of happiness in Chinese mythology; one of the SAN XING (San Hsing), or three Chinese gods of good fortune. He is identified with several historical people.

The most common is YANG CHENG (Yang Ch'eng or Yang Hsi-ch'i). Yang was a court official during the reign of Emperor Wu Di (520–50). At the time, it was customary for dwarfs to be presented to the royal family as jesters. This wasn't a request one could refuse, and the number taken from Yang Cheng's home region made it hard for their families to survive. Yang is supposed to have told the EMPEROR that dwarfs were not his slaves, at which point the practice stopped. Yang was then honored as the spirit of happiness.

He is also said to be the hero GUO ZIYI, or Kuo Tzu-i (A.D. 697–781), who defeated Turkish enemies during the TANG DYNASTY. A legend attached to the warrior says that he received a visit from a goddess, who predicted that great riches and honors would come to him. He was declared a "father of the empire" after his death.

In art, he is often shown alongside a child or as a BAT, a Chinese symbol of good luck.

FU YUEH A minister of the SHANG who is said to have lived around the 12th century B.C. According to legend, he was changed into a STAR because of his wise advice. In CONFUCIANISM, Fu Yueh was used as a model for a wise minister.

G

GAN JIANG AND MO YE (KAN CHIANG AND MO YEH) A married couple who made swords in ancient Chinese myth.

Gan Jiang was asked by his king to make two swords. But he could not manage to make them after three months of attempts. The iron and gold would not fuse properly in his furnace. Finally, Mo Ye, his wife, asked what was wrong.

Gan Jiang revealed that his master had used human sacrifice to make the process work. Mo Ye cut her hair and nails, then climbed into the furnace. From that point on, the smelting went without a problem. The swords that resulted were called Gan Jiang and Mo Ye, the YIN AND YANG of swords.

Some mythologists do not interpret the myth to mean that Mo Ye actually killed herself, only that she threw her hair and nails into the fire.

Mo Ye is alive in a later story involving Gan Jiang. In that version, Gan Jiang is called by the king, who is angry with him for taking so long to make his swords. Fearing the king will kill him, Gan Jiang takes one sword but leaves the other home with his wife, who is pregnant. She is to give the sword to his son when he is born.

Sure enough, the king chops off Gan Jiang's head. The son is born and named Chi Pi. A large man with red hair, he dreams of revenge as he grows. Meanwhile, the king has a dream and learns of him. Worried that the boy will kill him, the king offers a reward if his head is brought to him.

One day, a stranger meets Chi Pi. He tells him of the reward and promises that Chi Pi will have his revenge if he allows the stranger to take his head and sword to the king. Chi Pi agrees, then slits his own throat. The stranger takes the sword to the king along with the head. They put the head in a pot; while the king looks at it, the stranger chops off the king's head.

As it plops into the pot, the stranger lops off his own. All three heads are buried together.

His name is sometimes given as "Eyebrows Twelve Inches Apart" in English, a reference to his large size.

GAO XIN (KAO HSIN) A figure in Chinese myth whose old wife had a worm removed from her ear. The worm became a DOG named PAN HU. When Gao Xin's kingdom was invaded, he pledged one of his daughters to anyone who brought him the head of his enemy. Pan Hu soon presented the enemy's head to Gao Xin. Gao Xin hesitated to carry out his promise, but his daughter and all of his advisers urged him to do so. The girl went away with Pan Hu and became his wife.

In some traditions, Gao Xin is identified as DI KU.

GAO YANG (KAO YANG, ZHUAN XU, CHUAN XU, CHUAN HSU, CHUAN HO) A sky god and mythic emperor. His descendant, PO YI, was the ancestor of the Qin dynasty. Another descendant was KUN, who was killed by the gods after trying to stop a flood.

Gao Yang had several sons who were troublesome to humans. He had three sons who died in childbirth and became ghosts. He also had a son named Tao Wu (T'ao Wu), or "the Block." He looked a bit like a very large TIGER, except that he had a human face with a PIG's mouth and tusks. He wandered the woods causing mischief and trouble. Yet another son was a lean miser, often called the Wasted Ghost. People in ancient China sometimes took pity on him, throwing out old clothes and leaving small sacrifices of rice gruel for the mythic creature.

Gao Yang is also known as Chuan Hsu. He was not himself evil or particularly cruel.

GAO YAO (KAO YAO) In Chinese myth, often cited as a model for all judges because of his fairness and devotion to justice.

Gao Yao had a one-horned ram—QILIN—who could tell if a suspect was guilty or not. The mythological unicorn would not butt innocent people but would spear the guilty.

Traditionally, Gao Yao was said to have been a judge during the reign of YAO, a mythic emperor from the GOLDEN AGE. Scholars believe that the connection of justice to the *qilin* may have come from earlier rituals, perhaps involving the sacrifice of animals, or a trial by ordeal, where a defendant had to prove his innocence in a competition, contest, or some other test.

GEESE Used as a symbol of marriage in ancient Chinese art and folktales, since the ancient Chinese believed that wild geese mated for life.

During the ZHOU DYNASTY, geese were often given as an engagement gift. When a bridegroom went to fetch his bride from her father's house, the family and couple made a ceremonial toast to the wild geese. It was also said that if wild geese flew over someone's house, good news would soon follow.

GENIE A general term for a spirit that can take human form. SHAPE SHIFTING occurs often in Chinese myth (see CHIN KUANG HSIEN).

GHOST Spirit who haunts the EARTH. In Chinese myth and folklore, these are usually spirits who for some reason did not make it to HEAVEN. This could be because proper funeral services were not held or because they suffered a particularly violent or sudden death (see GUI). In Buddhist mythology, such souls were said to haunt the Earth as "hungry ghosts." Small offerings of food were made to them to keep a person from harm.

GOD There are several words for "god" in ancient Chinese.

Di (or *Ti* in the Wade-Giles Romanization) used both before or after a name, means "divine." It has been used as part of the Chinese EMPERORS' names since the JIN DYNASTY, demonstrating the link between the emperors and divinity.

T'ien Ti—which is also written in English as *Tian Ti, Tian Di,* and *Tiandi*—means "HEAVEN god." The term can describe the god of the skies or simply a god in heaven.

The term *Shang Di* is usually used to signify the highest god in heaven.

Shen and *Huang* are also used as parts of names to mean god or a deity. *Huang* means "yellow," but the color signifies royalty. Because of this, *Huang* is often used as part of an emperor's name, signifying both his rank and divinity. Feng Huang, for example, would mean the Emperor of the Birds or the holy Emperor of the Birds.

Nü or *O* attached to a name signifies a female god.

GODS IDENTIFIED WITH HUMANS It is common practice in mythology for heroes to be given mythic powers in stories written after their deaths. Over the years, such practices can lead to their being regarded as gods or semidivine beings. This happened often in Chinese history. All of the EMPERORS in the GOLDEN AGE, for example, are presented as godlike figures, even though the figures were originally based on real people.

In China, the practice was also reversed. After a person died, he or she was sometimes identified with a god who had existed before. This might happen in different ways.

One was by the emperor's appointment, in much the way a person was selected to a government post. An honored ancestor of an important family or a famous local deity might come to the attention of the emperor or the government ministers. That ancestor might then be named by decree to a place in the heavenly pantheon, perhaps to a spot in the MINISTRIES OF GODS. Such selections were often made for political purposes. Ancestors or gods were often asked for special favors—a safe passage, a good harvest, victory in war (see ANCESTORS AND ANCESTOR CULTS). If the ancestor delivered a favorable outcome, he or she might be honored again—and rewarded with a promotion (see QUEEN OF HEAVEN).

Followers of BUDDHISM also often considered a particularly saintly person as the reincarnation of an earlier deity. In this way, different historical figures were connected with earlier gods.

GOLDEN AGE A term used by mythologists to describe the time of the mythological three kings, SHUN, YAO, and YU, of Chinese prehistory. The kings at this time were thought to have godlike powers.

GONG GONG (KUNG KUNG) In ancient Chinese myth, a god who brings a disastrous FLOOD to ruin the EARTH. There are different versions of the tale. In most, though, the monster's vanity, anger, and humiliation are the root cause.

One tale has Gong Gong rashly deciding to ram the holy mountain BUZHOU (also called Mount Buxhou and Mount Buzhou) with his horn out of spite for his sworn enemy, Emperor YAO, one of the five legendary EMPERORS of prehistoric China. Buzhou was one of the EIGHT PILLARS holding up the sky; when Gong Gong impaled the mountain on his horn, the Earth tilted, and the rivers overflowed, flooding the land. To make more mischief against the emperor, he tore a hole in the sky, which caused the SUN to veer off its designated path.

In a different version of the tale, Gong Gong was so vain about his powers that he challenged ZHU RONG, the divine lord of fire, to a duel to see who was the more powerful. Over several days, the two monsters rolled around the heavens, causing great havoc among the gods. Eventually, they fell from the sky, with Gong Gong going down to defeat. Enraged at being beaten, Gong Gong tried to kill himself by running head first into Buzhou. But instead of killing himself, Gong Gong knocked off the top of the mountain, which tore a big hole in the sky and then crashed down, causing the Earth to crack open. Fire and water spewed out of the cracks, and everything and everyone was either killed in the floods or burned to the ground.

Gong Gong is portrayed somewhat less monstrously in one tale as a king who wanted to dam the waters. The gods opposed him, and the people saw that he would not succeed. They refused to help, and his rule was overthrown.

Bad weather and disasters are often said to be Gong Gong's doing, and his tirade against Buzhou was blamed for a peculiarity of Chinese geography. These legends say that when Gong Gong hit the great mountain, he caused the heavens to tilt toward the northwest, which, in turn, caused all the great rivers of China to flow toward the east.

Artists tend to show Gong Gong as a huge, black DRAGON of great strength with a human face. He has a horn on his head and is attended by a nine-headed SNAKE. He is said to be 1,000 li long (about 333 miles).

GOURD A common vegetable sometimes featured in myths and folklore.

Gourds come in various shapes and sizes. They have a hard, thick skin, which becomes hollow when dried. Gourds had many practical uses in ancient China. They served as containers for MEDICINES and powders, even as life preservers tied on the backs of children to help them float if they fell overboard into the ocean. Miniature figurines of old men carrying gourd-bottles on their backs were worn as CHARMS to bring the wearer longevity.

Artists show Li Tieguai, one of the BA XIAN, or Eight IMMORTALS, holding a gourd in his outstretched hand as smoke rises from his mouth into the HEAVENS. This was a symbol of his immortality, the smoke representing his spirit as it separated from his body. In the FLOOD story of FUXI, a gourd grown from a magic tooth cushions two children in their fall from heaven's door.

GREEN DRAGON OF THE EAST In Chinese myth, a DRAGON associated with spring. He brought regenerating rain and was seen as the embodiment of the YANG principle, positive and male (see YIN AND YANG). His element was wood.

The Green Dragon is sometimes used in art and decoration to symbolize the East or spring.

GUAN (KUAN) A mandarin, or official, of the QING DYNASTY.

GUAN DI (KUAN-TI, KUAN YU) A popular Chinese god who evolved from a real person to an important deity over the course of many centuries (see GODS IDENTIFIED WITH HUMANS). Guan Di was honored as a god of war, loyalty, wealth, and literature. He was said to protect temples, the government, and society in general.

Scholars say that the real person, whose name was GUAN YU (A.D. 162–220), was a bodyguard to one of the founders of the Three Kingdoms. Remembered and venerated over the centuries, his legend grew. He was said to have granted many favors when prayed to; temples in his honor became popular. In 1614 the Ming EMPEROR officially honored him by granting him imperial rank and a new name, Guan Di.

In 1725 the largest Guan Di temples throughout the country were made official Guan Di temples, under the control of the government. In 1856 Guan Di was given credit for helping Imperial forces during a battle. In recognition of his powers, the emperor decreed that Guan Di would receive the same sacrifices as CONFUCIUS, making the god officially as important or high-ranking as Confucius.

At first, Guan Di's most important quality was his loyalty, and this was one reason emperors liked to encourage his worship. But over the years, as he came to be considered more powerful, people attributed a wide range of qualities to him. As a god, his attributes became more general.

The process of Guan Di's evolution over the centuries shows how the nature of a deity can change through the years. It also demonstrates how the government might use a god's popularity to increase its own prestige and to control the god's followers.

Guanyin, the Buddhist and popular Chinese god of mercy, seen in one of his many guises (The Dragon, Image, and Demon, *1886*)

GUANGMU The Chinese Buddhist GUARDIAN KING of the West. Guangmu presides over the fall. His powerful eyes allow him to see all that happens in the universe. His Taoist equivalent is Moli Qing. He is called Mig-mi-bzang in TIBET and Sain Bussu Nidūdü in Mongolia.

GUANYIN (GUAN-YIN, GUANSHIYIN, KUAN-YIN, KUAN YIN, KANNON) The Chinese name for Avalokiteśvara or Kannon, the BODHISATTVA of mercy and compassion venerated by many Buddhist sects and associated with a wide range of qualities. Although Guanyin is most often considered male, Chinese artists sometimes show the bodhisattva as female, emphasizing the supposedly feminine qualities of mercy, compassion, and purity.

Some traditions say that Guanyin has 33 forms and that each one is related to a different manifestation or appearance of the divine being on EARTH. Groupings of eight (Banan) and 32 (Guanyin Sanshi'erxiang) representations of the divinity are also found in Chinese art.

Some traditions connect Guanyin as a female with childbirth. Many of his other manifestations are of warriors, commemorating the divine being's many battles on behalf of humans.

The Chinese name may be translated as "He hears the cries of the world," a reference to the bodhisattva's great compassion for humans.

Guanyin was also popularly considered the Chinese goddess of mercy or compassion, and could be asked to relieve suffering or grant a similar boon. Worship of the goddess, in this instance seen as female, was widespread.

In other popular legends about her, Guanyin is given credit for introducing the cultivation of RICE, which is said by some to derive its nutritional qualities from being filled with her own milk. She is mentioned in the 14th-century Chinese book XIJOU JI (Journey to the West), which shows how she interceded to protect the monkey who had stolen the PEACHES of immortality (see MONKEY KING).

The DALAI LAMA is considered the human reincarnation of the bodhisattva, who is also considered the original creator of TIBET.

GUAN YU The historic person (A.D. 162–220) later deified as GUAN DI (see GODS IDENTIFIED WITH HUMANS).

GUARDIAN KINGS (HUSHIZHE) In Chinese Buddhist myth, the four kings or deities who guard the compass points—north, east, west, and south. They protect the EARTH and Buddhist law. The kings are CHIGUO, DUOWEN, GUANGMU, and ZENGZHANG.

A number of myths are connected with the kings. According to one, they were present when BUDDHA's mother gave birth. When the Buddha was hungry, each king offered him a bowl of RICE; the Buddha held the bowls in his hand and created one bowl where there had been four.

The Guardian Kings are usually placed at the corners of altars; their ferocious bodies and faces thus guard the corners of Buddhist temples. Besides the directions, the kings are each connected with a different season, which itself is also connected with the direction. For example, Duowen guards the north, which is the region associated with winter. He therefore rules the winter. A believer might thank him for making the winter winds mercifully gentle.

GUCANG (KU-TS'ANG) An enchanted dog in Chinese myth who found the EGG containing KING YEN. When Gucang died, he was revealed to be a YELLOW DRAGON with nine tails and great horns. King Yen honored him with a respectful burial.

GUI (KUEI) Mythical DEMON spirits formed from the negative essence of people's souls. The *gui* were similar in some respects to Western GHOSTS, forced to wander or haunt the EARTH. While they were usually feared and thought capable of great harm, a few were not necessarily evil and could be helpful.

By many accounts, a *gui* was a soul that could not undergo REBIRTH AND REINCARNATION, often because the person drowned or committed suicide. A *gui* who had drowned could rejoin the cycle of life by finding another person to drown in her or his place. Suicides, however, apparently could never rejoin the cycle.

The souls of those who died violent deaths might become *gui* as well. These might also win release by getting someone else to take their place. For example, a man eaten by a TIGER might find another victim so that his own soul could be reborn. In the meantime, the *gui* would be the tiger's slave, hunting meals for him and doing his bidding.

A special type of *gui*, the TOUZIGUEI, stole babies from cribs. These *gui* could be repelled by nets or the smoke of burned sandals. *Gui* could also be repelled by *men shen*, or DOOR GODS, and a variety of CHARMS.

Some said that *gui* took revenge on people who mistreated them while they were alive. People also believed that the *gui* wore clothes with no hems and cast no shadows.

GUN (KUN) A descendant of the Huang Di, the YELLOW EMPEROR, and the father of YU, a great ancient Chinese hero. Both Gun and Yu played important roles in restoring the land after the devastation of the great FLOOD. Gun tried to save the world by stealing magic soil from HEAVEN in order to damn the rising flood waters.

ZHU RONG, an ancient fire god, executed Gun, but Gun's corpse did not rot. It remained intact for three years, then changed into a yellow BEAR. (In some versions of the story, it becomes a DRAGON or a turtle.) Dead, Gun gave birth to Yu, who was born from his belly button.

The fire god, apparently taking pity on humankind and thinking that what Gun had done was not that bad after all, allowed Yu to take soil and rebuild the EARTH.

Stories of Gun also sometimes show him as a rebel and evildoer. In one version of his legend, he is in charge of an irrigation system and fails to do his job, thus creating the flood.

GUNSHO MINGWANG The Chinese name for Mahāmāyūri, the "Queen of Magic" and "Peacock

Mother" of BUDDHA, honored in Buddhist mythology. She is one of the *RAKSAS*, or five "protectors," in Buddhist myth. These female divinities combat evil; their feminine power complements the male power of the FIVE GREAT BUDDHAS OF WISDOM.

Although Gunsho Mingwang protects believers from harm, her force is not aggressive. She can ward off snake bites, poisons, and other disasters. In TIBET, she is called Rma-bya Chen-no.

GUO ZIYI (KUO TZU-I) A historical person (697–781) often identified with the Chinese god of happiness, FUXING, one of the SAN XING, or with CAI SHEN, the god of riches.

Guo Ziyi fought for the TANG DYNASTY and defeated Turkish enemies during the reign of Emperor Xuan Zong (713–56). A legend attached to the warrior says that he received a visit from a goddess, who predicted that great riches and honors would find him. He was declared a "Father of the Empire" after his death. His son married the daughter of an emperor, and Guo Ziyi is often shown in art leading him to the court.

H

HAN DYNASTY The period from 202 B.C. to A.D. 220, which followed the breakdown of the JIN DYNASTY. The Han dynasty was established by Liu Pang after much fighting. He took the title of emperor in 202 B.C.

During this time, TAOISM and CONFUCIANISM thrived, and thinkers connected theories about how the universe worked to the Chinese state. The FIVE ELEMENTS, for example, were used to explain imperial rule and the rights and duties of the ruler and his subjects.

Large state bureaucracies developed to help oversee the imperial rule. Examinations were used to promote different officials, in some cases, allowing those from poor backgrounds to advance. The state also controlled the production of salt and iron.

The dynasty is often broken into three phases: Western or Former Han (202 B.C.–A.D. 9), which had its capital at Chang'an Xin; a time of disruption after the original Han rulers lost their authority (A.D. 9–23); and Later Han (23–220).

HAN PING AND HIS WIFE (HAN P'ING AND HIS WIFE) A popular love story in Chinese myth and folklore. It dates at least as far back as the fourth century A.D. and is a kind of Chinese "Romeo and Juliet" tale.

Han Ping was a servant of Prince Kang of the SONG DYNASTY. His wife was beautiful, and the jealous prince stole her for his own. The lovers were distraught and agreed through secret coded letters to commit suicide together. Han Ping went first. His wife was watched carefully, but she still managed to throw herself from the tower where she was kept.

The prince, angered, denied their wish to be buried together and ordered that their graves be kept apart. But at night a tree grew from each grave, and their branches came together. At the top, a pair of ducks sat, their necks together as they sang a sad song.

HAN XIANG (HAN HSIANG-TZU) One of the legendary Eight IMMORTALS, or BA XIAN. In the stories about him, Han Xiang was said to be the

Han Xiang, one of the Ba Xian, or Eight Immortals, in Taoist and popular Chinese myth (The Dragon, Image, and Demon, *1886*)

nephew of a TANG-DYNASTY philosopher. He became a disciple of LU DONGBIN, one of the original Eight Immortals. He had the power to make FLOWERS grow and blossom in the wink of an eye and was depicted as a young boy playing a flute so wonderfully that all animals would stop and listen. He was the patron of musicians.

The legends say he was a favorite student of Lu Dongbin, who was so pleased with his virtue that he took Han to HEAVEN and showed him a PEACH tree of the gods, which grew in the gardens of the palace of XI WANG MU and blossomed once every 3,000 years. The peaches of that tree were said to give or renew eternal life to anyone who ate one. Han Xiang climbed the tree at Lu Dongbin's request, but he slipped and fell to EARTH, achieving immortality a moment before he crashed.

Some tales depict him as having a wild, unpredictable temper as well as supernatural powers.

HARE   The hare, or rabbit, is a common animal in the Yangtze valley and northern China and was often used in myth and folklore as a symbol of longevity.

Ancient Chinese believed that they could see the face of a hare on the MOON, and the animal was connected with the Moon in many tales. A Taoist legend claimed that a hare spent his time on the Moon mixing the ELIXIR OF ETERNAL LIFE.

HEAVEN   Taoist conceptions of heaven varied greatly over time (and from sect to sect). As a popular notion, heaven is usually presented as having three parts or AZURES. They are YU QING ("Pearly Azure"), SHANG QING ("Upper Azure"), and TAI QING ("Supreme Azure"). Most sources give You Qing as highest, but some treat Shang Qing as the highest.

The heavens are associated with primeval gods and different Taoist ideas of the universe (see AFTERLIFE; IMMORTALS; SAN GUAN DADI).

HEAVENLY WEAVER GIRL   See WEAVER GIRL AND HEAVENLY OX.

HEAVEN'S MANDATE   Ancient Chinese rulers claimed the right to rule as a mandate from heaven. But this right was based on virtuous or proper behavior. If the EMPEROR did not behave properly, the disorder of his life would soon be seen in the disorder of his kingdom. This would be evidence that the mandate had been lost and a new DYNASTY would rise.

Written histories always showed how the last emperor of a dynasty was a bad person. This justified rebellion and the establishment of a new dynasty.

HE HE (HO HO, ERH HSIEN)   A pair of linked deities, Xiao Sheng and Cao Bao, who help merchants and bring them prosperity (see CAI SHEN).

By some accounts, especially in some popular traditions, He He is only one god, a generic spirit who brings wealth and great joy to those he favors.

HELL   See AFTERLIFE.

HENG O   See ZHANG.

HE QI (HO CH'I)   The Union of Breaths, rites practiced in TAOISM by followers of the teacher ZHANG DAOLING each new moon or month in the ancient Chinese CALENDAR.

The He Qi ceremony was supposed to be a sharing of energy among the community. It was conducted by a Taoist priest, though the details of exactly what it involved remain obscure. The rite was described by Buddhists who came later as a kind of sex orgy. Scholars believe that the ceremonies survived from earlier times and were merely absorbed by Taoism.

HERMIT   A holy man or woman who chooses to live alone to experience better his or her religious calling. Hermits are often seen as especially wise and holy and were used as characters in ancient legends and stories to demonstrate these qualities. In some cases, these figures were based on actual people, even though their stories contained fictional or mythological elements. Among famous hermits in Chinese BUDDHISM believed to be historical or based on real people was Budaishi (d. 917). Budaishi is honored by some schools of the ZEN sect, who believed he was a reincarnation of MILO FO or Maitreya.

HE XIANGU   One of the legendary Eight IMMORTALS, or BA XIAN. She has supernatural powers of flight and is known as the patron and protector of unmarried women. She was also invoked for her powers of housekeeping.

He Xiangu, one of the Ba Xian, or Eight Immortals, in Taoist and popular Chinese myth (The Dragon, Image, and Demon, *1886*)

Artists portray her as a demure young woman in flowing robes, holding a PEACH of eternal life or a LOTUS blossom. Sometimes she is standing on a floating lotus petal, with a FLY WHISK in her hand.

One story says she was a daughter of a shopkeeper who became immortal after grinding and eating a mother-of-pearl stone. In another version, she became immortal after eating the peaches of eternal life. A tale tells how she got lost in the woods and almost came to be eaten by a malignant DEMON, until LU DONGBIN came to save her with his magic sword. She was said to have disappeared when summoned to the court of the historical figure, EMPRESS WU.

HISTORICAL PERIODS   See DYNASTIES.

HO CH'I   See HE QI.

HO HO   See HE HE.

HO-PO   God of the YELLOW RIVER in Chinese myth. He was killed by YI, the divine archer. The rea-

sons vary, depending on the tale. In one version, Ho-po had been killing humans.

HO RIVER   See YELLOW RIVER.

HOU CHI   See HOU JI.

HOU I   See YI.

HOU JI (HOU CHI)   In Chinese myth, an AGRI-CULTURE god considered the father of the Zhou people. His descendants ruled as the ZHOU DYNASTY.

According to the stories, Hou Ji was born to Chiang Yuan after she made sacrifices to the gods. The birth was a virgin birth (though in some tellings JIANG YUAN is said to be a consort of DI KU, the legendary emperor).

Lacking an earthly father, Hou Ji was abandoned by his mother in a ditch. Wild animals cared for the babe until woodcutters found him. In another version, his own mother saw the reaction of the wild animals and realized that he was a god. She took him home and raised him.

Afterwards, he farmed. When he went to HEAVEN, he sent MILLET and other grains to EARTH.

In another version of the story, Hou Ji served under two legendary emperors of China. The emperor YAO promoted him to the master of agriculture after hearing of his skills as a farmer. Years later, when the people were starving, the emperor SHUN sent Hou Ji to show them how to farm. For his services, the emperor gave Hou Ji a fiefdom and called him "Lord Millet."

A few mythologists have raised the possibility that the mythical figure was originally a woman, questioning the traditional designation of *Hou* as lord, a male concept. Millet, a grain crop, was an important farming product in northern China.

HOU TU (HOU T'U)   A female EARTH deity, sometimes called the spirit of the earth, soil goddess, or simply earth. Because of the connection between the earth and fertility, Hou Tu had a succession of identities and was said to be one of several deceased empresses.

During the HAN DYNASTY, regular offerings were made to Hou Tu by the emperor and the dukes and lords answering to him.

HOU I See YI.

HSIA See XIA DYNASTY.

HSIA-HOU K'AI See KAI.

HSIA KUNG See XIAO GONG.

HSIANG See XIANG.

HSIANG LIU See XIANG LIU.

HSIANG QUEENS See XIANG QUEENS.

HSIANG TS'UNG See CAI SHEN.

HSIEH See XIE.

HSIEH T'IEN CHÜN See XIE TIAN JUN.

HSIEN See IMMORTALS.

HSIEN JEN See XIAN REN.

HSIEN NUNG See SHEN NONG.

HSIEN TS'AN See CAN CONG.

HSIEN WENG A spirit in ancient Chinese myth, the Ancient Immortal of the South, who helps LÜ SHANG remain loyal to WU in the battle against the last of the SHANG rulers. He has a deity named White CRANE Youth as one of his assistants.

HSI-HO See XIHE.

HSING T'IEN See XING WENG.

HSI SHEN See XI SHEN.

HSI WANG MU See XI WANG MU.

HSI-YU CHI See XIYOU JI.

HSÜAN-TIEN SHANG-TI See XUAN DIAN SHANG DI.

HSUAN TSANG See XUAN ZANG.

HSÜ CHEN-CHÜN See XU ZHENJUN.

HUA FU (HUA TUO) In Chinese mythology, the god of surgeons. Hua Fu is believed to be based on a real person who lived around the end of the second century A.D. and wrote about operating on stomach tumors, though he admitted external injuries were easier to cure. In the ministry of MEDICINE, TIAN YIYUAN, he was a specialist surgeon (see MINISTRIES OF GODS).

HUAINAN ZI (HUAI-NAN TZI) Text written 139 B.C., which includes information on a number of early Chinese myths. The work also illustrates TAOISM and other Chinese philosophies of the time.

HUA-KUANG FO A Buddhist deity who watches over goldsmiths and silversmiths. He also protects temples.

HUA MOUNTAIN (HUA SHAN) One of the FIVE PEAKS.

HUANG A word meaning GOD and used as part of an EMPEROR's name in Chinese mythology.

HUANG-CHUAN The YELLOW SPRINGS, where the YIN souls of the dead return to the underworld.

HUANG DI See YELLOW EMPEROR.

HUANG HE See YELLOW RIVER.

HUANG TI See YELLOW EMPEROR.

HUA TUO See HUA FU.

HUN According to later Taoist belief, the superior soul that separates from the lower soul when someone dies. The lower soul animates the body only during life. The superior soul is everlasting.

HUN DUN (HUN TUN) A being in Chinese myth, generally negative, if not evil, presented in several different ways.

In some sources, it is a mythical bird shaped like a yellow sack. In another, it is a red bird with six feet and four wings but no face (it lacks any bodily opening). Somehow it can dance and sing despite the absence of a mouth. It lives on the Mountain of the Sky, which is rich in ores and jade.

Hun Dun is also said to be the wicked son of Huang Di, the YELLOW EMPEROR, who was sent into exile. In these stories he is a destructive monster.

The term is also used to describe chaos or confusion.

HUO BU (HUO PU) The ministry of fire in Taoist myth (see MINISTRIES OF GODS). The ministry is headed by LUO XUAN, the "Stellar Sovereign of Fire Virtue." He has five assistants, who were identified with early Chinese ministers of the ZHOU DYNASTY. There are numerous other assistant FIRE GODS in the ministry.

The spirit of fire was honored for several days each year in the eighth month of the Chinese CALEN-DAR. The streets were hung with lanterns and lamps in his honor, and prayers were offered in hopes of preventing fires.

ZHU RONG, the "Governor of Fire," is another important member of the ministry of fire. He is identified with several legendary and historic figures; most commonly with a legendary emperor from the prehistoric period. It is said that ZHU RONG taught people how to set small fires to drive off beasts.

Zhu Rong is often depicted in art as riding on a TIGER. He presided over the South and helped break the link between HEAVEN and EARTH. After that, he was appointed to keep humans in their appointed positions in the universal order.

HU SHEN The Chinese god who protects against hail.

HUSHIZHE See GUARDIAN KINGS.

I CHING The *Book of Changes*, a manual used for fortune-telling in ancient China (see DIVINATION). The system it details is deeply connected to Taoist and ancient Chinese theories of the universe.

Its main part consists of a handbook for interpreting the BAGUA (Bagua) or the EIGHT DIAGRAMS (eight trigrams), which are formed by joining 64 hexagrams in specific combinations. The hexagrams themselves are traditionally formed by casting YARROW STALKS—modern practitioners in the West have substituted different methods—and building them into a comprehensive diagram.

The *I Ching* was a guide for Taoist and folk practitioners as they interpreted and, in some cases, attempted to control the future. Its use is ancient, and there is no consensus on where it was first used. According to stories associated with the *I Ching*, the legendary emperor FUXI first saw the trigrams on the back of a TORTOISE. Another tradition holds that

A woman prepares to throw the yarrow stalks so that they can be read according to the *I Ching*. (The Dragon, Image, and Demon, *1886*)

Wen Wang (c. 12th century B.C.) wrote the book. Wen Wang was cited by CONFUCIUS as a model emperor, and tradition connects Confucius with the *I Ching*, which is even considered one of CONFUCIANISM's recommended texts. A Confucian scholar, Zhou Dunyi (1017–73), used the *I Ching* as a starting point for an important work on Confucianism called *Taijitu shuo*, which means, roughly, "The Diagram of the universe or great ultimate explained." Most present-day scholars think that the connection between Confucius and the *I Ching* is dubious.

IMMORTALS *(HSIEN)* Also called Celestial Masters and Celestial Immortals, they are "supreme" or "perfect" humans in TAOISM. They can fly through the air, they eat air for nourishment, and the weather does not affect them.

The Immortals were first written of by ZHUANGZI, a writer and teacher of the fourth and third century B.C. Zhuangzi may have created the beings as allegories, trying to show the ideals for which humankind should aim. His Immortals are independent and free, able to exist beyond the cares of the world. But later followers of Taoism viewed them as actual beings.

When visitors from the eastern regions of China along the coast visited the EMPERORS during the QIN and early HAN DYNASTIES, they brought with them tales of Immortals who lived on islands in the East. One way of reaching these ISLANDS OF THE IMMORTALS, they claimed, involved magical ALCHEMY. The formulas included changing CINNABAR (mercuric sulfide) into gold. This gold, in turn, would be used to create special cups and bowls. By drinking from them, the emperor would increase his lifespan and be able to view the Immortals.

There are three classes of Immortals: SHENG JEN are the highest, living in the high HEAVEN; these are the saints. CHEN JEN live in the second heaven; these are the souls of heroes and other perfect beings in Taoism. XIAN REN are the most numerous and live in the lowest heaven. They are humans who have godlike powers. They include philosophers and magicians.

Humans who become Immortals appear to die, but they are actually simply changing in a process sometimes compared to a seed leaving its husk. After this point, their skin remains fresh, and they have the appearance of a "normal" living being.

Immortals are sometimes classified in texts as celestial or terrestrial. Celestial Immortals can change their appearances, have many special powers, and are said to live in the heavenly realms of the Taoist heavens. Terrestrial Immortals have no special powers, but they are considered wise beings or monks and are said to live in mythical forests and mountains on EARTH.

In many tales, there is little, if any, distinction between Immortals—who would have lived as humans and been adept at Taoist practice—and other deities.

The most famous of the many mythological beings said to have been given immortality in Chinese myth and lore are the BA XIAN, or the Eight Immortals.

ISLAM Muslims had settled in China by the time of the TANG DYNASTY in the eighth century. They were probably mostly merchants and traders who lived in separated areas where they could practice their religious beliefs. Muslim influence on the country and culture remained fairly small until the Yuan dynasty (also called the Mongol dynasty, 1279–1368), when the Mongol rulers used Islamic foreigners to help govern China.

Islam underwent a resurgence in China during the 19th century. It was estimated at the end of the 20th century that 1.4 percent of the country's 1.26 billion people practiced Islam.

ISLANDS OF THE IMMORTALS (ISLANDS OF THE BLEST, THREE ISLES OF THE GENII) Mythological islands said to be located in the Eastern Sea; home to the IMMORTALS, or *hsien*, spirits who drank from the fountain of life that sprang from a huge JADE rock and ate jewels that were scattered on the shores of these islands.

The islands were said to be the tops of mountains in the middle of a vast, bottomless pool in the ocean. There were once five mountains—Dai Yu, Yuan Jia, Fang Hu, Yingzhou, and Peng-lai. But they were not fastened to the bottom of the void (under the ocean) and thus moved around. This bothered the Immortals who lived there, and finally they asked the great god in HEAVEN to do something about it. He had YU QIANG secure them. Yu Qiang put the mountains on the backs of 15 sea turtles. But a hungry giant caught six of the turtles and took them off; Dai Yu and Yuan Jia eventually drifted north and sank.

The islands were supposed to be home to the BA XIAN, or Eight Immortals. Legends say that the first EMPEROR of the JIN DYNASTY in 219 B.C. sent a troop of men and women under the guidance of a Taoist mystic to find the islands. They spotted them, but a storm drove them back to China before they could land.

J

JADE The common term for a very hard mineral called nephrite. Ancient Chinese valued jade above every other gem or stone or even precious metals, including gold.

There are more than 100 varieties of jade in many different COLORS, including green, white, blue, clear, yellow, and CINNABAR red, the rarest of all. The color depends on the amount of iron the jade contains. In different regions of China, jade carvers specialized in a particular color: Cantonese jade carvers preferred apple green jade; Shanghai and Peking carvers preferred white.

Jade stones were often used for jewelry, small sculptures, official seals, and other pieces of art. Sacrificial bowls, incense burners, and other sacred objects, including the EIGHT BUDDHIST EMBLEMS on altars, were all made of jade.

Since it was such a rare stone, jade was a symbol of wealth, power, and excellence. EMPERORS in ancient China believed they could communicate directly with HEAVEN by praying to a perforated disk of jade, which was supposed to represent heaven.

CONFUCIUS was said to have compared the beauty of jade to the virtues all humans should aspire to. He compared jade's glossy surface to kindness, its strength to intelligence, its internal glow to a person's faith, its brilliance to heaven.

Jade is mentioned frequently in Chinese mythology. The god YU HUANG was called the Jade Emperor. The goddess XI WANG MU lived in a palace of jade in KUNLUN, where a fabled variety of red jade was believed to grow on a huge tree in the palace gardens.

Taoist alchemists believed jade was an ingredient in the ELIXIR OF ETERNAL LIFE, said to grant immortality. Some Chinese believed that jade could prevent a number of misfortunes. The wealthy drank out of jade cups, said to crack if any type of poison was poured into them. Riders would wear a piece of jade to protect them from being thrown off their horses.

Gold could be found in more parts of China than jade in the ancient period, and it was considered easier and cheaper to mine than jade. Gold's value increased, however, when BUDDHISM arrived, especially once it was used to make religious statues.

JADE EMPEROR See YU HUANG.

JASPER LADY (LADY YUN-HUA) A late Taoist figure said to have power over nature's forces. She was Lady Yun-hua, the younger sister of Princess Tai Zhen. She could cause tornados and use them to change the shape of the mountains. She also controlled a number of other deities who could also change the course of rivers and move earth.

The Jasper Lady is said to have lived in a JADE palace in the mountains. A tale in the 10th century had her appear to YU, a much earlier mythical hero still popular in Chinese folklore. The story showed that her powers were much greater than those of Yu, thus demonstrating the supremacy of Taoist doctrine.

JATAKA TALES Mythical tales of the historical BUDDHA's early life. The sources of these popular stories range widely. Some show up in different versions as part of Aesop's Fables. A number of the tales were used as teaching aides by monks to illustrate the ideals and values of BUDDHISM.

JEN I See YI.

JIANG YUAN (CHIANG YUAN) The goddess who bore HOU JI, mythic founder of the ZHOU

Buddha's childhood became the subject of a number of stories and mythical sagas known as the Jataka Tales (The Dragon, Image, and Demon, *1886*)

DYNASTY, through a virgin birth. She became pregnant after dancing in the footsteps of a giant god. Other sources say she became pregnant as a reward for her perfect sacrifices.

Jiang Yuan is said to have been the consort of DI KU, a legendary emperor. She abandoned her baby in a ditch; in some versions, however, she rescued him when she realized he was a god.

JIGONG LAOFO PUSA (CHANG-MEI) One of the historical BUDDHA'S DISCIPLES. He is known in the original Indian language as Mahākāśyapa. According to Buddhist tradition, Jigong Laofo Pusa was a very holy man and an excellent preacher. He is said to have taken over as head of BUDDHA'S monastery after the great Buddha's death, leading the community. Besides being one of Buddha's disciples, Jigong Laofo Pusa is con-

sidered a saint or sage, called an ARHAT or, in Chinese, a LUOHAN. In TIBET he is known as Od-srung Chen-po; in MONGOLIA he is called Gas-cib. Jigong Laofo Pusa is called the first in asceticism, which is the practice of self-denial and spiritual discipline.

JINNALALUO Divine beings with human bodies and horse's heads in Buddhist mythology. Their songs are said to fill HEAVEN. The *jinnalaluo* play a variety of instruments and are linked to very ancient Indian art, where they are shown as birds of paradise. They are also known as *kimnaras, feiren,* and *yishen;* they are called Mi'am-chi in TIBET. Some Buddhists claim that the Taoist god of the kitchen, ZAO JUN, was actually a *jinnalaluo* who came to EARTH as a monk.

JIU LI HU XIAN (CHI-LI-HU HSIEN) Nine brothers, the IMMORTALS of the Nine Carp Lake, who, according to a Taoist legend, were said to live in ancient China. The oldest brother was lame; the others were blind. Their father decided he would kill them. Their mother managed to have them taken out to a mountain known as the Mountain of the Nine Immortals. There they discovered how to make potions of immortality. When they drank them, a succession of red carps appeared in the nearby lake, and the brothers rode them away.

As an immortal, each brother had special powers. One could move mountains with his hands. Another could change trees into DRAGONS.

JOO-I See JU-I.

JO RIVER A river in western China said to be watched over by the Queen Mother of the West, XI WANG MU. The name is sometimes translated as "Weak River."

JOURNEY TO THE WEST See XIYOU JI.

JU-I (JOO-I) A ceremonial short sword and sword guard originally made of iron and used for self-defense by ancient Chinese warriors.

Artists have drawn this sword with many gods of the Buddhist pantheon. A round pearl is usually set into its center or handle. This pearl is said to shed a brilliant light on all nearby objects and is a symbol of

BUDDHA and his doctrines. The mystic LOTUS, another Buddhist symbol, is usually carved on one end the sword.

The 13th-century scholar Chao Hsi-ku, wrote that the sword was used for pointing the way in battles and for guarding against unexpected ambush. In more recent Chinese history, it was given as a present to wish someone prosperity.

JU LING (CHU LING, CHÜ LING HU) A powerful river god in ancient Chinese myth. The name itself means "Giant Divinity." Ju Ling is traditionally identified with the YELLOW RIVER in northern China.

In TAOISM, Ju Ling was said to have obtained knowledge of Tao and to know how the primal force could be used to create rivers. By using this force, he split a mountain to straighten a river's crooked course.

The imprint of his hand is said to be seen on Hua Mountain (see FIVE PEAKS), and the mark of his foot, on Shouyang mountain.

KAI (K'AI CH'I)   In early Chinese myth, the second ruler of XIA, son of YU.

Yu was able to assume the shape of a BEAR and so find the strength to continue to work longer than a normal person (see SHAPE SHIFTING). Later he would change back to a man and beat his drum so that his wife, NÜ JIAO, would bring him his dinner. One day Yu was working, breaking rocks as he made a path through the mountains. His pregnant wife mistakenly thought it was time to bring his dinner. Frightened by the bear, she ran away, with Yu running after her. She tripped and fell to the ground. There, because of her fright, she turned to stone. Yu had to split the rock to allow his son, Kai, to be born.

In a slightly different version of the story, Yu was about to marry Nü Jiao. He was so happy that he jumped up and began to dance. As he did this dance, his feet drummed on stone, and he was transformed into a bear. Nü Jiao ran away in fear and shame, fleeing to the mountains, where she was turned to stone. Yu followed and demanded that the boy be given to him.

Kai later went to HEAVEN and brought music back to the people. There is a connection between stone and music in Chinese history, since early drums were made with stone. Later writers used Kai's singing and dancing as an example of bad behavior, claiming that heaven was not pleased by music.

KAIGUANG   In Buddhist ritual, the consecration of a Buddhist statue. Traditionally, the statue's eyes are "opened" during the ceremony. This can be accomplished in a number of ways. In ancient times, a statue would be presented for the ceremony almost finished; only the eyes would remain to be done. The eyes were cut into the figure during the ceremony.

KAN CHIANG AND MO YEH   See GAN JIANG AND MO YE.

KAO HSIN   See GAO XIN.

KAO YANG   See GAO YANG.

KAO YAO   See GAO YAO.

KARMA   The idea that individual souls have a certain fate that cannot be escaped. Buddhists believe that actions, good and bad, can affect the soul's fate, but karma is unalterable and unavoidable.

A soul must pay for its sins, if not in this life, then in the next—or the next after that or the next after that. The only way for a Buddhist to escape the endless cycle of REBIRTH AND REINCARNATION is through ENLIGHTENMENT, though Buddhist sects disagree on how enlightenment may be achieved.

KING CHENG   See SHI HUANG DI.

KING CHIEH   The last ruler of the mythic XIA DYNASTY. He appears in Chinese myths and legends as a very evil man, one who by all rights should have been overthrown. He inflicted cruel punishments on his people, wasted money and treasure, and had many lovers.

It is common in Chinese accounts of DYNASTIES for the last ruler of the line to be shown as a great sinner or person of many faults. This showed that the overthrow and replacement of the old dynasty by a new dynasty was justified.

According to myth, King Chieh was overthrown by TANG THE CONQUEROR.

KING HAI (KING GAI, KING KAI)   According to Chinese legend, Hai was the seventh SHANG king. His sin of adultery was said to have doomed the Shang dynasty, eventually leading to its downfall under his successors.

According to the basic tale, Hai was visiting with another king named Mian-chen, the ruler of a country called You-yi. There he fell in love with the other king's wife. They had sex, and she became pregnant. In some versions of this story, King Hai is killed, and the cattle he has brought to the land of You-yi is stolen, because of his sin.

KING MIAO ZHONG In some Buddhist myths, the father of GUANYIN, who tried to stop his daughter from becoming a Buddhist monk, even trying to kill her. When his daughter returned from the underworld to heal her father's terrible illness, he finally realized that he had been wrong and ordered a statue made of his daughter to be worshipped by his people. (While Guanyin is often considered a male god, in these stories the deity is female.)

KING MU Legendary king of the ZHOU DYNASTY; traditionally said to have been the fifth king of the dynasty and probably in some way based on a real king. He is said to have visited the Queen Mother of the West, XI WANG MU. Mu had eight horses, each faster than the other. One was named Beyond Earth; its feet never touched the ground. The others were Windswept Plumes, Rush-by-Night, Faster-than-Shadow, Finer-than-Flashing-Light, Faster-than-Light, Rising Mist, and Wing Bearer.

KINGS OF THE GOLDEN AGE The three mythic kings who presided over China during ancient times: YAO, SHUN, and YU.

KING WEN See WEN.

KING WU See WU.

KING YEN A mythic king said to have ruled in the 10th century B.C. or the seventh century B.C., depending on the source. Xu was a mythic province whose exact location is now debated; scholars generally say it was in the Yangtze area.

According to the myths, Yen's mother was an attendant to the ruler of Xu. She became pregnant and gave birth to an EGG. She abandoned the egg by a river.

A dog named GUCANG found the egg and brought it to his mistress, an old lady who lived alone. The old lady, impressed by this odd-looking egg, covered it to keep it warm. Finally, out hatched a baby boy. She named him Yen.

Eventually, the attendant came to the old lady and asked for her son back. The boy was raised in the ruler's house and succeeded him as king. When Gucang died, he returned to his old form as a YELLOW DRAGON with nine tails and great horns; King Yen honored him with a respectful burial.

The myth continues, saying that King Yen did much to improve his kingdom. However, when the king of ZHOU went to war against him, Yen seemed not to have the heart for the fight. He was defeated and forced to flee.

KING ZHOU OF THE SHANG (KING CHOU OF THE SHANG) The last ruler of the SHANG; a legendary figure who appears in early Chinese histories.

Though there undoubtedly must have been a real last ruler of the Shang, the portrayal of Zhou in Chinese histories follows a general pattern that presents the final ruler of a DYNASTY as a villain. Though Zhou is said to have been very strong and smart, he was also very boastful and overtaxed his people. He indulged in music and did not properly honor the dead. He partied when he should have been working.

Zhou met his downfall when he wrongly persecuted WEN.

KITCHEN GOD See ZAO JUN.

KLU A Tibetan word for DRAGON.

KONGIUE DONGNAN FEI A popular Chinese folk ballad that dates from about the third century. It tells the story of a pair of star-crossed lovers who are unhappy with the conventional arranged marriage planned by their families. The lovers are separated; the woman drowns herself. When her lover finds out, he hangs himself. The grieving families finally give in to their children by burying the lovers in the same grave.

KONG JIA (K'UNG CHIA) According to Chinese legend, the 13th king of the XIA. Kong Jia is presented as a model of a bad king.

According to the ancient legends, HEAVEN sent him a pair of DRAGONS as presents during his reign. He brought a dragon tamer to his kingdom to take care of them. The tamer had different identities, depending on the tale. In one source he was Liu Lei. He did well until one of the dragons died. The tamer presented the dragon to the king as a meal. But when the king sent a messenger to ask why the dragon had died, Liu panicked and left the kingdom.

In another version, the tamer was Shimen. Kong Jia grew angry, because Shimen would not do his bidding, and murdered him. Afterward, a storm rose and left the mountain on fire. The king offered a sacrifice to Shimen, but Kong Jia fell down dead as he returned home.

KUAFU (K'UA-FU) In ancient Chinese myth, a braggart done in by his ego. According to the stories, Kuafu bragged that he could run faster than the SUN. He caught up to it in a race, but he was very thirsty. He emptied a river with his thirst; still needing water, he started toward a marsh. But he died of thirst along the way.

In another myth, Kuafu is killed by YING LONG, the Responding DRAGON, in a battle.

The Chinese name can be translated literally as "boasting" or "boastful man."

KUAN YIN See GUANYIN.

KUAN YU See GUAN DI.

KUCANG See GUCANG.

KUEI See GUI.

KUI (K'UEI) A storm god and beast in ancient Chinese myth; said to have only one leg. Huang Di, the YELLOW EMPEROR, captured the beast and made a drum from its skin. The sound could be heard for 500 leagues.

Later tradition said that Kui was the musician for the mythical kings YAO and SHUN.

KUI XING (K'UEI HSING, CHUNG K'UEI) An ugly dwarf in Chinese popular mythology who was discriminated against because of his features, even though he had earned excellent grades on the civil examination. He tried to commit suicide but was saved, in one version of the myth, by an enchanted FISH or turtle. (In some versions, he dies.) Kui Xing was worshipped by scholars studying for the imperial examinations. He assists WEN ZHANG, the god of literature. Artists portray him sitting on a giant sea turtle, holding an official seal and writing brush in his right hand to list outstanding scholar candidates. He lives in the STARS in the Ursa Major constellation.

KUN See GUN.

KUN (K'UN) In Chinese myth and folklore, a FISH that changes into a giant bird called Peng. The bird's wings are said to be thousands of leagues wide.

K'UNG CHIA See KONG JIA.

KUNG FU TZE See CONFUCIUS.

KUNG KUNG See GONG GONG.

KUNLUN (K'UN LUN) A sacred mountain paradise often mentioned in Chinese mythology and important to TAOISM and Chinese religious beliefs in general.

The mythic Kunlun was located in the real Kunlun (mountain range) in western China. The ancient Chinese believed that the mountain range was the source of the YELLOW RIVER and the home of the gods. The paradise stood at the top of JADE posts in the middle of a vast waste, a kind of heavenly void of perfect space. Nine gates were on each side, each guarded by a beast called Kai-ming, along with PHOENIXES and a luan bird. Pure humans could climb a tree ladder and speak with the gods there.

Kunlun was also said to be the site of XI WANG MU's fabulous palace and gardens and the shores of the Lake of Gems, where the PEACHES of immortality grew. Other trees there included the Tree of Pearls and the Jadestone Tree. Those who ate the fruits of these trees became immortal.

KUO TZUI-I See GUO ZIYI.

KU-T'SUNG See GUCANG.

L

LAI CHO The Guardian of Harvests in ancient Chinese myth. The god ensured a good growing season as well as a bountiful harvest (see AGRICULTURE).

LAMA A teacher and leader of BUDDHIST sects in TIBET. Legends and mystical powers are associated with some of the early lamas. Though these were historical persons, some of the tales include magic and supernatural events.

Among important lamas were Pad-ma Hbyung-gnas (an Indian monk also called Padmasambhava, who taught in Tibet in the eighth century), Grub-oa'i Dbyang-'phyug Mi-la or Mi-la-ras-pa (a lama and writer of sacred songs in the 12th century), and Tsongk-hapa or Blo-bzang Gras-pa (1357–1419). The DALAI LAMA is considered to be the reincarnation of the BODHISATTVA Avalokiteśvara and an earthly as well as spiritual leader.

LAN CAIHE (LAN TS'AI-HO) One of the legendary BA XIAN, or Eight IMMORTALS.

The legends say she began her life as the daughter of a family of herbalists. One day, when she was collecting medicinal herbs in her basket, Lan Caihe saw a filthy beggar who seemed to be in great pain. Taking pity on the man, she treated the boils on his body with herbs, then fed and cared for him. In return for her kindness, the beggar, who was really LI TIEGUAI in disguise, offered the girl immortality. She began wandering the world, singing songs and chanting poems that praised the eternal virtues of TAOISM and denounced the fleeting pleasures and illusions of earthly life. One day she shed her coat, boot, and belt and ascended into HEAVEN riding on a CRANE.

Lan Caihe is usually depicted as a woman dressed in a blue gown, with one shoe on and one

Lan Caihe, one of the Eight Immortals, or Ba Xian, in Taoist and popular Chinese myth, with her basket of herbs (The Dragon, Image, and Demon, *1886*)

foot bare. She waves a wand and chants poems as she begs in the streets. Sometimes she is shown wearing a heavy coat in the summer and a light frock in the winter; she also wears a belt made from a block of black wood. These are artists' ways of showing that she had renounced comfort and fashion for holier pursuits.

Alternate versions of her story depict her as a young man dressed to look like a woman.

LAN TS'AI-HO See LAN CAIHE.

LAO CHÜN See LAO JUN.

LAO JUN (LAO CHÜN) Called "Greatest Holy One" and "Supreme Pure," he is the third of the three gods in the Taoist SAN GUAN DADI. He dominated the third phase of the creation of the universe and inspired humans to establish TAOISM. He is the deified form of philosopher LAO-TZU.

LAO-TZU (LAO TZU, LAOZI) Known as the father of TAOISM (Daoism), Lao-tzu is said to have been a Chinese philosopher who lived in the beginning of the sixth century and wrote TAO-TE CHING, a collection of poems about the "Way that cannot be defined," a classic text for Taoism.

Lao-tzu was said in early accounts to have lived at the time of CONFUCIUS (551–479 B.C.), though he was a little older. Modern historians and scholars of Taoism have had great difficulty separating his actual life from legend, and some do not believe that he

Lao-tzu, traditionally honored as the founder of Taoism, in a 19th-century drawing (The Dragon, Image, and Demon, *1886*)

really existed. According to some legends, Lao-tzu disappeared to the West immediately after writing the *Tao-te ching;* he then reappeared at different times in history. Other legends claim that BUDDHA was actually Lao-tzu or one of his followers. Still others have Lao-tzu debating Confucius over various points of philosophy. A very popular legend has him teaching the principles of Taoism to LI TIEGUAI, who is considered to be the first of the Eight IMMORTALS, or BA XIAN.

LAOZI See LAO-TZU.

LAPIS LAZULI One of the seven precious things, according to Buddhist philosophy (see BUDDHISM). This blue mineral was used to tint porcelain a brilliant COLOR. The ancient Chinese physicians used to prescribe a potion made from dipping lapis lazuli in water, which was believed to cure fevers and soothe inflamed eyes (see MEDICINE).

LEANING MULBERRY TREE (FU-SANG) According to Chinese myth, the tree where the ten SUNS were hung when not in the sky (see YI). In some versions, the day's sun is placed on its top branch.

LEI BU (LEI PU) The ministry of thunder and storms in Chinese myth (see MINISTRIES OF GODS). The ministry was responsible for thunder and storms and included 24 high-ranking officials. Some of these were DEMONS from Buddhist myth. LEI ZU, the Ancestor of Thunder, headed the ministry and was one of the five thunder spirits responsible for most of the bureau's activities. The other thunder spirits included LEI GONG, the Duke of Thunder; Tian Mu, the Mother of Lightning; FENG BO, the Count of Wind; and Yu Shih, the RAIN MASTER.

LEI CHEN TZU See LEI ZHE ZI.

LEI GONG (LEI KUNG) A thunder god in Chinese myth. He is also called "My Lord Thunder" or "Thunder Duke."

Artists portray Lei Gong as an ugly beast. He might possess the body of a man, but his other features include a pair of wings, claws, and blue skin. Lei Gong usually carries a drum, mallet, and chisel, which he uses to attack human beings who are

Lei Gong, a thunder god (The Dragon, Image, and Demon, *1886*)

secretly guilty of a crime or who have escaped the law. He is depicted in many tapestries and prints as a fearsome presence who terrorizes animals and people with crashing thunder and bolts of lightning.

He is an important but menacing figure in the legends about the childhood of FUXI, a mythical sovereign in prehistoric China. Other myths show Lei Gong's benevolent side: In one story about a hunter who is out during a terrible storm in the middle of a forest, Lei Gong is diverted from his task of striking a tree by a DEMON lizard, who has assumed the form of a child waving a flag. In helping to kill the demon, the hunter is accidentally struck down by Lei Gong's might; when he wakes up, a message pinned to his body thanks him for assisting Lei Gong and rewards him with 12 extra years of life on earth.

Some legends say he has a wife, the LIGHTNING GODDESS, who carries a pair of mirrors that she uses to create flashes of lightning and sometimes to set fires.

LEI KUNG   See LEI GONG.

LEI PU   See LEI BU.

LEI ZHE ZI (LEI CHEN TZU)   The Son of Thunder in Chinese myth. He was supposed to have been born from an EGG after a thunderstorm and taken to Wen Wang, who already had 99 children.

Though Wen Wang adopted him, he was sent to a Taoist HERMIT to be raised as his disciple. When his adopted father was captured, Lei Zhe Zi sought a way to release him. He found two apricots; these changed him into a winged beast with a green face, pointy nose, and tusks. (In some art, he is shown with a monkey's head and three eyes.) The wings were tokens of the powers of wind and thunder, his birthright as the son of thunder. With his powers, Lei Zhe Zi freed his adopted father.

LEI ZU (LEI-TSU)   Lei Zu headed the ministry of thunder and storms, LEI BU in Chinese myth (see MINISTRIES OF GODS). Lei Zu is usually said to be the same as WEN ZHONG, the president of the ministry of thunder. Wen Zhong was a historical or semi-historical figure during the 12th century B.C., honored after death by being named to head the ministry of thunder. He was one of the five thunder spirits and, as Ancestor of Thunder, the top deity in the department.

Lei Zu is said to have three eyes. Light beamed from the third one in the middle of his forehead. He rode a black QILIN and was said to have been a minister during the ZHOU DYNASTY.

LEOPARD   Large, ferocious spotted CATS who appear in some Chinese stories. Leopards were embroidered on the robes of military officials of ancient China to suggest their superior combat skills.

Three varieties of leopards lived in the hills of the northern and far western provinces in China: the Manchurian leopard; the North China leopard; and the rarely seen snow leopard, which lived in the rugged, high-altitude, snow-capped mountains of upland Central Asia.

LI   The word *li* is a translation of three different Chinese words, and the concepts it describes are related. The different meanings are symbolized by different Chinese characters, but the difference is sometimes not so obvious to those who are not reading the original Chinese.

Li is used to describe the idea of a principle that underlies everything, a vital force that fills matter. The concept is important, especially for NEO-CONFUCIANISM.

Translated into English as the Chinese word for "manners" or "rituals," the concept of *li* includes the idea of proper behavior in all things. In order to live properly, a person must observe and follow *li*, conducting the proper rituals, honoring ancestors, knowing his or her place in the community, living a proper life. *Li* was very important to Confucius and his followers as well.

Li is also the word for a measurement roughly equal to one-third of a mile. The measurement is sometimes used in Chinese myths, legends, and other ancient stories. The English measurement "league" is often substituted in translations.

LIANG WU DI (LIANG WU-TI) Historical EMPEROR of China who lived from A.D. 502 to 549.

According to legend, he had a jealous and evil wife who had wasted her life. When she died, she haunted his dreams. Finally, the emperor realized that he must have special prayers and ceremonies performed to put her at peace. When they were read, his wife's soul ascended to HEAVEN as a Buddhist deity. The prayers became known as the "Water Litany of King Liang."

LI BING (LI PING) A historical figure (third century B.C.) whose story tells of his vanquishing a local river god in Shu and ending the practice of human sacrifice there.

According to the account, Li Bing was sent to the province of Shu by King Chao of QIN. It was customary there to offer two young girls to the river. Li Bing substituted his own girls instead. He brought them to the river and made his offering, asking the god to show himself and drink with him before taking the girls. When the god did not, Li Bing took his SWORD and declared that he had been insulted. He challenged the god to a fight.

It is said that he then vanished, reappearing as one of two fighting OXEN on the river bank. A short while later, he reappeared as a human, saying that the remaining ox nearby was now his. That ended the practice of human sacrifice.

A somewhat similar story is told of Xi Men Bao, an official around 410 B.C. In that incident, Xi Men Bao confronted a group of officials who were profiting from the practice of offering a girl to the YELLOW RIVER god. Xi Men Bao exposed their frauds and ended the practice.

LIGHTNING GODDESS Wife of LEI GONG, a god of thunder, according to some legends. The Lightning Goddess is one of the earliest of Chinese nature gods. She accompanied her husband and the spirits of wind and rain on their stormy travels. In each hand, she carried a brass mirror, which she would flash to create jagged bolts of lightning or even fire. She was prayed to in hopes of preventing or relieving drought conditions.

LIN CHÜN See LORD OF THE GRANARY.

LING CHIH See PLANT OF IMMORTALITY.

LING XIAO BAO DIAN The mythological celestial palace; the place where the main Chinese gods gather to discuss events, reports on earthly matters, and other duties. In one myth, the palace was in chaos for a while, after the MONKEY KING stirred up mischief among the gods who lived there.

LING ZHI See PLANT OF IMMORTALITY.

LI NO CAH See NAZHA.

LION In ancient China, statues of lions often appeared in Buddhist temples, where they symbolized faithful beings and protected the temple. When two lions were paired at the entrance to the temple, the lion on the right guarded the treasures of the temple, as well as Buddhist law. The other, with its mouth closed, guarded all the hidden powers of BUDDHISM and the universe—as symbolized by its closed jaws.

Lions were often called BUDDHA's DOGS, or *bofo*.

Statues of lions were also erected to guard tombs during the second century A.D. Popular figures in art, they were imported from Africa as gifts to the EMPEROR. The lion was also embroidered on the court robes of second-grade military officials.

LI PING See LI BING.

LI SZU (LI SI) As a minister of Emperor Shi Huang Di, Li Szu proposed in 213 B.C. that all books except for technical manuals and handbooks should be burned, especially those connected with history and mythology. The emperor agreed, and many early books about Chinese religion and mythology were lost.

LI TIAN (LI T'IEN) The Chinese god of FIRECRACKERS. Li Tian is said to have discovered that firecrackers would scare away a giant devil in the West, leading to their use in ceremonies and celebrations.

LI TIEGUAI (LI T'IEH-KUAI) The first of the legendary Eight IMMORTALS, or BA XIAN, of the Taoist pantheon. Li Tieguai, also known as "Li with the Iron Crutch," is often depicted in art as a beggar leaning on a crutch, carrying a MEDICINE GOURD in his hand or around his neck. He is considered the patron of pharmacists.

According to Taoist tradition, Li Tieguai was the first to become immortal, with the help of LAO-TZU, who taught him the principles of TAOISM and the secrets of nature. Li Tieguai's adventures are featured in many different stories. He was supposed to be able to leave his body and wander around the world in spirit, then return to his body without harm. In one tale, Li Tieguai decided to visit a mountain sanctuary, taking only his soul. He asked a disciple to take care of his human body for seven days, saying that if he had not returned by then, the disciple should burn the body. Unfortunately, the disciple decided to burn the body a day early so that he could visit his mother, who was dying. When Li Tieguai arrived back from the sacred mountain on the seventh day, his soul could not find his body and began to wander around looking for a body to inhabit. The only one he could find was a filthy corpse of an ugly, crippled beggar who had died of hunger. Li Teiguai did not really want to live in the beggar's body, but Lao-tzu gave him an iron crutch to walk with and persuaded him to inhabit the body. (In other versions, the gods gave him the crutch and a gold band to tie back his tangled hair.) When Li Teiguai went to find the disciple and heard why he had burned the body, he felt great compassion and used medicine from the gourd around his neck to bring the disciple's dead mother back to life.

In yet another version of the story, Li Teiguai was wounded and given a crutch by XI WANG MU, the

Li Tieguai, one of the Ba Xian, or Eight Immortals, in Taoist and popular Chinese myth with his iron crutch (The Dragon, Image, and Demon, *1886*)

Queen Mother of the West. After healing his leg, she taught him the secret of immortality.

Many stories tell of how Li Teiguai spent his life hobbling through the land, teaching Taoism and looking for people to convert into disciples. Some stories show Li Teiguai walking through a lighted furnace or across a pool of water; he even shrinks himself small enough to fit inside his gourd.

Li Tieguai is said to have helped ZHONGLI QUAN become one of the Eight Immortals.

LI T'IEN See LI TIAN.

LIUHAI XIAN (LIU-HAI HSIEN) A Taoist IMMORTAL said to have left his EMPEROR's service after realizing that the emperor was corrupt.

According to this story, Liuhai Xian received a visitor who was an Immortal. The visitor took 10 EGGS and began stacking them up toward the ceiling.

Each was balanced on the other by a gold coin. Liuhai pointed out that this was a risky thing to do. His visitor told him it was nowhere near as dangerous as working for his master, the emperor. Liuhai understood and left.

During his travels, Liuhai was said to have learned the formula for turning gold into the PILL OF IMMORTALITY (see ALCHEMY). One of the stories told about him is that he searched for years for a magical, three-footed toad that had escaped from heaven. When he found it, he ascended to HEAVEN overjoyed.

LIU MENG JIANG ZHUN (LIU MENG CHIANG-CHUN, VALIANT MARSHAL LIU MENG, LIU-MENG) *A mythic and legendary figure; one of the many gods of* AGRICULTURE *and one of several connected with grasshoppers. Liu Meng Jiang Zhun was worshipped early each year so that he would prevent hordes of locusts (also known as grasshoppers and* CICADAS*) from flying into the village and eating the crops.*

Liu Meng Jiang Zhun, or "the Valiant Marshal Liu Meng," a god of agriculture, who helps ensure a good harvest by driving off grasshoppers (The Dragon, Image, and Demon, *1886*)

This figure was also associated with various legendary military leaders and sages throughout China's history. Some of these include Liu I, a marshal of the SONG DYNASTY; Liu Jia, who was sent to fight the invading Mongols in A.D. 1126 and committed suicide when captured; and Liu Zai, the superintendent of imperial estates under the emperor Li Zong of the Song dynasty.

Liu Meng Jiang Zhun's legendary victories were the subject of plays and pageants. Concerned that the figure might inspire rebellion, King Xi of the QING DYNASTY (who reigned from 1662 to 1723), ordered the people to stop worshipping him. But many of his early temples continued to draw worshippers for centuries afterward. Some scholars believe that Liu Meng Jiang Zhun and BAZHA, a spirit protector against grasshoppers, are the same deity.

LO An ancient capital city mentioned in myth as a capital of WU; located near the LO RIVER. It is known today as Loyang, Honan.

LOBIN (LO-PIN) A river goddess in one of the stories about YI, the divine archer. Yi takes her after killing her husband, the lord of the YELLOW RIVER.

LO HSÜAN See LUO XUAN.

LONG A Chinese word for DRAGON.

LONG SHAN (LONGSHAN, LUNGSHAN) The "Dragon mountain," located near Chengziyai, Shangdong. The name is used by archaeologists and other social scientists to refer to findings of a prehistoric culture discovered in the area.

LONG WANG (LUNG WANG) Chinese myth and folklore use "Long Wang" as the generic name for a variety of DRAGON kings that brought rain to the land. They include those who rule the four oceans with the help of an army of sea creatures, those who rule the HEAVENS, and those who sit on the five cardinal points of the world.

In some stories, these dragon kings serve the Jade Emperor, YU HUANG; in others, they serve YUANSHI TIANZONG, the "Celestial Venerable of the Primordial Beginning."

Some myths gave dragon kings the authority over life and death, because they were responsible for the rain and funerals. They were also the protectors of ferrymen and water carriers and were said to punish anyone who wasted water.

LO-PIN See LOBIN.

LORD OF THE GRANARY (WU XIANG, LIN CHŪN, LIN JUN, WU-HSIANG)   The hero who founded the mythological city of Yicheng in SHU, modern Sichuan (Szechwan) in south-central China. He is the father of the BA tribe, who inhabited the region. He was the son of Chengli and descended from Da Hao; his name was Wu Xiang.

According to the story, five CLANS in the region lived in a pair of mountain caves on Mount Wuluo. Until Wu Xiang's time, they had all been subjects of another god. Then they decided to rule themselves, and Wu Xiang competed with champions from each of the other clans to see who would gain the right to rule. The contest consisted of throwing swords at a rock. His was the only one to hit.

The others were disappointed, and Wu Xiang suggested a new contest. They would all make boats of clay and see whose floated. Again, his was the only winner, and the others accepted him as their lord, calling him the "Lord of the Granary," Lin Jun.

Later the Lord of the Granary sailed his boat down to the Salt River. There he was met by the beautiful SALT RIVER GODDESS. She asked him to stay with her forever, but the Lord of the Granary declined. However, that night as he slept, she came and lay with him. In the morning, she turned into a bug. The goddess then gathered other bugs together, blocking out the sky so that the Lord of the Granary could not find the direction home. He also could not see which one of the many flies was she, so there was no way of dispelling the insects.

Finally, the Lord of the Granary announced that they should get married. He gave one of her servants a green SILK belt, saying that the goddess should wear it as a token of their engagement. As soon as she put it on, he knew where she was and killed her with an arrow (see ARCHERY). His path was then clear to return home.

LORD OF THE RIVER See HO-PO.

The Lord of the Granary, an important hero in Chinese mythology (The Dragon, Image, and Demon, *1886*)

LORD OF THE WEST See WEN.

LO RIVER A tributary of the YELLOW RIVER.

LOTUS The lotus is a beautiful water FLOWER in the same family as water lilies. It symbolizes many things in art, myth, and legends around the world. For Buddhists and many others in Asia, the lotus represents immortality and purity, as well as ENLIGHTENMENT. Scholars trace the symbolism to India, where the lotus is included in the depictions of early myths.

Some Buddhists believe that the appearance of a new BUDDHA on EARTH is marked by the blossoming of a special lotus. Lotus flowers are included in many pieces of art and literature describing NIRVANA and paradise. Paintings of the Buddha, for example, often show him sitting on a lotus flower.

It is also the emblem of one of the BA XIAN, or Eight IMMORTALS; HE XIANGU is frequently shown holding a lotus flower in her hand.

The ancient Chinese used the plant as an ornament, for food, in cosmetics, and in MEDICINE. Lakes and pools were planted with lotus stems for beauty. The stems were sliced and boiled or grated and powdered to make the thickening powder called arrowroot. Chinese grocers would wrap items in dried lotus leaves. Lotus seeds were used in desserts. The kernels were used in soups or roasted to eat like nuts.

LOTUS SUTRA The important texts of Buddhism are called SUTRAS. These contain the teachings of the BUDDHA or commentaries on his teachings. Different sects place varying emphasis on the sutras. MAHAYANA, ("Greater Vessel" or "Greater Vehicle") Buddhists put special emphasis on the *Lotus Sutra.*

The *Lotus Sutra* teaches that Buddha's essence permeates all things. It suggests that the way to become enlightened is through wondrous apprehension rather than logic. According to these teachings, Buddhas-to-be, or BODHISATTVAS, work to help others reach ENLIGHTENMENT.

LU BAN (LU PAN) The Chinese god of carpenters. Lu Ban heads the celestial ministry of public works (see MINISTRIES OF GODS). In one story, Lu Ban made a wooden kite so large and strong that his father used it to fly. Unfortunately, the people in Wuhai, where the kite landed, thought his father was a devil and killed him. Lu Ban was so angry that he built an IMMORTAL from wood and used it to cause a drought in the town.

LU DONGBIN (LÜ TUNG-PIN, LÜ YEN, OR LÜ TSU) One of the legendary Eight IMMORTALS, or BA XIAN. He is said to punish the wicked and reward the good.

One story tells of Lu Dongbin's decision to devote himself to TAOISM and a life of holiness. He met ZHONGLI QUAN (another of the Eight Immortals) at an inn. While his host warmed up a pot of wine, Lu Dongbin fell asleep and had a vision of his future: 50 years of good fortune, followed by a skirmish with bandits who would ruin his family and murder him. When

Lu Ban, a heavenly carpenter (The Dragon, Image, and Demon, *1886*)

he awoke, Lu Dongbin decided to renounce earthly ambition and become a disciple of Zhongli Quan.

Another story says that when he was still a young student, he met a DRAGON who gave him a magic SWORD that would conceal him when he visited HEAVEN. Another says that, after successfully overcoming 10 temptations, he won a sword that had supernatural powers to fight evil. Others say that Lu Dongbin traveled the world for 400 years, mixing with ordinary people and using his magic sword to slay evil dragons, help the good, and conquer ignorance.

Artists show him holding a FLY WHISK in his right hand and wearing a sword slung across his back. He was a popular patron of scholars and barbers and the guardian of ink makers.

LU HSING See LUXING.

LUNGSHAN CULTURE See LONG SHAN.

LUNG WANG   See LONG WANG.

LUOHAN   Buddhist saints or sages; also known as ARHATS. Buddhist tradition holds that there are a large number of these saints, and different texts list varying numbers, from 50 to thousands. (The numbers are often given as multiples of 500, which was probably used originally merely to indicate "a great many.")

Despite the large numbers cited in texts, scholars have identified only a handful of saints who are generally worshipped.

Outside of China, a group of 16 saints are commemorated: Ajita (Ashiduo); Angaja (Yinjietuo); Bhadra (Botuoluo), Chudapanthaka (Zucha Bantojia), Jivaka (Jubaka), Kalika (Jialijia), Kanakabhadra (Biliduoshe), Kanakavatas (Jianuojia Facuo), Nagasena; Nakula (Nuojuluo), Panthaka (Bantuojia), Pindola Bharadvaja (known as Bintouluo in China), Rahula (Luohuluo); Subinda (Supinte), Vajraputra (Fasheluofuduoluo), Vanavasin (Fanaposi); Chinese Buddhists added two more in the 10th century, probably from TAOISM. The names of these two saints are different according to region and sect, but names and attributes mean "DRAGON Tamer" and "TIGER Tamer." Various sects and locales add their own two figures to the 16; most, if not all, are believed to be based on historical people.

In TIBET, Dharmatala and Huashan—believed to be actual monks—are included with the traditional 16.

LUOHULUO   The Chinese name for Rahula, the son of the historic BUDDHA. Luohuluo was one of BUDDHA'S DISCIPLES. Traditions about his birth vary. Some hold the Luohuluo was born before his father began to look for ENLIGHTENMENT. Others say that he was born the day the historical Buddha achieved enlightenment.

Luohuluo died before his father. He is honored as a saint (in Chinese, a LUOHAN). Luohuluo is said to watch over novice monks as they begin their quest for enlightenment.

LUO XUAN   The head of the fire ministry, HUO BU, in Chinese myth (see MINISTRIES OF GODS). Luo Xuan is called the "Stellar Sovereign of the Fire Virtue."

According to the stories told about him, Luo Xuan was a Taoist priest. During a battle, he changed himself into a three-headed giant and held a magic weapon that could create a sword of fire (see SHAPESHIFTING). He sent the fire against the city of Xigi, setting it ablaze. The DRAGON Long Ji arrived, coaxing rain from the clouds. Luo Xuan tried to escape, but he was crushed by a flying pagoda sent by a god named the Pagoda Bearer.

LU PAN   See LU BAN.

LUS   A Mongolian word for DRAGON.

LU SHANG (CHIANG TZU-YA)   A legendary general who fought with King WU in the battles that established the Zhou dynasty. He is said to have lived from 1210 B.C. to 1120 B.C.

After the battles, he is said to have visited Kunlun, the paradise in the western mountains. There he visited the Jade Palace, where he was tempted by the evil magician Shen Gongbao, who tried to trick him into changing sides. To dazzle Lu Shang with his powers, Shen Gungboa claimed he could chop off his head and throw it into the air, promising that it would return without damaging his neck. Lu Shang agreed to join Shen Gongboa's forces if the magician could really do this trick. But Hsien Weng, a Taoist spirit of the South (also called the Ancient Spirit of the South) interfered. He ordered a crane to snatch the head of Shen Gongboa, so it could not return to the magician's neck. Lu Shang, realizing he had been tricked, returned home in time to save Wu's forces from a fresh attack.

As described in the annals, the battles include mythical beings who could control the rain and animals such as qilins or unicorns.

Lu Shang was also worshipped as the god of fishermen. According to a legend, after his battles were over, he spent his time fishing until he was 80, when he became prime minister for the emperor.

LUTE   A stringed musical instrument with a pear-shaped body and a long, narrow fingerboard. The lute was said to have been invented by FUXI. The *qin* (or *chin*) lute is a seven-stringed instrument; the *se* lute has 25 strings. The *se*, also called a zither, was popular in ancient China, though it is rarely seen today.

Played together, the two lutes produce a wondrous harmony said to be a symbol of happiness in marriage. The music was included in ancient ceremonies.

LU TUNG-PIN See LU DONGBIN.

LUXING (LU HSING, LU XING) One of the three Chinese gods of good fortune (see SAN XING).

M

MAGICIAN In ancient China, the study of TAO-ISM included learning about different formulas and processes that gave a devoted Taoist power over the elements. It was thought to be possible for a Taoist to change materials from one element to another, a process called ALCHEMY in the west.

Taoists believed that the devout could obtain other powers, especially once they became IMMORTALS. These powers included floating in the air and changing body shape or form (see SHAPE SHIFTING).

MAGPIE A bird used to symbolize joy in Chinese folklore and art. Slightly smaller than the CROW, the magpie has a black body, a white underbelly, and a tail that seems to shine blue-green.

Some people believed that living near a magpie's nest would bring good luck. The bird's song was also supposed to guarantee success.

MA GU The name of three different Taoist IMMORTALS, all women, who figure in Chinese myth and legend.

According to one tradition, Ma Gu was a kind-hearted woman and devout Taoist who lived in the second century A.D. She was responsible for reclaiming a large, flooded coastal area of Kiangsu and converting it into a MULBERRY orchard.

A second tale tells of a girl named Ma Gu whose father, Ma Hu, was so mean that he made her work morning and night. Finally, she left home and went to the mountains. He realized his mistakes and cried over her loss so bitterly that he became blind. She returned and cured him with some special wine from the mountains. But she did not stay, turning into a bird instead and flying to the heavens.

The third Ma Gu was a holy HERMIT who lived during the reign of Emperor Huicun (Hui T'sun) (r.

1101–26). The emperor declared that she was a CHEN JEN, a type of Immortal, after her body died.

MAHAYANA BUDDHISM Mahayana ("Greater Vehicle" or "Greater Vessel") BUDDHISM is a term used to describe a group of Buddhist sects that have similar beliefs. Among the most important belief from a mythological point of view is that it is possible for people to achieve ENLIGHTENMENT through the works of others, especially BODHISATTVAS and other religious figures.

According to this school of Buddhism, BUDDHA was one manifestation, or human form, of a force that lives beyond ordinary human knowledge. Mahayana Buddhism distances itself from older, more conservative sects, which it calls the Hīnayāna, or "Lesser Vessel," Buddhism. This older branch—which calls itself THERAVADA, "the Way of the Elders"—holds that enlightenment can be achieved only by the means outlined in the conservative texts.

According to Mahayana teachings, there is an eternal Buddha without beginning or end. Different manifestations of this force live as people, and there is always one present in the world. The founder of Buddhism, Shāka or Siddhartha Gautama (as he was known before reaching enlightenment), was one of these Buddhas.

Those who reach NIRVANA and become enlightened can choose to stay on EARTH and help other people. Those that stay are called bodhisattvas, or Buddhas-to-be. According to Mahayana beliefs, this selfless action is more worthy than simply reaching Nirvana. Many of the stories of bodhisattvas were adapted from earlier stories, legends, and myths.

Many sects of Buddhism are included in the Mahayana branch of Buddhism. In general, Mahayana sects are accepting of supernatural phenomena that often accompany myths and legends.

MAITREYA See MILO FO.

MANDARIN The word used in the West for officials in Chinese government. There were nine grades of officials. They dressed in special clothes and carried tokens of their office. The word *mandarin* came from Portuguese words meaning "counselors." The word today is also used for the Chinese language, once used at court, and to describe the main Chinese dialect, known inside China as Putonghua.

MANG SHEN (NIV MANG) A Chinese god of AGRICULTURE represented by a clay figure who is said to beat an OX at a spring ritual.

According to myth, Mang Shen beats a heavenly ox with a willow branch every year at the end of winter to wake up the earth so that spring will come. The ancient Chinese held a yearly spring sacrifice reenacting the scene with clay statues of Mang Shen and the Spring Ox.

MANY-SPLENDORED BIRD A mythical bird whose eyes were each said to have two pupils. It was supposed to look like a rooster but make the sound of a PHOENIX. A strong flier, it could swoop like a hawk.

At different times in ancient China, the many-splendored bird was thought to be either an omen of bad luck or a bringer of bad luck. But it could also keep bad luck away. Some said that offering the many-splendored bird pure red JADE would keep it coming back, and thus it would continuously ward off evil. Images of the bird were hung in display at New Year celebrations.

MARA (MARA) According to Buddhist myth, Mara was the prince of DEMONS. The historical BUDDHA was said to have fought Mara and defeated him. The term *Mara* as well as the original stories come from India.

MARICHI An Indian Buddhist goddess sometimes identified with the Chinese Taoist goddess QUEEN OF HEAVEN.

MA SHIHUANG (MA SHIH HUANG) A deity in ancient Chinese myth who helped veterinari-ans and cured the ills of animals. He was said to have been named Han Shuai in life and had worked during the prehistoric period helping investigate herbal MEDICINES. It is also said that he once cured a DRAGON; the dragon then carried him on his back in gratitude.

MASTER YEN The hero of an ancient Chinese legend who was said to have created a human robot.

According to the tale, Master Yen was visited in his land beyond KUNLUN by King Mu of the ZHOU. Master Yen showed the king a person who began to sing and dance. The king had never seen such an entertainer, as this person could sing and dance better than anyone and never grew tired. But then, just as the show was about to end, the entertainer insulted the king by flirting with his attendants very rudely.

King Mu became furious. He declared that he would put Master Yen to death for bringing someone so rude into his presence.

Master Yen quickly grabbed the performer and ripped his body apart, showing that he was not a person at all but a perfect machine, constructed of wood, leather, and all sorts of other things.

The king examined the machine very carefully. All of the miniature organs seemed very lifelike and were intricately connected. He was so pleased that he not only spared Master Yen's life but took him back to his palace with great honors.

MA TSU P'O See QUEEN OF HEAVEN.

MA WANG The king of horses in Chinese myth. People prayed to him, along with Ma She, the riding master, to make horses tame.

MAYA See MOYO.

MA YUAN-SHAI (GENERAL MA, GENERAL OF THE WEST) A mythic figure in both Buddhist and Taoist lore. General Ma fought a number of DRAGON kings, including the Blue Dragon, and spirits of the wind and fire. He is said to have been reincarnated as a punishment for being too cruel to evil spirits he had been sent to exorcise (see EXORCISTS).

Ma Yuan-Shai is shown in art with three eyes. He is said to intercede with other gods on behalf of anyone who prays.

MEDICINE Healing practices in ancient China evolved along with the growth of TAOISM, FOLK RELIGION, and knowledge about different healing practices. Cures changed as the concepts of how and why one got sick changed.

Myth and religion played a role in early medical procedures. At the time of the SHANG DYNASTY, angry ancestral spirits were thought to cause many illnesses. People tried to cure these ailments by appeasing the dead souls, generally with sacrifices (see ANCESTORS AND ANCESTOR WORSHIP). Scholars call this procedure ANCESTRAL HEALING.

ZHANG DAOLING was said to have begun practicing Taoist medicine after receiving a vision from LAO-TZU in the second century A.D. Zhang saw disease as a punishment for sins, imposed by the GUAN DADI, or "Three Judges of the Dead." Ceremonies were needed to remove it. During the ceremonies, the Taoist priest made *chang* (petitions or prayers), which were said to go to officials in one of three Taoist HEAVENS. Each one had a special responsibility for a specific ailment and its corresponding DEMON.

There were many ways for this appeal to be made. One involved *FU*, written talismans that were burned and then ingested with water by the sick patient. A person tried to stay healthy by using CHARMS to keep evil demons away or by forming an alliance with a positive power.

Some Taoist practitioners saw illnesses largely as the result of conflicting powers or of forces that were out of balance. They used the concepts of YIN AND YANG, along with the FIVE ELEMENTS, to restore balance and banish unwanted forces from a certain area of the body. For example, a pain in the liver area might be cause by too much fire; a way would then be sought to bring water there. The study of different natural substances led Taoist doctors to supply patients with a wide range of medicines. Followers of CONFUCIANISM and other Chinese philosophies that emphasized practicality and real-life results added more medicines based on trial and error, or what we might consider a scientific basis.

Medical practices that developed as the civilization grew were varied and complicated; some remain mysterious and yet powerful today. Acupuncture and herbal cures, to name two, are considered by many to be more effective in certain situations than Western medicine.

MENG HSI See MENG SHU.

MENG NIA See MENG SHU.

MENG PO (MEN P'O) According to Buddhist myth, Meng Po greets the souls of those who have died and are ready to be reborn in a special hall of the AFTERLIFE or Buddhist hells. She gives a bowl of soup to each soul. This makes them forget their past. Her reception area is often called "the Hall of Oblivion."

MENG SHU (MENG HSI, MENG K'UEI, MENG NIA, MENG SHUANG) The name of a country said in Chinese myths to lie outside of China. The people there have human heads and the bodies of birds.

MENG SHUANG See MENG SHU.

MEN K'UEI See MENG SHU.

MEN SHEN See DOOR GODS.

MIAO A tribe mentioned in some ancient Chinese myths, usually as a troublesome group. In the YU myths, they are said to bring jewels in tribute to YAO.

MIAO ZHONG See KING MIAO ZHONG.

MILLET A grain cultivated in ancient China. It was especially important in the northern areas of China and is often mentioned in myths.

MILO FO (MI-LO FO, MILUO-FO) The Chinese name for Maitreya, a BUDDHA-to-be, or BODHISATTVA. Milo Fo is the only bodhisattva generally recognized by sects in both branches of Buddhism, THERAVADA and MAHAYANA. The deity is popularly known as "the laughing Buddha." In art, he smiles or laughs and looks very round and plump.

According to some Buddhists, the time of Buddhist law can be split into three periods, growth and dominance, deterioration, and absence. Milo Fo will reappear at the end of the 3,000-year time of absence, once more establishing the law. Until that time, he waits in HEAVEN.

Artwork often shows him sitting in heaven, waiting for his time to return as Buddha and the "turner of the wheel" of law.

MINISTRIES OF GODS In later Chinese myth, the gods responsible for different natural and supernatural events were often spoken of as belonging to a large bureaucracy of gods. This may have been partly a reflection of Chinese society and the government. Because of its size, China was ruled by a complicated bureaucracy, so perhaps it was natural to believe that the universe was also run the same way.

The function of thunder, for example, had its own department, with a head god (WEN ZHONG) and a group of other gods to help him with his duties. Medical matters were particularly complicated, with gods for each organ and ailment.

Historians point out that there was not actually a one-to-one correspondence between the real departments of the government and the celestial ministries.

Here are some of the main celestial ministries: thunders and storms (LEI BU), MEDICINE (TIAN YIYUAN), smallpox (DOU SHEN), waters (SHUI FU), fire (HUO BU), epidemics (WEN BU), time (TAI SUI), Five Sacred Mountains (WU YUE), exorcisms (CHU XIE YUAN), and public works (LU BAN). Finances are identified with the god CAI SHEN. The ministry of literature is often connected with WEN ZHANG and war with the god of war, GUAN DI.

MO HSI See MO XI.

MOLIZHI According to Chinese Buddhist myth and popular belief, Milizhi is the mother of the North Star.

In Buddhist mythology, Molizhi is the Chinese name for Marici, who protects warriors and is a goddess of fire. In China, she was one of the few women recognized as a divinity by Buddhist sects. She is known by several names, including Tiannu in Chinese and Hod-zen Chan-ma in Tibetan. The divinity was especially important to the Chan, or ZEN, BUDDHISM sect.

MONGOLIA The historic home of the Mongol people, Mongolia lies in Central Asia, between China and Russia.

Scientists have found evidence of human settlements in the area dating back to prehistoric times. Much of the area in South Mongolia is a vast, uninhabitable desert.

In ancient times, Mongolia and China often interacted. During the Liao dynasty (907–1125), China effectively controlled Mongolia. Later, Genghis Khan (c. 1162–1227), ruler of the Mongol CLANS, ravaged northern China. Genghis Khan's descendant, Kublai, defeated China's armies; Mongolian leaders then ruled China until the Ming dynasty rose in 1368.

Partly because of internal strife, the Mongolian homeland was split into two parts by the beginning of the 18th century. The southern portion—Inner Mongolia—was closely aligned with the Chinese and eventually became part of the country.

The association between China and Mongolia over the centuries led to exchanges of culture and myth. BUDDHISM provided another common heritage, although Mongolian Buddhist practices were more closely aligned with those in TIBET, another neighbor to the south.

MONKEY KING (SUN WUKONG, SUN HOU-TZU, SUN WU-K'UNG, STONE MONKEY) A mythological and popular figure who appears in many Chinese tales under a variety of names. Mythologists see him as a TRICKSTER figure. (Tricksters trick humans or others in myths and often take the shape of animals. They are common to many cultures.)

According to his basic story, the Monkey King was born from a stone EGG during the beginning of creation. At first, the Monkey King looked exactly like a monkey. Then he gained more powers and looked more human. Finally, he could change into any shape he desired (see SHAPE SHIFTING). He became king of the monkeys and lived for 300 years before searching for the secret of immortality. According to some, the Buddhist monk Xuanzang taught the monkey the path to immortality and named him Sun Wukong, which means "Enlightened monkey."

But the monkey's behavior was anything but enlightened. He crossed his name off the list of the

The Monkey King doing battle in heaven

dead, then stole a magic weapon from the DRAGON King and used it to beat off the spirits from hell who came for his soul. The Dragon King and the king of the underworld complained bitterly about the monkey's behavior, so the Jade Emperor, YU HUANG, decided that the monkey should be taken to heaven, where he might be controlled. But the monkey only became more brazen, committing many sins before drinking the ELIXIR OF ETERNAL LIFE.

It is said that the Monkey was released after 500 years of imprisonment on the condition that he journey to India. The story of the journey is told in *XIYOU JI, Journey to the West*, the classic Chinese epic celebrating the exploits of XUAN ZHANG.

Monkeys often appear in Chinese myth and folklore as mischievous creatures, often tricking humans.

MOON The Moon is included in several ancient Chinese myths, but, unlike in some cultures, it is not a major figure in Chinese mythology.

According to one belief, there were 12 moons, one for each month. Eleven would wait in a tree while the other did its job of illuminating the night. CHANG-XI was the mother of the 12 moons.

ZHANG E, the wife of YI, the divine archer, is said to live on the Moon, in some versions as a toad. She shares the moon with an old musician called WU

KANG, fated to labor at the impossible task of chopping down the cinnamon tree of immortality, as well as a HARE. The hare in some versions is mixing a Taoist ELIXIR OF ETERNAL LIFE, which produces immortality.

An unrelated Chinese tale speaks of two shy sisters who lived on the Moon. The sisters did not like being stared at by Moon gazers and persuaded their brother, who lived on the SUN, to change places with them. The sisters ensured their privacy on the Sun by arming the Sun's rays with 72 embroidery needles to stab the eyes of those foolish enough to stare at them.

Some myths say that eclipses are caused by the Heavenly Dog STAR eating the Moon. Mythic archer Yi is said to stop the Heavenly Dog with his arrows, ending the eclipse.

It was customary in ancient China during an eclipse to follow the archer's example by ringing bells, clanging gongs, and setting off FIRECRACKERS, scaring the Heavenly Dog into giving back the Moon.

MOTHER OF METAL Mythological figure said to be the ancestor of the JASPER LADY.

MOTHER OF THE TEN SUNS See XIHE.

According to some Chinese myths, the moon is inhabited by a hare and the wife of Yi, the divine archer (The Dragon, Image, and Demon, *1886*)

MOTHER OF THE TWELVE MOONS See CHANGXI.

MOUNT BUXHOU See BUZHOU.

MOUNT YEN In Chinese myth, the place where the SUN sets.

MO XI (MO HSI) Concubine of KING CHIEH in Chinese myth and legend. After the king got rid of Mo Xi, she helped YI YIN. This, in turn, led to the downfall of the XIA (see TANG THE CONQUEROR).

MOYO The Chinese name for Maya, the mother of the BUDDHA. She is also known as Zhende Pusa. In TIBET, she is called Sgyv̄-phrul-ma. According to Buddhist legend, Moyo had a dream that prophesied the coming of the Buddha.

MU See KING MU.

MUCLINDA According to Buddhist myth, Muclinda is a seven-headed king of the serpent gods, or water spirits, called NAGAS. Muclinda sheltered the BUDDHA from bad weather by spreading the cobralike hoods of his seven heads over him during a seven-day downpour. When it stopped raining, the serpent king was transformed into a young prince, who proceeded to pay homage to the Buddha.

In Tibetan Buddhism, the legends say the *nagas* guard the Buddhist scriptures.

MULBERRY Mulberry trees are sometimes mentioned in ancient myths and legends. They were plentiful in ancient China and played an important part in the SILK industry. The trees' leaves were eaten by silkworms, which produced silk thread used for cloth and fine clothes.

An ancient story describes how the mulberry tree got its name, which means "mourning." The tale concerns a girl and a horse and has been told and collected in different forms. Mythologist Anne Birrell calls the story "The Silkworm Horse" in her book, *Chinese Mythology.*

According to the tale, there was once a sad girl who missed her father. Left all alone, she told her horse that if he could go and bring her father home, she would marry him. The horse immediately bolted.

Her father found the horse, which was clearly saddened. He mounted it and rode it home. But after they arrived, the horse continued to act strangely, never eating. Whenever he saw the girl, however, he became quite excited. Finally, the father asked the girl what was going on. She told him. Worried and ashamed, he killed the horse with his bow and arrow, then skinned it.

While he was away, the girl kicked the horse skin. She laughed at the dead animal, telling it that it had been killed because it wanted a human for its wife. As she spoke, the horse skin rose up, grabbed her, and went off.

A neighbor saw what had happened and told her father. A few days later, they found the girl and the horse skin wrapped as a cocoon on a tree. They called the tree a mulberry tree. Silkworms eating on the tree did much better than on any other tree, and its seeds were soon used to grow many others.

The girl is identified as CAN NÜ, the goddess of silkworms, in some tales.

MULIAN (MU LIEN) One of the 10 great disciples of BUDDHA (see BUDDHA'S DISCIPLES). He is known as the disciple who first had supernatural powers.

Mulian is known as Mu-dga-li-bu in TIBET. Artists sometimes show Mulian with a LOTUS FLOWER, which symbolizes ENLIGHTENMENT.

MUSICAL INSTRUMENTS Different accounts credit different legendary Chinese EMPERORS with the invention of musical instruments. FUXI was supposed to have invented musical instruments during his reign around 2953 B.C. SHUN was credited with inventing a wind instrument called the *shao,* which could be used to summon a PHOENIX, but only when there was a virtuous emperor sitting on the throne.

MYSTIC KNOT A symbol of long life seen in Buddhist art. The knot has four intertwined strands. One of the Eight Treasures, or the EIGHT BUDDHIST EMBLEMS, the symbol was said to appear on the bottom of the BUDDHA's foot.

N

NAGA A mythological creature that could change its shape to become a serpent. Stories about *nagas* originated in India and spread throughout Asia along with BUDDHISM and Buddhist mythology. In various legends, they served the BUDDHA and the Indian god Vishnu. In Tibetan Buddhism, they are said to guard the scriptures.

NAN-CHI LAO-JEN See SHOUXING.

NARCISSUS The narcissus FLOWER is a symbol of good luck in Chinese folklore. The flower was often cultivated to bloom in time for the New Year, when it signaled good fortune for the coming year.

NAZHA (NO CHA, LI NO CAH, SAN T'AI TZÜ) Mythological Chinese figure known as "the Third Prince." He was a Chinese folk hero and a particular favorite in rural villages. His tales include numerous pranks and misadventures, and he appears in many popular stories.

According to his basic story, YU HUANG, the Jade Emperor, was concerned that there were too many DEMON spirits wrecking havoc on EARTH. He summoned Nazha to discuss the problem. Nazha agreed to take on the task of chasing them away. He was incarnated as the third son of Li Jing (Li Ching), a legendary general who served the Western ZHOU DYNASTY in the 12th century B.C. (Li Jing is also called the Pagoda Bearer.)

Nazha was said to be born with a magic gold bracelet on his right wrist, which he later used as a weapon. He also wore a pair of red silken pants that gave off golden rays of light. At age seven, he stood six feet high. His earliest fights were as a boy, when he encountered the son of the DRAGON king, AO BING.

On his many heroic missions, Nazha carried his spear and his gold bracelet, which he could make larger or smaller as needed. He drove from place to place in a CHARIOT with wheels of fire. He had the power to exorcise spirits and was a cunning adversary.

Artists portray him as a young boy, wearing elaborate robes and armor and spearing demons, serpents, and other evil spirits.

NEO-CONFUCIANISM A term used to describe CONFUCIANISM following its revival in the 11th century in China. Among its most important thinkers was ZHU XI.

NINE An important NUMBER in ancient Chinese mythology and popular beliefs. The number was used to symbolize the sky and HEAVEN, among other things.

NINE CAULDRONS Large metal containers cast by YU as he warned the people against different dangers. The cauldrons can also judge the righteousness of an EMPEROR's rule.

The pots have special, magical qualities that enable them to change shape and size in the mythical accounts in which they appear. For example, when the pots are small and heavy, it is a sign that the emperor's rule is good. Large and light means the rule is bad.

NINE SONGS According to Chinese myth, the music KAI received (or in some versions, stole) from HEAVEN. Also called the Nine Summons, which is believed to be a reference to songs used at funeral rites (because the soul is being summoned to the afterlife).

NIRVANA A term used to describe the state of ENLIGHTENMENT, the goal of devout Buddhists.

Because Nirvana can only be properly understood by those who achieve it, it is difficult to describe. However, it is usually talked of as a release from the cycle of endless REBIRTH AND REINCARNATION that all souls must go through. It might be thought of as a blissful state of knowledge, where one finally understands all there is to understand about the universe.

NIU WANG   The god of OXEN in Chinese myth. Niu Wang is also said to protect against epidemics and sickness (see MEDICINE).

NO CHA   See NAZHA.

NÜ   A word often used to indicate a divine woman in Chinese myth.

NÜ CHIAO   See NÜ JIAO.

NÜ CHOU (NÜ CH'OU, DIVINE WOMAN CHOU)   A deity in ancient Chinese mythology who can overcome drought. She does this by setting herself on fire. She is then reborn, and she never truly dies (see REBIRTH AND REINCARNATION). Her burned face is hidden by her hand or a sleeve in depictions. She wears green clothes, a COLOR often connected with spring in Chinese myth.

One story connects her with the crab, which the Chinese believed could also regenerate itself.

NÜ GUA (NÜ KUA)   A Chinese mythological figure who appears, in slightly different form, in several myths. Nü Gua is often depicted as a woman with a serpent's body beneath her human head.

The traditions concerning Nü Gua mostly involve CREATION MYTHS and FLOOD stories. Following a flood started by GONG GONG, Nü Gua took five colored stones from the river and melted them down to patch the hole in the sky to stop the flow. Another version of this story has her damming the flood with reed ashes and resetting the four corners of the EARTH with the legs she had cut off a giant turtle.

When her repairs were done, she set out to bring life back to Earth. She created the human race by taking clumps of yellow earth and sculpting them into people, with a human head like her own, but with feet and legs, instead of her tail. When she stood the little figures on the ground, they immediately came alive, which made Nü Gua very happy.

After a while, though, the process seemed to be taking too long, and she became impatient, so she took a rope, dipped it into the mud, and trailed it about so that drops fell off. It was said that the carefully sculpted specimens became the noble and rich, while the drips from the muddy rope became the humble, poor, and crippled.

Realizing that these humans might die, Nü Gua divided them into male and female so that they could bear children.

In another set of stories, she and her brother were said to have been the only two people to survive a great flood started by the wrath of LEI GONG, the thunder god. They lived together on KUNLUN and thought that they might marry, but they were not sure if this was all right. So they prayed to heaven asking for a sign. When the sign was granted, they became married. But they did this with some shame, making a fan to shield their faces. (A fan was used in wedding ceremonies, possibly as a reminder of this myth.)

The two had children in one version of the tale. In another, Nü Gua gave birth to a ball of flesh that her brother hacked to pieces and scattered on the winds to become human beings wherever the pieces landed.

In some versions of her story, Nü Gua is the sister/wife of the legendary King FUXI, said to have ruled in prehistoric China. Her name and symbol comes from the words for "GOURD" or "melon," symbols of fertility. She is sometimes known as "Gourd Girl" or "Dark Lady of the Ninth Heaven." (*Ninth heaven* is a reference to Taoist belief and represented the highest heaven.)

The goddess is also said to be the patron of wedding arrangers, or "go betweens." Her name is given as NÜ WA in some stories. Artists have portrayed her and her brother as having human bodies and entwined DRAGON tails. She is often shown playing a flute.

NÜ JIAO (NÜ CHIAO)   The wife of YU, a mythic Chinese hero. She came from the Tushan CLAN, and Yu met her after asking HEAVEN for a sign. After their marriage, Nü Jiao became pregnant with his child, KAI, but things did not go well for the hero and his bride.

NÜ KUA   See NÜ GUA.

NUMBERS   Many numbers had special significance for the ancient Chinese, especially those steeped in TAOISM. They saw them as omens or expressions of underlying forces. Two was an essential number, for example, since it expressed the YIN AND YANG relationship. FIVE was a very important number—there were FIVE ELEMENTS, five COLORS, five senses, and five known planets. Some groupings were natural—the five senses, for example—but others corresponded to a preconceived notion of the significance of the number.

NÜ PA   See DROUGHT FURY.

NU WA (CHING WEI)   Mythological daughter of the Flame Emperor, YAN DI, of Chinese myth. She drowned in the sea and was changed into a spirit called the Ching Wei, a bird. According to the myth, the bird must carry wood and stones to dam up the eastern sea. It is not clear why, though some scholars believe that she is being punished, perhaps by the sea for trespassing in its realm. The story has some parallels to one of the tales of NÜ GUA, but mythologists have generally seen it as a separate myth.

ODD-ARM COUNTRY A name given in ancient Chinese mythology to a strange land, apparently north of China. There the inhabitants have only one arm, but they are said to be able to make kites that can carry people.

OFFERINGS TO ANCESTORS See ANCESTORS AND ANCESTOR CULTS.

OLD MAN OF THE SOUTH POLE See SHOUXING.

OMITU FO (AMITABHA, AMIDA) The Chinese name for Amitabha, popularly known as Amida, one of the FIVE GREAT BUDDHAS OF WISDOM.

Omitu Fo represents the idea of the historic BUDDHA in the AFTERLIFE (though not the historic Buddha himself). According to Buddhist tradition, the historic Buddha took a vow to save all beings after a long period of meditation. Amida represents this moment in the historic Buddha's life.

Followers of the PURE LAND SECT OF BUDDHISM believe that Amida reigns in a paradise in the West. According to the sect's beliefs, he will deliver a true believer to that paradise if the believer says his name when he dies.

Besides Omitu Fo, Amida was known by several other names in Chinese, including Benshi Heshang (which means "Master"), Xitian Jiaozhu ("Sovereign" or "Lord Master of the Western Paradise"), and Daci Dabei ("Great Compassion and Sympathy").

ORACLE BONES Animal bones used in fortune-telling, DIVINATION, and religious practices. Archaeologists have found such bones when excavating ruins from the SHANG DYNASTY, where they were used in elaborate ceremonies to ask questions of the gods.

Omitu Fo, also known as Amida (The Dragon, Image, and Demon, *1886*)

The ruler's question would be inscribed on the bone, usually in a yes-no format, with the possibilities also inscribed on the bone. A heated bronze point would then be pressed against the bone, creating small T-shaped cracks. The crack would then point to the proper answer.

A typical question might be asked in this form: We will have a good harvest? We will not have a good harvest? Scholars say that the questions could be very specific or more general. There were even questions about the weather.

Animal sacrifices to please the immortal spirits were also part of the ceremonies. TORTOISE shells were used as well in some of the ceremonies.

Scholars point out that the use of writing indicates a very advanced society. In fact, as far as is known, the Shang were the earliest to use writing east of the Indus River. About 800 of the 3,000 Shang characters are still recognizable in modern Chinese writing.

ORAL TRADITION The handing down of myths or legend through stories told but not written down. Scholars note that while oral traditions are often accurate, they are subject to much change as the story is passed on. Details, therefore, can be unreliable. It is believed that many early Chinese myths were passed along through oral tradition for centuries until they were written.

ORANGE Fruit native to China. It was a custom for many centuries that the EMPEROR of China would offer large quantities of oranges to the gods of HEAVEN each year during the official imperial sacrifices. During the Chinese New Year, families give oranges to friends and relatives, a custom believed to bring happiness and prosperity for the coming year.

OWL Seen as an evil omen, even a symbol of death, in Chinese folklore. The ancient Chinese believed that young owls ate their mothers.

Many superstitions about these nocturnal predators encouraged the idea that the owl was a DEMON or evil spirit. Some people thought owls could snatch away the soul. The harsh hoot of a screech owl was said to sound like a Chinese phrase that means "to dig someone's grave."

OX Oxen and water buffalo were important animals in ancient China. Farmers used them to pull plows. They could also be used to turn the millstones used to grind grains into flour. The animals were a source of food and hides.

Water buffalo are members of the ox family and were used primarily in southern China. The two terms—*water buffalo* and *ox*—are often interchanged in myth and folklore, especially in translation.

Oxen were seen as a symbol of the coming of spring, a natural connection because of their use.

The "Beating of the Spring Ox" was an ancient ceremony conducted each spring at the start of the farming season. A huge clay sculpture, called the Spring Ox, was brought out to the fields to be beaten with sticks or willow branches under the supervision of a clay figure of MANG SHEN ("the Herdsman," one of the Chinese gods of AGRICULTURE). It was said that Mang Shen woke up the earth each spring by beating the Spring Ox.

ASTROLOGERS and other officials of the ancient Chinese court decided what COLOR and position of the tail each year's clay ox would have. It was said that the people who came to the ceremony could tell what the weather and harvest would be by the look of the clay ox—a yellow ox predicted a bumper harvest.

P

PA   See BA.

PA CHA   See BA ZHA.

PAGODA   A special tower seven to nine stories high, with the roofs of each story curving upwards like horns. The buildings are often connected with Buddhist temples or have a religious function.

In China pagodas were usually built to honor a special act of devotion by a Buddhist, to correct the FENG SHUI of an area, or to pay tribute to a member of the royal family. They are believed to have been first built in China around the third century A.D.

When BUDDHA died, his ashes were said to be divided into 84,000 holy portions. These were distributed throughout the known world and marked by building a pagoda on each spot.

PA HSIEN   See BA XIAN.

PAI CHUNG   See BAI ZHONG.

PAI HU   See WHITE TIGER OF THE WEST.

PA KUA   See BA GUA.

PALUSHENA   The Chinese name for Vairocana, one of the most important of the FIVE GREAT BUDDHAS OF WISDOM and one revered by many northern Buddhist sects, especially those that follow the Yogacara school. According to the teachings of this school, a Buddhist student should attempt to unite with BUDDHA through spiritual union.

According to Buddhist legend, Palushena was a great teacher who lived in an iron tower in southern India before the eighth century. He inspired three Buddhist disciples who brought the doctrines of Yogacara BUDDHISM to China, where it mixed with and inspired other sects in the MAHAYANA ("Greater Vessel" or "Greater Vehicle") branch of Buddhism.

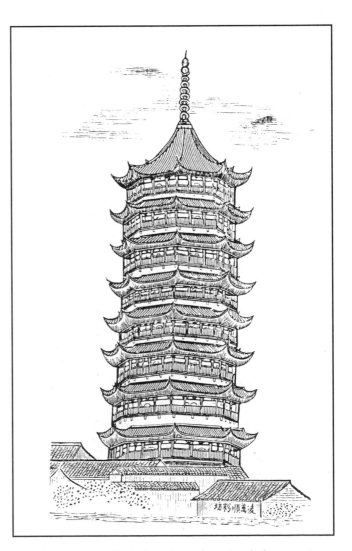

A 19th-century artist's drawing of a pagoda he saw in China during his stay there (The Dragon, Image, and Demon, *1886*)

Palushena is envisioned in a wide variety of ways, especially in Japan, where he is sometimes identified with the monk Kobo Daishi (774–835), who founded the Shingon sect after a visit to China. In general, he is seen as a reincarnation of the first Buddha and identified with the Sun at the center of the universe. In TIBET he is known as Rnam-par-snang-mdsad; in MONGOLIA Nasi Geigülün Djogiaqchi.

PANGU (P'AN KU, P'AN-KU) In Chinese mythology, the creator of the world.

According to this CREATION MYTH, Pangu was the child of the vital YIN AND YANG forces, hatched from the great COSMIC EGG of CHAOS in the beginning of time. He slept in the shell for 18,000 years, until one day he rose and stretched. As the shell broke, YIN, the heavy elements, fell down and created

Pangu, shown here chiseling the universe from chaos (The Dragon, Image, and Demon, *1886*)

the EARTH. YANG, the lighter elements, rose and created HEAVEN.

At first, the distance between these two places was very slight. But each day they moved apart another 10 feet, until after 18,000 years, the space was vast. Pangu grew proportionately. When he died, his body became the surface of the Earth, his breath became the wind and clouds, and his voice became the thunder and lightning. His head was the mountains; his eyes were the SUN and MOON. The insects on his body became human beings.

In some versions of his story, Pangu is said to have chiseled the world from chaos over the span of 18,000 years.

Mythologists have long sought to find the origin of this story. The idea of a creator god forming the world from chaos or even an EGG in the midst of chaos is not unique to China. Brahma, a key figure in Indian and Hindu mythology, for example, was born from a cosmic egg. Since Pangu does not appear in Chinese mythic texts until the third century C.E., one theory holds that the story came from India; another that the myth of Pangu came from what is now Thailand in the sixth century C.E. and was inserted into an earlier story.

In art, Pangu is sometimes shown as a dwarf wearing a bearskin. He may have the Sun and Moon or a hammer and chisel in his hands. He is accompanied by a *QILIN*, RED BIRD (or PHOENIX), TORTOISE, and DRAGON.

PAN GUAN (P'AN KUAN) A term used to describe an officer or aide to a god in Chinese myth. Pan Guan is also mentioned as a mythological character, recording people's fates in a large book, consulted when the soul arrives in the AFTERLIFE.

PAN HU (P'AN HU) A divine DOG in Chinese myth said to have been born from the ear of the wife of GAO XIN (also sometimes known as DI KU). The woman raised him, naming him Pan Hu, which means "Plate-GOURD."

According to the tales, when Gao Xin's kingdom was invaded, he pledged one of his daughters to whatever hero could bring him the head of his enemy. Pan Hu went off and soon brought the enemy's head to Gao Xin. Gao Xin hesitated to carry out his promise, but his daughter and all of his advisers urged him to do so. The girl went away with Pan Hu and became his wife. They had six children; their descendants founded the YAO clan.

This myth is one example of how many Chinese believed that gods could exist in many forms and have supernatural powers that allowed them to do things that would not be possible for humans. The physical impossibility of humans and animals producing children is one of those supernatural acts.

P'AN KU   See PANGU.

PAN KU   Pan Ku (A.D. 32–92) was an important early Chinese writer and historian. He authored the history of the HAN DYNASTY, the *Han shu*, with his father, Pan Piao, and sister, Pan Chao.

P'AN KUAN   See PAN GUAN.

PANTAO   See PEACH.

PAO HSI   See FUXI.

PARADISE   According to one Taoist belief, there are numerous earthly paradises, which are inhabited only by IMMORTALS. The best known are PENG LAI and KUNLUN.

PEACH (*PANTAO, P'AN-T'AO*)   Seen often as a symbol of long life and immortality in Chinese myth and folklore.

The peach tree sometimes appears as a ladder tree between HEAVEN and EARTH (see CHIEN-MU). Some believe that evil spirits and DEMONS can use it to pester humans.

The most famous tree of KUNLUN, or PARADISE, was the fabled peach tree of immortality (the peach tree of the gods), which blossomed once every 3,000 years. It is mentioned in tales of XI WANG MU.

It was a popular custom at one time in China to hang branches of peach blossoms over the front door at the New Year to stop evil from getting through the door.

Because of its connections with ideas of immortality, peachwood was used in TAOISM for exorcisms (see EXORCISTS).

PEACOCK   Though not native to China, the peacock was widely raised throughout the country in ancient times and was prized for its richly colored tail. The feathers, with iridescent COLORS and one to three spots, or "eyes," were worn by high officials in the Ming dynasty (1368–1644).

PEACOCK MOTHER OF BUDDHA   See GUNSHO MINGWANG.

PEARLY EMPEROR   An all-powerful Taoist and Chinese GOD often called or identified in legends with YU TI, Yu Di, or YU HUANG, names ordinarily associated with the Jade EMPEROR.

Some books and scholars treat the Pearly Emperor as a separate god. The name also sometimes used to refer to the Taoist philosophical concept of the god rather than to the popular attributes attached to it. *Pearly* refers to the highest level of Taoist HEAVEN, sometimes called the "Pearly AZURE."

PEI TOU   See BEI DOU.

PENG   See KUN.

PENG LAI (*P'ENG-LAI, P'ENG-LAI SHAN*)   A mythical island in the East China Sea that is said to be the home to the BA XIAN (the Eight IMMORTALS) and other Immortals. It is one of the ISLANDS OF THE IMMORTALS, also called Islands of the Blest.

Many explorers tried to locate the islands and their mythical treasures. Peng Lai, along with the islands Fangchang and Yingzhou, was said to be made of jewels and gold. Its trees were made of pearl and coral, its animals and birds were glittering white, and in its fields grew the PLANT OF IMMORTALITY, *ling zhi*.

There were five original islands. Two drifted away after a giant took away the TORTOISES holding them up. The islands later sank.

PENG MENG   See BENG MENG.

PENGZU (*P'ENG-TSU*)   An old man in Chinese myth and folk tales. "Peng the Ancestor" is a figure of long life. There are different versions of how he got to live so long; in most cases it is said that he pleased the gods with his perfect sacrifices.

PHOENIX Said to rule over the southern quadrant of the HEAVENS in Chinese myth. It is also called the "EMPEROR of all birds" and symbolizes warmth, peace, and prosperity. It is only supposed to appear during the reign of a virtuous ruler, after being summoned by a MUSICAL INSTRUMENT called the *shao*. The phoenix was said to nest in the palace of Emperor YAO, considered one of the kindest of all emperors.

Buddhists consider the phoenix a sacred bird, since it is not a flesh-eating predator.

While the phoenix is often mentioned in myth, scholars cannot decide whether the bird was meant to refer to a real bird, and, if so, which one. Some think it was actually a PEACOCK or an argus pheasant;

Many artists have drawn their own depictions of the mythological Chinese phoenix. It generally looks like a cross between a peacock and a bird of prey.

artists have represented it as both. The bird is sometimes identified as the RED BIRD.

In some Egyptian myths, the phoenix is said to rise from its own ashes after a fiery death. This idea is not present in Chinese myth.

PIEN CH'IAO See BIAN QIAO.

PIG There are several gods of pigs or related beings in ancient Chinese myth. ZHU BAJIE was said to be half pig, half man, due to a mistake he made when he was exiled to EARTH by YU HUANG. ZHUZI ZHEN was known as a god of pigs, the essence of pig, or the perfect pig. And ZHU JUAN SHEN was the god of pigsties.

PI-HSIA YÜAN-CHÜN See SHEN MU.

PILL OF IMMORTALITY According to Taoist belief, a special pill that will make a human become an IMMORTAL. It is manufactured through ALCHEMY. Usually one of its base materials is gold.

PINGHUA *(P'ING-HUA)* Chinese popular narratives, often folklore or legends, from the early 14th century. These prose works deal with heroic themes.

PLANT OF IMMORTALITY From ancient times, the Chinese diet has always included a wide variety of mushrooms and other fungi. The Chinese believed that mushrooms were very healthy and could help people live long. The most important of all fungi was said to be the mythic *ling zhi (ling chih)*, or the plant of immortality (also called the plant of long life), which grows at the roots of trees only during the reigns of a virtuous EMPEROR. It is said that the mystics of the Taoist religion ate the seeds and were able to become IMMORTALS.

Artists show the plant being eaten by the BA XIAN, or Eight Immortals. The design of the Buddhist scepter called *ju-i* is said to be based on the shape of this fungi. According to myths, the *ling chi* grew on an island in the Eastern Sea, also called the East China Sea (see ISLANDS OF THE IMMORTALS). Near it lay a JADE fountain overflowing with sacred wine, offering immortality to whoever ate the fungi and drank the water.

PLUM Aside from being a very popular fruit in China, plums were connected with various legends and myths.

One declared that the philosopher LAO-TZU had been born under a plum tree. Some people believed that just looking at a plum could quench their thirst: A folktale tells how an artist traveling through the desert painted a plum so lifelike that it made his mouth water and helped him survive. A similar story has General Cao, who lived around A.D. 163, advising his thirsty soldiers to gaze on a distant grove of plum trees in order to refresh themselves.

POMEGRANATE Introduced to China during the HAN DYNASTY around 126 B.C., the brilliant red pomegranate, filled with hundreds of sweet-tasting, pearly seeds, was used in making everything from hair dye to MEDICINE.

Buddhists saw the fruit as the essence of good luck and sometimes used twigs of the pomegranate tree to sprinkle water during ceremonies. They substituted pomegranates if PEACHes, the symbol of longevity, were not available for temple ceremonies.

Pomegranates also symbolized the hope that a family would have many generations of children—as many as there were seeds in the fruit.

PO YI In ancient Chinese myths, the tamer of animals and descendant of GAO YANG, a sky god. He is also said to be the controller of floods for YU and an ancestor to the QIN people, originally named Ta Fei.

Po Yi's identity is somewhat confusing, and the name is connected with a number of different figures.

PO YI AND SHU CHI Two brothers in Chinese myth. They refused to take the throne after their father, Guzhou, died. The brothers went into exile, living under the protection of Chang, afterward known as WEN. When Wen and his son WU went to war against the SHANG, the brothers refused to help Wen or Wu and found that they were once more exiles. They eventually starved to death.

Their story was used as an example of the ideal of nonviolence by CONFUCIUS. The Taoist philosophers, on the other hand, pointed out that they had caused their own deaths by refusing to choose sides or fight.

PRETA Evil spirits in Buddhist mythology. They could take over a dead body if certain precautions were not taken. These "hungry GHOSTS" were fed in a special ceremony to keep them away.

An ancestor's ghosts were also fed to keep them from becoming hungry ghosts (see ANCESTORS AND ANCESTOR CULTS).

PROTECTORS OF THE DHARMA In Buddhist myth, gods who fight enemies of the law, or Buddhist DHARMA. The number and names vary from sect to sect. The most popular in ancient China was YANLUO WANG, the fifth king of hell. The ancient Indian term for the divinities is Dharmapālas.

PU-CHOU See BUZHOU.

PURE LAND BUDDHISM According to this school of BUDDHISM, Amitabha BUDDHA (Amida or OMITU FU) reins over a PARADISE called *Qingtu*, a land in the West. If at the point of death, a believer says the Buddha's name, her or his soul will be transported there. The idea was present in China by at least the fifth century and enjoyed great popularity during the TANG DYNASTY and afterward. It also became very popular throughout Japan.

Adherents sometimes use stringed beads to keep track of the many times they say the name during devotions.

PURNA One of Buddha's ten great disciples, known as "He who is first explaining the good law" (see BUDDHA'S DISCIPLES). According to Buddhist legend, Purna was a businessman who heard the historical BUDDHA preach in Sravasti, India. After his conversion, he preached far and wide. Some believe he protects sailors on their voyages.

PURPLE PALACE According to a late Taoist belief, the Purple Palace is the highest home in HEAVEN, reserved for the king of heaven.

The heaven of Pure Land Buddhism promised an afterlife of joy (The Dragon, Image, and Demon, *1886*)

PU XIAN (P'U HSIEN, PU K'UNG) A Buddhist BODHISATTVA and historical figure (d. A.D. 774) who popularized Tantric BUDDHISM in China. (Tantric Buddhism uses special rituals and meditation as part of its practice.)

The monk is said to have come from Ceylon (present-day Sri Lanka) around A.D. 719 and was held in high regard by EMPERORS of the TANG DYNASTY. He brought with him a collection of holy books of Buddhist teachings. He is said to have worked many magic spells during his time in China.

One legend about him tells of how he fought with and conquered a magical white ELEPHANT who could turn into a man (see SHAPE SHIFTING). Another tells of how he produced rain by making clay figures of DRAGONS and reciting prayers over them.

Pu Xian was a popular bodhisattva figure in China, and many Buddhist temples were dedicated to him. He is often shown riding a placid white elephant with long tusks and is often portrayed with a green face, wearing a yellow robe with a red collar and holding a LOTUS stalk with a SUN on top.

He is also called Amogha, O-mo-K'a, and Po-che-lo.

QI (CH'I) A Chinese term for natural energy, positive forces flowing through the earth that can help humans. The concept is especially important in FENG SHUI.

QIAN FO (DINGGUANG FO) The "Thousand BUDDHAS," a term for the Buddhas who have lived in the past, according to Buddhist belief and myth.

According to some Buddhist sects, there has been an infinite number of Buddhas in the past. Scholars generally interpret the NUMBER 1,000 as symbolizing the uncountable number of Buddhas. Caves at Dunhuang in China commemorate these past Buddhas.

Besides the historical Buddha, only a very few past Buddhas are revered as individuals by different Buddhist sects. The best known in China is DINGGUANG FO, the Chinese name for the past Buddha also called Dapankara. Dingguang Fo is known as Mar-me-msdad in TIBET and Chula Choqiaqchi in MONGOLIA.

QI GU-NIANG See SHENG MU.

QI GUZI (CH'I KU-TZO) The "Seven Young Ladies," mountain spirits honored in Fujian Province in ancient times. They were said to help avert droughts, floods, and disease.

QILIN (CH'I-LIN, KILIN) A mythological Chinese beast, similar to a unicorn and usually called one in translations of Chinese stories. Its body was like a deer's, except that its hoofs were like a horse's. On its head was an enormous horn that looked like a spear. This horn could be used as a weapon to banish evil spirits. The *qilin* would not attack the innocent (see GAO YAO).

The *qilin* was used in art to symbolize justice. According to legend, a *qilin* would appear in a court where the ruler was especially good or just.

QIN (CH'IN) An independent state on the eastern coast of China. During the third century B.C., its ruler King Cheng conquered six of its neighbors to form an empire, the basis for the Chinese kingdoms that followed. The name China comes from Ch'in, the Wade-Giles Romanization of Qin.

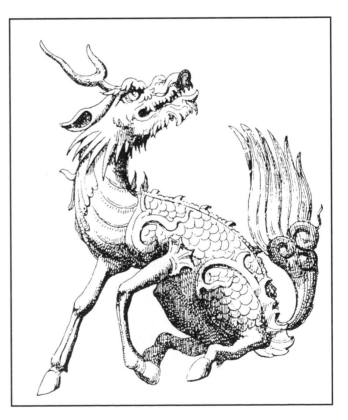

Though often called a "unicorn" in translations, the *qilin* is not as horselike as the unicorn of Western myths, as seen in this illustration.

QIN DYNASTY (CH'IN DYNASTY) The historical rulers of the early Chinese Empire. The emperors of Qin claimed to have descended from the sky god GAO YANG through PO YI.

QING DYNASTY (CH'ING DYNASTY) The period of Chinese history from the Manchurian conquest of China in 1644 to the revolution in 1911. The Qing rulers came from Manchuria, slowly extending their control after a period of chaos. They employed a variety of methods, including the use of Confucian doctrines and popular gods, to maintain their political authority. They encouraged the more obedient forms of Tibetan BUDDHISM and rural rituals.

QING LONG (CH'ING LUNG) The Blue DRAGON. He is one of the guardians of Taoist temples with Bai Hu, the WHITE TIGER OF THE WEST. Qing Long is identified with Deng Jiugong, a legendary general for the SHANG DYNASTY.

QING LONG PA JIANG JUN The mythical "Green DRAGON General" in Chinese myth. He guards the entrance to the hall of the Jade Emperor, YU HUANG.

QINGQUI (CH'ING-CH'IU) A mythic marsh of the East sometimes mentioned in ancient Chinese myths.

QIN GUANG WANG (CH'IN KUANG-WANG) The president of the first court of the Taoist AFTERLIFE.

According to this set of beliefs, Qin Guang Wang reviews the weight of a soul's sins when the soul arrives in the afterlife. If the soul's good outweighs the bad, the soul goes straight to the 10th court, where it will be reborn. On the other hand, bad sinners go to Yejing Tai, or Mirror Tower, where they see what is in store for them—reincarnation as a cow, mule, DOG, or reptile (see REBIRTH AND REINCARNATION). Then they work off their sins in a series of courts as they travel to the 10th court to be reborn.

QING WA SHEN (CH'ING WA SHEN) Frog spirits, thought to have power to prevent or cure illness in ancient Chinese folk belief and myth. Frog spirits were also thought to bring success in business. There were a number of such spirits around the country. Many were said to be the spirits of actual people who were able to assist the living.

QUEEN MOTHER OF THE WEST See XI WANG MU.

QUEEN OF HEAVEN A mythical goddess who is said to control the sea. Mythologists have connected her with a number of different traditions, including BUDDHISM and TAOISM, as well as popular belief.

In ancient China, seafarers worshipped her just before the first trip of the fishing season, prayed to her when making or mending their fishing nets, put her image on their boats, and kept a lamp burning to illuminate her image throughout the voyage. Seafarers often made models of fishing boats as tokens of their gratitude, which they placed next to her image. Her temples were found along shores, harbors, and centers of fishing towns and trade ports. When a long sea voyage was planned, the whole town joined in a procession in her honor.

In Buddhist myth, the deity was identified with the goddess of the dawn or light, Maritichi. Taoists, influenced by Buddhist portrayals, called her Zhun Di (or Chun Ti in old style) and made her more warlike. In the seventh and eighth centuries, she gained her own collection of gods to serve her.

Popular stories connect the mythic figure with a woman of the Lin family known as Aunt Lin, who lived in Fujian, China, during or before the 10th century (see GODS IDENTIFIED WITH HUMANS). It is said that her mother and father went out fishing every day, while she stayed on shore, chanting prayers for her parents' safe return. One day she had a vision: The entire fishing fleet was floundering on the high seas. She ran to the shore and, with her prayers, guided her parents' boat back to shore; it was the only boat to return.

For the rest of her life, Aunt Lin cared for mariners. Her concern for them was said to continue after her death, and gradually she came to be considered a significant local deity in an area where fishing and seafaring were important.

In 1156 the EMPEROR officially recognized Aunt Lin's contributions to mariners and the country in general. As her fame grew, so too did the things she was said to do as a deity. By the beginning of the 15th century, she was considered a protector of all Chinese. The emperor declared her a concubine, or wife of HEAVEN.

As the QING emperors moved to control the Fujian coast, they sought to gain popularity by aligning themselves with the goddess and to elevate their own status by simultaneously making her more important. In 1737 the emperor declared her the empress of heaven, at the top of the pantheon.

Artists often portray her sitting on a throne, with her two female assistants, Thousand Mile Eyes, who carries a sword, and Fair Wind Ears, who carries a long horn.

QUEEN OF MAGIC   See GUNSHO MINGWANG.

QUESTIONS OF HEAVEN   A Chinese text collected in *Songs of Chu*. Dating from about the fourth century B.C., it is an important source of ancient Chinese myth; in some cases, it gives the oldest record of the tales. It is written in a unique question-and-answer style, which accounts for its title. The author's name is not recorded but is believed to have been a member of the Chu state during the late ZHOU DYNASTY.

Aunt Lin, the Queen of Heaven (The Dragon, Image, and Demon, *1886*)

R

RABBIT   See HARE.

RAIN GOD (RAIN SPIRIT, YÜ SHIH, YU SHIH)   An early nature god who appears in Chinese myth and legends. The rain god is a generic god, one of several who can work together to produce storms, including the Thunder God (LEI GONG), the LIGHTNING GODDESS, and the Wind God (FENG BO). As the concept evolved, later versions of these myths refer to more specific forms of a rain god, such as the RAIN MASTER, the son of GONG GONG.

RAIN MASTER (YU SHIH)   In later Chinese myth, the son of GONG GONG. His power is so great that a drop of water from his cup will bring a week's downpour.

In the legends of the battles between Huang Di, the YELLOW EMPEROR, and the rebellious CHIYOU, god of rain, the Rain Master and FENG BO, a wind god, agreed to bring a major storm against the Yellow Emperor's armies.

Artists depicted the Rain Master as a human figure holding either a vial of water or a DRAGON sitting on a platter, since the dragon can also be a symbol of rain.

RAKSAS   The five "protectors" in Buddhist myth. These female divinities combat evil; their feminine power complements the male power of the FIVE GREAT BUDDHAS OF WISDOM. The best known in China was GUNSHO MINGWANG, the Chinese name for Mahamayuri, the "Queen of Magic" and "Peacock Mother" of BUDDHA. While Gunsho Mingwang protects believers from harm, her force is not aggressive. She can ward off SNAKE bites, poisons, and other disasters. In TIBET, she is called Rma-bya Chen-no.

REBIRTH AND REINCARNATION   The idea that a soul returns to life in another body. Rebirth is an important element of Buddhist and later Taoist belief.

According to BUDDHISM, during each life, a soul can seek to advance through the different spheres of existence, until finally it reaches ENLIGHTENMENT or NIRVANA. The cycle of life and death is known as *samsara*. Exact beliefs about rebirth differ depending on sect, but, in general, a soul must do good deeds and follow its KARMA, or destiny, to move toward a higher level of existence.

RED   The COLOR red is often used by Chinese artists and writers to symbolize luck and joy. The color's symbolism was widely recognized, beyond myth and legend. For example, a bride's wedding robe was traditionally red, bringing luck and joy to the marriage.

RED BIRD (SCARLET BIRD)   A mythical bird of prey that symbolized the South in Chinese myth and folklore. It was later identified with the pheasant and the mythical PHOENIX. It was also connected with summer and the element of fire, and it represented drought and the YIN principle, negative and female. It also represented the empress.

RED CHILD DEMON   A monster who was a friend of the MONKEY KING but taunted him and his companions (see XIYOU JI.)

REINCARNATION   See REBIRTH AND REINCARNATION.

RESPONDING DRAGON   See YING LONG.

RHINOCEROS HORN   Before the historic era, a species of rhinoceros lived in Sichuan (Szechwan).

In the years that followed, fossilized rhinoceros teeth were excavated and sold as "DRAGON's teeth." Sometimes they were ground up and used in MEDICINE. Horns were also carved in elaborate designs for use in ceremonies or as decorations in temples and palaces. A pair of horns was considered one of the Eight Treasures or lucky tokens of China. The other treasures included pearls, coins, mirrors, books, jade stone gong, a faceted stone or jewel, and a healing artemesia leaf.

RICE An important crop in southern China during ancient times up to the present. Images of rice appeared on clothing and belt buckles of government officials and naval officers.

RUYIZHU According to Buddhist myth, the *ruyizhu* is a special jewel that can bring ENLIGHTENMENT. In art, it is usually depicted as a glowing ball with a pointed top. While the jewel can bring enlightenment and freedom from desire, it can also grant wishes.

S

SA CHEN JEN   See SA ZHENREN.

SALT RIVER GODDESS   A deity in Chinese mythology. She tries to trick the LORD OF THE GRANARY into marrying her and staying in her kingdom near the river. The story is part of a FOUNDING MYTH.

The Lord of the Granary sailed his boat down the river from the mountain of Wuluo to the Salt River. There he was met by the beautiful Salt River Goddess. She tempted him to stay with her forever, but the Lord of the Granary declined. However, that night, as he slept, she came and lay with him. In the morning, she turned into a bug. The goddess then gathered so many other bugs together that they blocked out the sky, and the Lord of the Granary could not find the direction home. He also could not see which one of the many flies was she, so there was no way of dispelling the insects.

Finally, the Lord of the Granary announced that he had decided to marry her. He gave one of her servants a green SILK belt, saying the goddess should wear it as a token of their engagement. As soon as she put it on, he knew where she was and killed her with an arrow. His way was then clear to return home.

SAN BAO (SAN PAO)   The three jewels or precious objects honored in Buddhist myth: BUDDHA, his law, and the priesthood.

SANG-LIN   A MULBERRY forest in Chinese myth. It is where the divine archer, YI, kills Fengxi. The forest is also mentioned in the tales of TANG THE CONQUEROR.

SAN GUAN DADI (SAN KUAN TA-TI, SAN KUAN, SAN GUAN, SAN YUAN DADI, SAN QING DAOZU, SAN QUING DAOZU)   A grouping of three gods who personify the three elements that rule the entire universe according to some Taoist beliefs: the elements of breath, vital essence, and spirit. The figures became entwined with different beliefs and attributes as time went on, but they remained generally popular for centuries.

Zhang Heng, a Taoist philosopher who lived during the reign of Ling Di (A.D. 168–90), is credited with explaining how the GODS divided up their responsibilities. The system was based on a concept that divided the universe into three spheres, with each god presiding over one sphere. The three gods are as follows:

Yuanshi Tianzong (Yüan-shih T'ien-tsun): He is also known as "Perfect One" or "JADE Pure." This eternal being has the power of invisibility and represents the world's origins. He dominated the first phase of creation and was credited with creating the HEAVENS and the EARTH. He is in charge of the highest layer of Taoist heaven.

Lingbao Tianzong (Ling-pao Ta Fa-Shih): He is called the "Highest Holy One" or "High Pure," because he represents the elements of energy and activity. He invented the calculations of time and controls YIN AND YANG. He dominated the second phase of creation and is in charge of the second layer of heaven.

LAO JUN (Lao Chün): He is called "Greatest Holy One" and "Supreme Pure." He represents the human race. He dominated the third phase of the creation of the universe and inspired humans to establish TAOISM. He is said to be the deified form of philosopher LAO-TZU, who founded Taoism. He is in charge of the lowest layer of heaven.

They are also called the "Three Supreme Rulers" or "the Venerable Three Rulers."

In later variations of the basic mythological beliefs, the deities were referred to as the "Three Officials." Here their names were TIEN GUAN (the official of heaven and bringer of happiness), DI GUAN (the official of earth and forgiver of sins), and SHUI GUAN, (the official of water and diverter of misfortune). They were said to have been sent by the Jade Emperor, YU HUANG, at that time considered the highest authority in heaven, to observe the thoughts and deeds of humans.

In general, the trio was believed to forgive sins, prevent disasters, and ward off the spirits that brought on illness. Some texts also refer to them as the controllers of heaven, earth, and the waters. Others refer to them as the rulers of three periods, or epochs, of universal history. The gods were said to control a different part of each year as well as a historical period.

Those who believed that the gods forgave sins followed a threefold ritual to earn forgiveness. Sins were written on three pieces of paper. One piece was burned; its smoke reached the gods in heaven, where it was read and the sin was pardoned. Another was buried; the essence of earth absorbed it and forgave the sin. The last was thrown into water, where the sin was washed away.

The three figures were popularized in a short play, called *The Official of Heaven Brings Happiness*, which was traditionally shown before theatrical performances. Artists portrayed them as three long-bearded emperors wearing royal robes and crowns that sometimes bear the yin and yang symbol.

SAN HSING   See SAN XING.

SAN KUAN TA-TI   See SAN GUAN DADI.

SAN PAO   See SAN BAO.

SAN QING DAOZU   See SAN GUAN DADI.

SAN T'AI TZÜ   See NAZHA.

SAN XING (SAN HSING, SAN-HSING)   The "Three Stars of Good Luck"; popular figures in Chinese myth and lore.

These three Chinese gods of good fortune are connected with the stars of the constellation of Ursa Minor. They were said to have started out as human beings who were given the gift of divine status, because of their special merits or deeds (see GODS IDENTIFIED WITH HUMANS). Artists portray them in various ways, but the most common is as three happy old men, surrounded by symbols of good fortune and immortality.

The three gods are FUXING, or Fu Shen, the god of happiness; LUXING, or Lu Hsing, the god of salaries and honors; and SHOUXING, or Shou Hsin, the god of longevity.

The three are identified with a number of historic figures. Fuxing is usually identified with YANG CHENG, who won fame for protecting the rights of dwarfs at the imperial court. He was alternatively identified with a minister of the EMPEROR WEN ZHANG (535–52) and a famous historical general, GUO-ZIYI.

Luxing was said to be a servant of the founder of the HAN DYNASTY in the beginning of the second century B.C. named Shi Fen.

Shouxing is also called Shou Lao, Nan-chi Lao-jen, and "the Old Man of the South Pole." He is in

The three popular Chinese gods of good luck, personified as (clockwise, from left) the god of happiness, the god of honors, and the god of longevity (The Dragon, Image, and Demon, *1886*)

charge of determining the date that someone will die. He was connected with Peng Zu, a distant descendant of Emperor Zhuan Xu, who claimed to be 2,000 years old.

SAN YÜAN   See SAN GUAN DADI.

SA ZHENREN (SA CHEN JEN)   A mythic Taoist doctor and MAGICIAN said to have lived in SHU. He had the power to bring lightning. According to one legend, he ascended to become an IMMORTAL while his body was being carried in a coffin. His mourners noticed that the coffin was very light and opened it to discover that he was gone.

SCARLET BIRD   See RED BIRD.

SCULPTURE   Chinese sculpture dates to prehistoric times. At times, its subjects have concerned myth, state religion, and FOLK RELIGION.

Early on, Chinese artists mastered the carving of ivory and JADE, as well as wood, stone, and other materials. Early prehistoric sculpture was mostly on a small scale. BUDDHISM, however, encouraged the use of bronze and the casting of large statues, often of BUDDHA.

Stone sculpture has been found from the SHANG DYNASTY. Among the figures that have survived from this time are TIGERS, buffalo, and OWLS. During the HAN DYNASTY, stone LIONS were erected as guards to tombs. *Ming qi* or *ming ch'i* were objects made from pottery ceramics specifically to be buried in tombs with the dead. These objects included animals, buildings, gods, foods, utensils, and other examples of contemporary life.

Early wood carvings of figures have been found in tombs from the TANG DYNASTY. Much smaller figures of different GODS and IMMORTALS also survive. These were apparently very popular during the Ming period, when they were carved in great numbers. Buddhist divinities were also popular. Larger than a person, these statues were covered with plaster and painted. Some had bits of gold applied to them.

SEN SHIN   The "Noxious God" in TAOISM and popular belief. The Sen Shin takes the soul when a person dies and brings it back to the deceased's home. A

The Sen Shin brings a soul home after the body has died. This spirit must be treated very carefully. (The Dragon, Image, and Demon, *1886*)

Taoist priest would perform a ceremony to rid the house of the being, who in art looks like a rooster. The ceremony was performed two to three weeks after death and was one of the most important funeral services.

(In some English texts, the god's name is given as SAN XING or San Hsing, but this god is different from the popular gods of happiness also known by that name.)

SERPENT   See SNAKE.

SHA   A Chinese term for the evil energies that flow through the EARTH, often taking humanmade paths, such as roads or ditches. The idea is important in FENG SHUI.

SHAMAN   A shaman communicates with the spirit world, usually through ritual or other special means. Many ancient religions and folk practices involved the use of shamans as priests and healers (see ORACLE BONES). Shamans date to prehistory in China and were not completely displaced by newer religions or philosophies, such as TAOISM or BUDDHISM (see SHANG DYNASTY).

The term *wu* is sometimes used for a female and *xi* for a male shaman in Chinese (see KUNLUN).

SHANG CH'ING   See SHANG QING.

SHANG DI (SHANG TI)   A mythological being known as the "Supreme Being," sometimes simply called "Di" or "Ti," meaning "lord" or "GOD." Shang Di was considered to be the father of China's SHANG DYNASTY, which lasted from 1550 B.C. to 1027 B.C. He ruled HEAVEN and controlled the gods of thunder, lightning, wind, and rain. People of ancient China believed that he determined their fates, and he was also regarded as the god of AGRICULTURE.

SHANG DYNASTY (YIN DYNASTY) An

early Chinese period, until recently believed to be mostly legendary. However, archaeological discoveries in the late 20th century have shown that it was real and have uncovered much information about it.

Historians and archaeologists believe that the dynasty thrived from around 1550 B.C. to 1027 B.C. It is mentioned in the SHIJING, the first history of China, but little was known of this early Chinese civilization until the beginning of the 20th century, when archaeologists began important excavations.

Centered around the YELLOW RIVER, the people who lived during the Shang period had elaborate architecture, arts, and culture. They used a 10-day week and regarded their ancestors as deities who could help or harm the living (see ANCESTORS AND ANCESTOR CULTS). Ancestor worship rites that honored the Shang dynasty continued in Sun (now Shantung) long after the DYNASTY fell from power. Animal sacrifices were made to gain the favors of the departed souls or to avoid their curses.

The Shang people's religious practices apparently included human sacrifices. Hundreds of victims have been found in tombs and building foundations, though scholars continue to study the practices and their meanings.

Among the most interesting archaeological discoveries have been ORACLE BONES, which were used to gather information and advice from ancestral spirits and gods.

Ancient texts say that there were 31 Shang EMPERORS, whose family name was Zi. They were replaced by the ZHOU DYNASTY.

By the 1990s, scholars had identified 30 kings and seven capitals, including one near Zhengzhou and another, YIN, at Anyang in present-day China. Approximately 1,000 towns had been identified from writing on oracle bones.

In Chinese myth, the Shang were said to have descended from CHIEN DI and could therefore trace their origins to the gods. The dynasty itself was said to have been founded by TANG THE CONQUEROR.

Accounts of the Shang in ancient Chinese texts mix myth with history, and it is often difficult to separate the two. As a general rule, the later the period mentioned, the closer historians believe the information is to being accurate.

SHANG QING (SHANG CH'ING) One of

three parts in the Taoist HEAVEN. Each part is called an AZURE. They are YOU QING ("Pearly Azure"), Shang Qing ("Upper Azure"), and TAI QING ("Supreme Azure").

SHAO HAO (CH'ING YANG) The mythical

ruler of the kingdom of Niao in Chinese myth. The kingdom is said to lie in a waterfall pool beyond the Eastern Sea.

The kingdom's name means "bird." Shao Hao chose the name, because when he came to the throne, PHOENIXES appeared. Each minister and government agency had the title of a bird. The "Hawks," for example, were police.

SHAPE SHIFTING Many early Chinese myths

featured creatures with the characteristics of many different beasts. The Chinese QILIN, for example, though usually called simply a "unicorn," is said to have a deer's body, a horse's hooves, and a cow's tail, and an enormous spear or pointed horn growing out of its forehead. Serpent tails are common. Sometimes the beasts are presented as half-human.

According to Taoist belief, a learned scholar of TAOISM could master a wide range of arts. Among the most mysterious—but also the most powerful—was the ability to change shapes. Taoist priests often change shapes in myths. XU ZHENJUN, for example, became a DRAGON then an OX, during one of his battles.

SHEJI (SHE CHI) Gods of the soil and harvest in

Chinese mythology. Each god helps farmers in a local area. A large collection of important historical figures came to personify these gods, both locally and nationally (see GODS IDENTIFIED WITH HUMANS).

SHEN NONG is honored as the patron of AGRICULTURE and the first farmer.

SHELI FO (SHELO-ZI) One of the historical BUDDHA's disciples (see BUDDHA'S DISCIPLES). According to tradition, he was a regent and law giver. In TIBET he is known as Nid-rgyal. His ancient Indian name is Sariputra, and he is known as the first in wisdom.

SHEN A term usually translated as "spirit" or "soul," used in connection with Chinese myth and religious beliefs. Scholars say that there are two kinds of *shen*. One lives in human bodies during life. The other lives on after DEATH. Those blessed with abundant life *shen* can be powerful enough to rule over others, including gods.

SHENG GU (SHENG-KU) A legendary female Taoist MAGICIAN said to have lived during the TANG DYNASTY. She could walk on water. After a disagreement, her husband tried to have her killed. Instead, her body stayed in its perfect state for 700 years. In the meantime, her soul had shed its hull and become an IMMORTAL.

SHENG JEN The highest level of Taoist IMMORTAL, the saint (see TAOISM).

SHENG-KU See SHENG GU.

SHENG MU (BIXIA SHENGMU, PI-HSIA YÜAN-CHÜN, SHENGMU) The mythological daughter of the powerful DONGYUE DADI, the god of the eastern peak, who supervised all areas of human life on EARTH. She looked after the welfare of women and children and was the goddess of childbirth.

She was also known as Tai Shan Niangniang and called "the Celestial Immortal Who Brings Children," "the Saintly Mother," "the Matron Who Brings Children," and "the Goddess of the Varied Clouds." She was venerated by many and eventually compared to GUANYIN, considered the Buddhist goddess of mercy in China.

SHEN I See YI.

SHEN NONG (SHEN NUNG) Also called "the Divine Farmer" and "the Divine Husbandman," Shen Nong was a mythical emperor of China's prehistoric period (2838–2698 B.C.) and was said to be the sec-

Sheng Mu, the daughter of the eastern peak (The Dragon, Image, and Demon, *1886*)

ond ruler, after FUXI. (Some early sources vary his position.) Ancient Chinese myths honor him as a god of MEDICINE, health, AGRICULTURE, and forestry. He is said to have taught humans to farm. He is one of the Three Nobles.

Shen Nong is often portrayed wearing green leaves, since he was considered a primitive god who lived before clothes were invented. While he was a good and kind god, he ruled with the assistance of the agent of fire and was sometimes called "the God of the Hot Winds," which could bring harm to the crops.

According to the myths, Shen Nong was the son of a princess named Andeng. She conceived her son through the influence of a heavenly DRAGON. He was born near the Chiang River and belonged to the CLAN of the Lieshan.

Shen Nong was said to live very simply. He invented the plow and grew grain in a field he plowed and cultivated himself. He analyzed the useful and harmful qualities of many plants. He taught others to farm. He also invented markets where farmers could trade for what they needed. His wife was said to grow MULBERRY trees. He ruled without laws, and his kingdom existed in complete harmony. War was unknown.

A group of Chinese scholars known as "the Tillers" wrote about the emperor during the third and second centuries B.C. Their works have been lost, but they used Shen Nong's mythical kingdom as an example of a utopia, or a perfect agrarian society.

Scholars of Chinese mythology note that the stories of Shen Nong are unusual, because they show the emperor and his wife doing manual labor in the fields. Ordinarily, manual labor was looked down upon and was considered to be beneath an emperor. Another interesting aspect of the Shen Nong stories is the emphasis on what might be called scientific method. Shen Nong tastes different fruits to determine their qualities. Rather than possessing infinite knowledge, he is an experimenter and a learner.

These experiments also connect him with early medicine and medical knowledge, because of the ability of different herbs discovered through trial and error to cure ailments. Early texts on the power of medicinal herbs are credited to him.

In some works, Shen Nong is confused with YAN DI, the Flame Emperor.

SHENO WANG   A spirit of fire that appeared as a SNAKE.

SHEN TU   DOOR SPIRITS said in folk belief to protect the doors of Chinese homes. In ancient times, they appeared as pictures or small statues near the walls of many homes.

The most popular door gods are a pair of mythic brothers said to have lived on Mount Tu Suo, Shen Tu (or She T'u) and Yu Lei (or Yü Lei). The older Shen Tu stands to the left, and Yu Lei patrols on the right. They were said to have power to tie up any evil spirits and feed them to the TIGERS. The popular name, *shen tu*, was taken from the elder brother's name.

These brothers are the poor man's version of the more powerful *shen meng*, or door gods, since they can only tie up the spirits, not slay them.

SHE WANG   The king or god of SNAKES (or serpents) in Chinese myth.

SHI GAN DANG   A special stone in Chinese myth and folk belief said to keep away bad spirits. A TIGER's head is carved in the stone. On the forehead of the tiger is the character for *Wang*, meaning king.

The stones are said to have the spirit of a brave person within them.

SHIH-JOU   See SHIROU.

SHI HUANG DI   King Cheng (d. 210 B.C.) of QIN, the historical ruler who emerged as the victor in the period of the Warring States. Shi Huang Di called himself the "first EMPEROR" of unified China and set the pattern for many leaders who followed. In fact, the name China is said to derive from the name Ch'in (now spelled Qin in pinyin), the country he started from.

Cheng took over as king of Qin in 246. At the time Qin was a small but important state on the coast of China. But the king conquered nearby Han, Wei, CHU, Chao, Yen, and Qi, combining them into an empire covering the eastern portion of China.

When he established the empire, King Cheng declared himself Shi Huang Di. (*Shi* means "first," and *Huang Di* means "emperor.") He instituted a strong central government, standardized measurements, and issued consistent laws. He also established strong defenses. He started the Great Wall, drafted and maintained an army, and traveled throughout the kingdom. He also ruthlessly suppressed rebellions. Shi Huang Di's prime minister was a scholar named Li Szu (or Li Ssu), who believed that the state must have a strong central government to thrive.

Shi Huang Di was succeeded by a son who proved to be a very weak leader. Rebellions followed, and the country broke back into independent states amid much conflict and chaos. The Western HAN DYNASTY, started by Liu Pang (256–195 B.C.), eventually succeeded in reuniting the empire.

SHIJI   (SHIH-CHI)   The *Historical Records* written by Han court historian, archivist, and astronomer SIMA QIAN (145 B.C.–c.90 B.C.). The work became the model for official histories that followed. It had 130 chapters and began with the creation of humans. Much of the early material is myth or legend. It also included information on astronomy, economy, and proper rules of behavior.

Sima Qian said that his father had started the work and that he merely finished it.

SHIJING   (SHIH-CHING, MAO CHIH, MAO SHIH)   This collection of ancient poems, the *Classic*

of Poetry, first published in 600 B.C., was used by CONFUCIUS as an example of great writing and literature. It has more than 300 poems, including ballads and songs. They cover a wide range of topics and include more formal hymns sung at religious rituals. According to tradition, the anthology was burned by order of SHI HUANG DI during the period of Warring States, but it was recovered and rewritten. The version that survived includes a commentary by Mao Chang (also written as Mao Ch'ang) and is sometimes called the *Mao Shih*.

SHIROU (SHIH-JOU) A mythological creature said to be one of the guards of KUNLUN. It looks like an OX's liver.

SHOUXING (SHOU HSING, SHOU-HSING LAO T'OU-TZU) The Chinese god of longevity, connected with a STAR located in the constellation of Argo. The star is known to many in the West as Canopus, the second-brightest star in the sky.

Shouxing is a popular figure, especially as a member of the SAN XING, or San Hsing, the gods of happiness and wealth also known as "the Three Stars of Good Luck." He was also called "the Old Man of the South Pole," under whose influence the nation enjoyed peace.

Artists show him as an elderly man with a long white beard, a bald head, and a sweet expression, riding or leaning on a male deer and usually holding one of the PEACHES of eternal life and a long staff with the ELIXIR OF LIFE hanging from the top. This is a reference to his early identification as a Taoist IMMORTAL.

Shouxing is in charge of determining the date that someone will die and of writing it down in his ledger. The digits of the appointed date can never be changed, but one legend hints that he might juggle them in someone's favor. According to this tale, a child called Zao Yan found out that he would die in 19 years. A monk told him to go to a field where two men were playing a board game and offer them something to eat and a jug of good wine. But he was warned not to answer any of their questions.

While he waited quietly, the two old men argued about how they should thank him. One of the old men was Shouxing, who decided he would swap the number of years the boy would live, giving him 91 instead of 19.

SHU The ancient state of Sichuan (Szechwan), in south-central China. The Shu kings traced their ancestors to CAN CONG, a god who taught humans how to make SILK.

SHUBOJIA (SUBHUTI) One of BUDDHA'S DISCIPLES, Shubojia is considered in many Buddhist schools to be the historical BUDDHA's spokesman. He is the first in expressing emptiness or in talking about the need to empty oneself of desire. In TIBET he is known as Rabhbyor.

SHU-CHING See SHUJING.

SHUI FANG In Chinese mythology, a god of AGRICULTURE, specifically, the god of embankments and dikes. These manmade structures are part of an irrigation system and keep water from flooding fields and villages during heavy rains.

SHUI FU The celestial ministry of water in Chinese myth; also called the treasury (or palace) of water. This was an especially large ministry, with a council headed by a DRAGON god, dragon kings who functioned as ministers of the four seas (one for each DIRECTION OF THE COMPASS), a ministry of salt waters with many departments, and separate bureaus for lakes, ponds, wells, and every other imaginable body of water. There were even roaming spirits not specifically in charge of anything.

The MINISTRIES OF GODS in Chinese myth were beneficent deities who could use their powers to help people in various ways. The members of Shui Fu might help bring a good harvest of pearls or save a land from FLOODS.

SHUI GUAN (SHUI KUAN) The "Official of Water and Diverter of Misfortune"; one of a trio of Taoist and popular gods called the SAN GUAN DADI. The gods forgive sin and bring happiness. The others are TIEN GUAN (HEAVEN) and DI GUAN (EARTH).

SHUI KUAN See SHUI GUAN.

SHUI YONG (SHUI YUNG) A god of agriculture in Chinese myth, specifically the deity of canals and rivers.

SHUJING (SHU-CHING) The *Classic of History*; an early history of the Chinese DYNASTIES.

Scholars say much of the book comes from the fourth century B.C. or earlier. Though presented as a history, the book includes much mythological information. The first five chapters deal with the GOLDEN AGE, the next three with the XIA DYNASTY (the dates given are roughly 2205 to 1766 B.C.), and the rest with the SHANG DYNASTY and Western ZHOU.

The book contains documents, speeches, proclamations, and orations and is presented as history, though the early events are legendary and mythic.

Copies were burned under the ruler SHI HUANG DI, but, according to legend, a copy was found hidden in the wall of CONFUCIUS's own house. Confucians included the book among the FIVE classics all scholars should study.

SHUN (CH'UNG HUA, YU TI SHUN, YU YU) The second of three great legendary kings who ruled in the GOLDEN AGE of China's prehistory. He came after YAO and before YU.

Shun's stories often show him as a faithful son and celebrate this important virtue. In these tales, he is a hero who has to fight off the tricks of his half-brother and his blind (and usually evil) father, who favored his half-brother. In one story, Shun was sent to fix a shed—only to have his parents pull the ladder away and set fire to it. Then he is trapped in a well while digging it out. But Shun miraculously survives all trials. When his half-brother comes to him, Shun forgives him and even asks him to help him govern the land.

Shun was chosen by EMPEROR Yao, first as an aide and then as his own successor, because of his great loyalty and ability. It is said that the emperor felt that Shun would make a wiser ruler than his own evil son. Shun married the emperor's two daughters, Nu Ying and O Huang. Eventually, he was given the honorary title of *Chong Hua*, which implied that he had surpassed Yao in virtue.

Shun was said to have been buried in the mountainous wilderness of ZANG WU, a place in the South where eagles, ELEPHANTS, and TIGERS roamed. His half-brother, having repented of his evil, watches over the grave. The nearby mountain is known as the "NINE Doubts."

SILK The ancient Chinese are believed to have discovered silk threads and learned how to weave them into strong and beautiful cloth before the middle of the third century B.C. For hundreds of years, the methods used in creating the material remained a secret; even after silk was exported to other countries, China had a monopoly on its production.

In ancient times, the process began with silk worms that were carefully cared for, fed on MULBERRY leaves, and then killed in larvae stage so that their filament thread could be harvested.

Silk thread's natural strength and versatility allowed it to be used to create beautiful garments, which were worn by the wealthy and powerful. The cloth is often cited as a sign of status and wealth in Chinese legend and myth. Its trade was an important source of income and contact with outside cultures, and it was a valued gift in early diplomacy.

SIMA QIAN (SSU-MA CH'IEN) HAN court historian, archivist, and astronomer, Sima Qian (145–c.90 B.C.) wrote the SHIJI, or *Historical Records*.

SKU-INGA A Tibetan name for the FIVE GREAT KINGS.

SKY GOD See TIAN DI.

SKY RIVER Another name for the Milky Way galaxy, used in Chinese myth. To the ancient Chinese, this broad, curving band of STARS was a heavenly river, sweeping across the terrain of HEAVEN in the same way the YELLOW RIVER flowed across the Chinese land.

The Sky River plays an important role in the myth of the WEAVERGIRL AND HEAVENLY OX.

SNAKE (SERPENT) The sixth creature of the TWELVE TERRESTRIAL BRANCHES.

In Chinese myth and folklore, snakes were often seen as deities in disguise, often bad ones that could inflict harm even when appearing innocent. They were considered self-serving and cunning, using flattery and misdirection to get what they wanted.

SONG DYNASTY (SUNG DYNASTY) Chinese historical period, 960 to 1280, during which the empire was ruled by EMPERORS known as the Song. The period is sometimes split into the Northern Song DYNASTY from 960 to 1127 and the Southern Song dynasty from 1127 onward. It replaced the TANG DYNASTY.

The head of the dynasty was Zhao Kuangyin (Chao K'uang-yin), a military commander under the Tang. He took over after what most historians describe as a military coup. As emperor, he was a master politician and diplomat, as well as soldier, and established a long line of powerful emperors who would rule the new Song dynasty for 300 years.

This was a time of great creativity in the arts and technology, with the development of coal mining, siege warfare, gunpowder, naval technology, wood-block printing of books, and paper. Foreign trade with Europe for spices, silks, and other luxuries boomed. The population doubled in size from 60 million to 120 million people by the end of the Song dynasty. Cities grew and agricultural methods improved.

During the 12th century, a northern clan named JIN that ruled Manchuria rebelled against Song rule in the North. The Jin forced the Song to abandon North China in 1126 and to retreat to the southern part of China, which they ruled until 1279. Mongolians under Genghis Khan conquered the Jin and later toppled the Southern Song dynasty, uniting all of China under Mongolian rule (see MONGOLIA).

SONGS OF CHU Second-century collection of ancient Chinese poems, some dating as far back as the fourth century B.C. They are used by scholars to study myths.

SPRING AND AUTUMN (*SPRING AND AUTUMN ANNALS, CHUN-QIU*) A history, or chronicle, of Lu covering 722–481 B.C. It is an important work of early Chinese history. Scholars also use this phrase to describe an important period during the ZHOU DYNASTY.

SSU-MA CH'IEN See SIMA QIAN.

SSU-MING-FO-CHUN See ZAO JUN.

STARS By the fourth century B.C., Chinese astronomers had identified 809 stars and grouped them into 122 constellations; by the fifth century A.D. they knew of 1,464 stars and placed them in 284 constellations. Of these stars, a total of 72 were thought to have an evil influence. These were called the DI SHA. Another 36 were good stars, or Tiangang.

Stars were identified with a variety of legendary and historical figures in China. Most have little obvious connection to the stars now, but there are exceptions. One story told of the ancient SHANG and their connection with a star called the Chen star, which is in the constellation known today as Orion. According to the story, the mythical emperor Gao Xin (also known as Kao Hsin and DI KU) had two sons, Yan Bo (or Yen Po) and Shi Chen (or Shih Ch'en). The boys did not get along and every day threatened to come to blows. Finally, Gao sent Yan to the land of the Shang, where he would be in charge of the Chen star. The TANG followed Yan Bo to the YELLOW RIVER and settled in the North. Shi had his own star in the constellation—a good distance away.

The story of the WEAVERGIRL AND HEAVENLY OX is another popular Chinese tale relating to stars.

SUI DYNASTY Historical DYNASTY (581–618) in ancient China. It is important because it reunified China and set the stage for growth in art, philosophy, and culture in general.

After two centuries of division, China was reunited by Wen Di, known before his death as Yang Chien (541–604). He ruled from 581 until his death. The emperor strengthened and reorganized Chinese government bureaucracy. He also used BUDDHISM, CONFUCIANISM, and TAOISM to help unite the country. He brought the different legal systems of North and South China together and raised standards for government office. He was succeeded by his second son, Yang (also known as Yang Di, Yang-ti, and Prince Yang Kuang [569–618]). Yang continued the improvements his father had made. In the end, however, the dynasty collapsed. Later historians blamed this on Yang, calling him self-indulgent and generally using him as a model for the "bad last" emperor. (See FOUNDING MYTHS.)

The Sui dynasty was succeeded by the TANG DYNASTY.

SUI-JEN See FIRE DRILLER.

SUN   Several Chinese myths concern the Sun and explain its rising and setting. Two versions in particular are popular and have been told and retold as folktales, children's stories, and myths.

According to one myth, each day a charioteer drives one sun across the sky. (Ancient China had a 10-day week, and thus each sun ventured out once a week.) Things proceeded very well for a while, until the suns became jealous and wanted to ride in the sky every day. Finally, one morning, they crowded into the CHARIOT together.

The people of the EARTH suffered great hardship, because now there were 10 suns where there should have been only one. Drought threatened. Strange beasts and monsters ran wild. Finally, the people begged for help. The father of the suns called the divine archer, YI, and gave him a vermilion bow and arrow. Yi shot nine of the suns from the sky.

The father of the suns in the original myth is TAIYANG DIJUN, who is sometimes described as the god of the eastern sky. In the *CLASSIC OF MOUNTAINS AND SEAS*, an ancient text relating myths, the charioteer is XIHE, who is married to Taiyang Dijun and is the mother of the suns. (In some later versions of the tale, the charioteer of the suns is not the mother; in other versions, she is not named.)

This basic story has been told in many different ways, with slightly different details as each storyteller retold the story and added drama and color.

According to another sun myth, a large MULBERRY tree stands in the Tang valley near the river. Each day, a different sun takes a turn at the top of the tree, while the others stay at the bottom.

The sun is also said to pass through 15 different stages in the sky every day. Three of these times mark meals—breakfast, lunch, and dinner. According to this tradition the sun rises from Yang, or "Sunny," valley after bathing in the Xian Pool, brushing past the LEANING MULBERRY TREE to mark dawn. It sets in the Meng valley.

SUN BI (SUN-PI)   The Chinese god of shoemakers.

SUNG DYNASTY   See SONG DYNASTY.

SUN HOU TZU   See MONKEY KING.

SUN SSU-MIAO   See YAO WANG.

SUN WUKONG   See MONKEY KING.

SUPERINTENDENT OF LIVES   See ZAO JUN.

SUTRAS   Important texts of BUDDHISM, which contain the teachings of BUDDHA or commentaries on his teachings. Different sects place varying emphasis on individual sutras.

SWORD   The swords mentioned in Chinese myths and legends are usually not specially named or venerated. One exception, however, occurs in the tale of GAN JIANG AND MO YE, a married couple who make swords in ancient Chinese myth. *JU-I* is another sword important in Chinese myth.

In Buddhist myth and art, swords symbolize wisdom, which cuts down ignorance and evil.

TABUN QAGHAR   A Mongolian name for the FIVE GREAT KINGS.

T'AI CH'ING   See TAI QING.

TAI HAO (T'AI HAO)   A god of light in ancient Chinese myth. The name was also applied to FUXI.

Tai Hao is also one of the Four EMPERORS defeated by the YELLOW EMPEROR.

TAI QING (T'AI CH'ING)   One of three Taoist HEAVENS. Each part is called an "AZURE." They are YOU QING ("Pearly Azure"), SHANG QING ("Upper Azure"), and Tai Qing ("Supreme Azure").

TAI SHAN (T'AI SHAN)   The sacred eastern mountain, one of the FIVE PEAKS of Chinese myth, was the home of the god DONGYUE DADI, who ruled the Heavenly Ministry of Five Peaks, Wu Yo. The word "shan" means mountain.

One story explaining Tai Shan's status as the holiest of all the Five Peaks says that the souls of all creatures, including humans, leave the mountain at birth to inhabit a new earthly body, and return at death. Taoist priests built a stairway of 7,000 steps up to the summit of Tai Shan, erecting shrines, temples, and a huge monastery at its peak. These mountain shrines draw thousands of pilgrims and tourists even today.

TAI SUI (T'AI SUI)   The ministry of time in Chinese mythology (see MINISTRIES OF GODS). It is also the name of the president of the ministry.

Scholars have connected the god Tai Sui with the planet Jupiter because of its movements through the HEAVENS. Tai Sui has also been connected by some to the MOON. His worship seems to have begun during the Yuan dynasty (1260–1368), perhaps because of Mongolian influence.

Tai Sui is called the "Lord of Time," the "President of the Celestial Ministry of Time," and the "Ruler of the Year." He kept a staff of 120 lesser Tai Sui who were in charge of the individual years within each 60-year cycle. The ministry presided over dates and times, good and bad, and could decide human destiny.

Tai Sui was often worshipped and prayed to in hopes of preventing disasters.

TAIYANG DIJUN (TI CHÜN)   According to the *CLASSIC OF MOUNTAINS AND SEAS*, an ancient text relating myths, Taiyang Dijun is a supreme god who is father of the SUN and MOON. But elsewhere he is cited as the ancestor of craftspeople and of musicians. His identity has been a subject of debate for scholars.

In perhaps the best-known tradition, Taiyang Dijun is father to the 10 suns and husband to XIHE, their mother. He is also father to the 12 moons and the husband of their mother, CHANGXI. He is said elsewhere to be the only bird of PARADISE, which watches over the EMPEROR's altar, and to have given arrows and bow to YI so that he could shoot down the suns. He also has a large BAMBOO grove where the plants grow so large that each one could be used on its own as a boat.

Some mythologists connect him to a general named Xu Gai who lived during the ZHOU DYNASTY. He is also called "the God of the Eastern Sky."

The references to him that have survived seem to indicate that he was an important god in prehistoric times, but he was eventually displaced or forgotten for some reason.

TAN CHU   See DANZHU.

TANG DYNASTY (T'ANG DYNASTY) The Tang dynasty (618–907) followed the SUI DYNASTY. It was started by Li Yuan (566–635), who had been a government official under the Sui rulers and was related by marriage to them. As the Sui rule collapsed, Li rebelled and took power, proclaiming himself emperor in 618. The dynasty was named after his fief in Shansi. Rebellion and chaos reigned until roughly 627, when the Tang dynasty emerged victorious.

TANG THE CONQUEROR (T'ANG THE CONQUEROR) Tang is the mythic or legendary founder of the SHANG DYNASTY, the line of rulers in early Chinese history.

According to legend, he fought and defeated KING CHIEH, the last ruler of the XIA DYNASTY. He was helped by YI YIN, one of his counselors. Tang pretended to have an argument with Yi Yin and shot arrows at him. Yi Yin pretended that he barely escaped with his life. Hearing of this feud, the Xia rulers welcomed him. While in the kingdom, Yi Yin gathered information from a former mistress of the king.

Yi Yin returned to Tang with his information after three years. Then he went back to gather more information.

According to the legends, Tang marched with his army, wielding a large ax. In one battle, he fought with a man name Keng, striking him so hard that he cut off his head. The headless GHOST—"the Corpse of Xia Keng"—vanished in Mount Wu.

As the final battle loomed, Chieh's army refused to fight. Tang sent Chieh into exile, and he was said to have died on the mountain of Nanchao.

While the accounts of Tang the Conqueror are legendary, archaeologists have found ample evidence of the existence of the Shang.

TAODIE (T'AO-T'IEH) A mythical Chinese monster who has a head but no body. The monster symbolizes gluttony. The creature appears as a mask in a variety of art forms.

TAOISM (DAOISM) An ancient Chinese combination of religion, philosophy, and folk beliefs, including ritual healing. Its different strands of belief date far back in history. Taoism is deeply entwined with Chinese culture and history. It evolved and changed over many centuries but is still important today, both in China and in the West, where its more philosophical elements are emphasized.

Tradition holds that Taoism was founded by LAO-TZU, who wrote the TAO-TE CHING (Daodejing), or *The Way of Power*, as it is often translated in English. (The title is also sometimes translated as the *Classic of the Way of Power*.) A very short and poetic book, it instructs kings to rule almost invisibly and not to interfere with their subjects or their ways of being. In this way, all will prosper. War should be a last resort. The action most completely in tune with this philosophy is complete passivity, or doing nothing.

The Tao, or "Way," is a basic, primal force that cannot be seen or even named. It existed before creation and continues to exist. It cannot be placed in a category. The Tao includes the nameless and the named, the being and the nonbeing. Things start in the Tao and return there. A person's highest goal should be to return to the thingness and nothingness of the Tao.

Several other ideas about the makeup of the universe are important to Taoism and to Chinese thought in general. The most important is YIN AND YANG, a set of opposing but connected forces that underlie everything. Another important idea is that of the FIVE ELEMENTS, or five agencies, the powers that animate the universe. This idea implies that change is constant, as the energy of the five elements flows through many transformations, or changes, in an endless cycle.

Another major Taoist thinker was ZHUANGZI (c. 369–286 B.C.). In the book that bears his name, he wrote of the immortal celestial masters who are beyond care and can fly. These are also known as the IMMORTALS, or *hsien*. It is possible that he meant them as allegories, or models, for humans to follow, but they eventually came to be treated as deities as well as models of behavior.

Taoist priests' duties included performing rituals to cure illness. Disease was seen as a punishment for sins, imposed by the SAN GUAN DADI, or the three gods of the universe. Ceremonies were needed to remove it. During the ceremonies, the priest made *zhang* (petitions or prayers), which were said to go to officials in one of three Taoist heavens. There were many of these officials, or *guan jiang*. Each one had a special responsibility for a specific ailment and its corresponding DEMON. There were many ways for this appeal to be made. One involved FU, written talismans that were burned and then ingested with water by the sick patient.

Another important duty of a Taoist priest was to officiate at the *jiao*, a community festival of renewal celebrated at a temple. These ceremonies might last more than a week and involve a number of private as well as public rituals; they were very elaborate and were celebrated according to a cycle that is more than 60 years long. The ceremonies continue in many communities today.

ALCHEMY, the mystical practice of changing material from one element to another, was also an important part of Taoist belief. ("Making dust fly in the ocean" is a Chinese saying that refers to this ability.) Magic and mysticism in general were important to the Tao practitioners, who wielded great influence at court until the second century when Taoism finally began to be seen as a kind of official religion (see MAGICIAN).

Taoism continually integrated different ideas and beliefs as it evolved. In the fourth century, Taoism was once more revolutionized by Taoist leaders Xu Mi and his son Xu Hui. They incorporated some ideas from BUDDHISM, which had been growing in influence in China for some time. They also encouraged alchemy and other special Taoist practices. In the fifth century, Emperor Tai Wu Di of the Northern Wei dynasty made Taoism the empire's official religion. When the Tang reunified the northern and southern parts of the empire, Taoism's influence and prestige grew even greater. The founder of the TANG DYNASTY claimed that he had descended from Laotzu. To hold a government position, an official had to pass an exam on one of the Tao literary classics. Taoist works were sent throughout the kingdom and to neighboring countries, including TIBET and Japan.

Among other branches that were formed in later years was the Quanzhen, "the Perfect Realization," which Wang Chongyang started in 1163. The monks of the sect founded the White Cloud Monastery in Beijing in the 20th century, before the arrival of communism. The monastery remains famous worldwide.

A Taoist priest, drawn in the 19th century (The Dragon, Image, and Demon, *1886*)

Taoism is still practiced, especially in Taiwan, and its influence on Chinese culture will no doubt continue to be felt for many years. The importance of the written word in Taoist practices had a dramatic effect on Chinese society, both in encouraging literacy and in demonstrating literacy's importance. Likewise, Taoist investigations into alchemy and MEDICINE helped advance the study of science in general.

TAOIST FOLK BELIEFS Over the centuries, TAOISM has combined many folk religious practices in its beliefs (see FOLK RELIGIONS). While mythologists and other specialists tend to view such beliefs separately from Taoism, for many Chinese there was no hard dividing line. The religion of the spirits (*shen chia*) included a wide range of practices and deities similar to Taoism and probably influenced by it. In the same way, Taoism, its practices, and its mythology were inspired by and, in some cases, grew from these basic folk beliefs. The practices of a *fa shi*, or folk priest, may be called "little rites" by Taoist priests, who practice the "great rites," or rituals, but they are not seen as blasphemy.

Experts sometimes separate Taoism artificially into two parts, "philosophical Taoism" and "religious Taoism," to make it easier to discuss its different ideas. The division has fallen out of favor among recent scholars, but it does show the different elements of Taoism.

TAO T'ANG See YAO.

TAO-TE CHING (*DAODEJING*) One of the central texts of TAOISM. The title is generally translated into English as *The Way* or the *Classic of the Way of Power*. The text consists of a collection of poems. They use metaphors to describe the "Tao" or way of the universe.

Traditionally, LAO-TZU is considered the author of *Tao-te ching*, though scholars have cast doubt on this.

T'AO T'IEH See TAODIE.

TAO WU (T'AO WU) Also known as "the Block," Tao Wu is a DEMON or evil spirit in ancient Chinese myth who looks a bit like a very large TIGER, except that he has a human face, a PIG's mouth, and tusks. He wanders the woods causing mischief and trouble. He is one of the sons of GAO YANG, a sky god.

TEA Tea is an important drink throughout much of Asia. It has been drunk in China since the TANG DYNASTY.

The beverage's connection to BUDDHISM is celebrated in a legend that claims it was discovered in India by a monk named BODHIDHARMA, generally known as Damodashi in China. According to the leg-

end, the monk nearly fell asleep several times during his meditation, which would have ruined his proper preparation for becoming a BUDDHA. To keep his eyes from closing, he cut off his eyelids and threw them on the ground. Tea bushes grew where they fell.

TEN CELESTIAL STEMS (SHIH T'IEN KAN) Part of a complicated system used in ancient China to divide units of time and to show that everything on EARTH corresponds with everything in HEAVEN. The Celestial Stems worked with the TWELVE TERRESTRIAL BRANCHES and corresponding FIVE ELEMENTS to produce a system known as the CYCLE OF SIXTY, which was said to govern and explain all events. It was connected to the art of Chinese DIVINATION, or fortune-telling, through various means, including the I CHING and astrology (see ASTROLOGER).

The 10 Celestial Stems, in order, are as follows:

- Jia (Chia), the first stem, is an energy or essence that lives in trees and corresponds to the element of wood.
- Yi, found in hewn timber, also corresponds to the element of wood.
- Bing, the energy found in lightning, corresponds to the element of fire.
- Ding, the fourth stem, which is found in burning incense, is also a fire element.
- Wu, the fifth stem, is an essence that resides in the hills. It corresponds to the element of earth.
- Ji is found in earthenware or pottery; it also corresponds to the element of earth.
- Geng, the seventh stem, is an energy found in metallic ores and corresponds to the element of metal.
- Xin, found in metal objects, also corresponds to the element of metal.
- Ren, the ninth stem, resides in salt water and is connected to the element of water.
- Gui, the 10th stem, is found in fresh water and also corresponds to the element of water.

TEN GREAT DISCIPLES OF BUDDHA See BUDDHA'S DISCIPLES.

TEN KINGS OF HELL According to some Buddhist sects, souls are judged for their sins after their death by the kings of hell. They are then sent for appropriate punishment before being allowed to be reborn into the world (see REBIRTH AND REINCARNATION). A wide range of DEMONS torture and inflict punishment in the Buddhist hells, according to the popular myths associated with them.

In China DIZANG is generally considered the first lord of hell, and he is assisted by the other kings. Elsewhere, YANLOU WANG (also known as Yama and Yamaraja) is considered the chief king.

TEN SUNS   See YI.

TEN THOUSAND   A NUMBER often used in TAOISM to symbolize the entire universe or the full range of creation.

THAO WU   See TAO WU.

THERAVADA BUDDHISM   The conservative branch of BUDDHISM, which can be contrasted to MAHAYANA.

Known as "the Way of the elders," the Theravada schools hold that ENLIGHTENMENT can be achieved only by the means outlined in the conservative texts of Buddhism. In general, Theravada Buddhists do not consider it possible to achieve enlightenment without becoming a monk.

THREE ERAS   A term usually used in Chinese mythology to refer to the XIA, SHANG, and ZHOU DYNASTIES, or periods, the earliest times with which written myth and legends are concerned.

THREE KINGS OF THE GOLDEN ERA   See GOLDEN AGE.

THREE OFFICIALS   See SAN GUAN DADI.

THREE STARS OF GOOD LUCK   See SAN XING.

THU (SHE)   A god of the EARTH in Chinese mythology.

THUNDER GOD   See LEI GONG.

TI   See DI.

TIAN (T'IEN)   The word for "heaven" in Chinese mythology. Scholars say the original sense of the word refers to the physical sky above, which was seen by the ancient Chinese as a rounded or arched dome. But the word was also used to describe the places where GODS or IMMORTALS were, then to describe the gods themselves, and, finally, simply refer to them.

TIAN DI (T'IEN TI, TIANDI)   Literally, "Heaven God" or "Sky God." The term can describe the specific GOD of the skies or simply a god in HEAVEN. A different term, SHANG DI, is usually used to signify the highest god in heaven. These distinctions are not always followed, especially when the myths are translated or retold.

TIAN FEI (T'IEN FEI)   The "Heavenly Concubine" or "Empress of Heaven" in late Chinese myth.

Just as an EMPEROR had to have a wife, so too did the king of HEAVEN. Several humans are identified with this goddess, and mythologists have connected her to a variety of guises, including Indian water spirits. Tian Fei was worshipped by navigators for help on journeys. Women seeking a child would also pray to her.

TIAN HOU   See QUEEN OF HEAVEN.

TIAN LONG (TIAN-LONG)   One of two mythological servants of WEN ZHANG, the Chinese god of literature. Tian Long was deaf, and his companion, DIYA, was mute. Since they helped Wen Zhang prepare and mark his examination papers, there was no fear of either being bribed to give out the questions in advance.

A second myth mentions Diya and Tian Long as the mother and father of all the creatures and human beings of the EARTH.

TIANONG DIJUN   See TAIYANG DIJUN.

TIAN SHI DAO (TIEN SHIH TAO)   The "Way of the Celestial Masters," a name used to describe the style of TAOISM that came to dominate in China around the second century and strongly influenced all that followed.

The celestial master is the hero of a book by Taoist Gan Zhongke called *Taiping Jing*, or the *Classic of Great Peace*, written at the end of the first century B.C. That work called for a renewal of the HAN

DYNASTY. Its author was put to death for criticizing the EMPEROR.

TIAN YIYUAN (T'IEN I-YUAN)

The bureau or celestial ministry of MEDICINE in Chinese myth (see MINISTRIES OF GODS). This large ministry is responsible for providing cures and warding off diseases. It has many members, including PANGU and FUXI, as well as other ancestral Chinese gods. There is some disagreement in the traditions about precisely who are the chiefs, but the king of remedies is YAO WANG.

TIANYU YUANSHUAI (T'IEN-YU YUAN-SHUAI)

In Chinese myth, the son of the Green DRAGON.

According to his story, the boy was born with a human body and a dragon face. While Tianyu Yuanshuai was raised by friends, his father was chased for many years by a hero named Ciji Zhenjun. Tianyu Yuanshuai wished to get revenge but was stopped by 12 devils. Then he was told by Yu Ti that must not slay his enemy and instead was given the devils as his followers.

The deity was a member of the celestial ministry of exorcisms (see EXORCIST; MINISTRIES OF GODS).

TIBET

This mountainous region that includes Mount Everest, borders on Qinghai, Sichuan, and Yunnan Provinces in China. Now an autonomous region of China, Tibet's status and relationship with China has been controversial for centuries and remains so. Tibet and China shared parts of their culture as well as religious beliefs for many centuries.

Srong-brtsan-sgam-po (c. 608–50) ruled Tibet and formed an alliance with China, marrying a royal princess. A successor, Kri-srong-Ide-brtsan (755–97), waged war on China and captured its capital in 763. Kri-srong-Ide-brtsan also brought BUDDHISM to Tibet, inviting teachers from both India and China to the country during his reign.

After the 14th century, the Dge-lugs-pa, or "Yellow Hat," sect of Buddhism grew to dominate the country. In the 16th century, the title of DALAI LAMA was first given to the head teacher of the sect. The title meant "Oceanwide" or "Worldwide holy man." The Dalai Lama's powers grew to include the leadership of the government as well as religion. The Dalai Lama's status was greatly enhanced by the belief that he was the human reincarnation of the BODHISATTVA Avalokiteśvara (GUANYIN in Chinese), who is considered the original creator of Tibet.

During the Chinese Revolution of 1911–12, Tibet asserted its independence. It remained a separate country until the rise of the Communists following World War II. China sent troops to Tibet in 1950. The Dalai Lama was exiled after an unsuccessful revolt in 1959.

TI CHÜN See TAIYANG DIJUN.

T'IEN See TIAN.

TIEN FEI See TIAN FEI.

TIEN GUAN (T'IEN KUAN)

The "Official of HEAVEN and Bringer of Happiness"; one of a trio of Taoist and popular gods called the SAN GUAN DADI. The gods forgive sin and bring happiness. The others are DI GUAN (EARTH) and SHUI KUAN (water).

T'IEN I-YÜAN See TIAN YIYUAN.

T'IEN KUAN See TIEN GUAN.

TIEN SHIH TAO See TIAN SHI DAO.

T'IEN-YÜ YÜAN-SHUAI See TIANYU YUAN-SHUAI.

TIGER

Popularly called the "king of the wild beasts," the tiger often appears in Chinese myths.

The tiger is a symbol of ferociousness in Chinese myth.

Tigers were seen as emblems of the West and the third creature of the TWELVE TERRESTRIAL BRANCHES.

Folklore held that tigers lived to be 1,000 years old, turning white at 500. Painted tigers on the walls of cities and villages were believed to scare away evil spirits. Mothers embroidered tiger heads on children's shoes to keep them from harm. Ashes from burning a tiger's skin were carried in a necklace vial as a CHARM to keep sickness away.

The WHITE TIGER OF THE WEST, Bai Hu, was considered a guardian of Taoist temples, and its image was painted on the temple doors.

TI K'U   See DI KU.

TI KUAN   See DI GUAN.

TING-JIAN   See GAO YAO.

TI-SHA   STARS of evil in Chinese myth. By one count there are 72, all said to influence events on EARTH.

TI-TSANG WANG   See DIZANG.

TI YU   The Chinese Buddhist hell or AFTERLIFE where souls work off their sins. The Buddhist underworld has a number of different parts, depending on the sect's beliefs. In China the number of parts was said to range from eight to 138—including a special hell for women. Ti Yu is not a final stopping place but a station before REBIRTH AND REINCARNATION.

TORCH DRAGON (CHU LUNG) The DRAGON said in Chinese myth to bring light to the northern lands not reached by the SUN. The dragon had a human head and a serpent's tail. Light flowed from the dragon's eyes; when he closed his eyes, the world became dark.

The Torch Dragon may be an older or foreign GOD barely remembered from the early historic period of China.

TORTOISE   The tortoise (often written as "turtle" in translation) is a symbol of stability in Chinese myth and literature.

Tortoises hold up the ISLANDS OF THE IMMORTALS and, in some mythic tales, are said to hold up the foundations of the universe. In some accounts of the PANGU creation story, a tortoise keeps Pangu company while he chisels out the world.

Tortoises are kept in tanks at Buddhist temples; feeding them brings good luck. Some Buddhists believe that the tortoise is one of four spiritually endowed creatures.

One legend holds that the markings of a tortoise's shell inspired the original characters of Chinese CALLIGRAPHY. Tortoises' long lives make them a symbol for longevity.

TOU MU   See DOU MU.

TOU SHEN   See DOU SHEN.

TOUZIGUEI   A DEMON spirit that stole babies from cribs. A *touziguei* was the soul of a woman who died before marriage. Denied the chance to have babies of her own, the GHOST-like spirit haunted the world, trying to steal the children of others. The spirits could be repelled by nets or the smoke of sandals.

TRICKSTER   Characters in myth who trick humans or others and who often take the shape of animals (see SHAPE SHIFTING). They are common to many cultures. The MONKEY KING is an example in Chinese myth.

TS'AI SHEN   See CAI SHEN.

TS'ANG-WU   See ZANGWU.

TS'AN NÜ   See CAN NÜ.

TS'AN TS'UNG   See CAN CONG.

TSAO CHÜN   See ZAO JUN.

TS'AO KUO-CHIU   See CAO GUOJIU.

TSAO SHEN   See ZAO JUN.

TUNG WANG KUNG   See DONG WANG GONG.

TUNG-YUEH TA-TI   See DONGYUE DADI.

TU-SHAN GIRL   See NÜJIAO.

TU YU   See DU YU.

TWELVE TERRESTRIAL BRANCHES
Part of the system of designating hours, days, months, and years in ancient China. They were combined with the TEN CELESTIAL BRANCHES in calculating the CYCLE OF SIXTY.

The 12 Terrestrial Branches and their corresponding animals and zodiac signs, as well as the times and directions these signs influence, are as follows:

TWELVE WARRIORS   According to BUDDHIST MYTH, YAOSHI FO is accompanied by 12 warriors or guardians, who also guard the four directions of the EARTH. They are Andira, Catura, Indra, Khumbira, Mahoraga, Mihira, Paja, Sandilya, Sindura, Vajra, Vikarala and Anila.

TZ'U-HUA   See CIHUA.

Terrestrial Branch	Animal	Zodiac Sign	Time	Direction
Ci	Rat	Aries	11 P.M.–1 A.M.	North
Chou	Ox	Taurus	1–3 A.M.	North-Northeast
Yin	Tiger	Gemini	3–5 A.M.	East-Northeast
Mao	Hare	Cancer	5–7 A.M.	East
Chen	Dragon	Leo	7–9 A.M.	East-Southeast
Si	Serpent	Virgo	9–11 A.M.	South-Southeast
Wu	Horse	Libra	11 A.M.–1 P.M.	South
Wei	Goat	Scorpio	1–3 P.M.	South-Southwest
Shen	Monkey	Sagittarius	3–5 P.M.	West-Southwest
You	Cock	Capricorn	5–7 P.M.	West
Xu	Dog	Aquarius	7–9 P.M.	West-Northwest
Hai	Boar	Pisces	9–11 P.M.	North-Northwest

U, V

UNICORN See QILIN.

UPALI One of BUDDHA'S DISCIPLES. Upali was a barber by trade, according to Buddhist legend. He is called the first disciple of discipline; according to tradition, he recorded the important rules first followed by Buddhist monks and the devout. In TIBET he is known as Nye-var-khor; in MONGOLIA he is called Chikola Akchi.

VAIROCANA See PALUSHENA.

VEDAS Early religious texts from India, originally passed along by oral tradition. The religious ideas contained in the vedas helped influence later Buddhist thought (see SUTRAS).

VERMILION BOW The special bow given to the divine archer YI so that he could shoot the 10 SUNS from the sky. Vermilion is the color RED, a COLOR of good luck.

VIDYARAJAS In BUDDHIST MYTH, the mystic kings or warriors who battle the DEMONS. According to Chinese Buddhist myth, the Vidyarajas combat the evil that comes from Kimon, the gate of demons in the Northeast.

Each of the five Vidyarajas can be viewed as a form of the FIVE GREAT BUDDHAS OF WISDOM. They are Budong Fo (Acalanatha), Jianganjie (Trailokyavijaya), Jingang (Vajrayaksa), Kundali, and Yanmandejia (Yamantaka).

W

WANG   See DU YU.

THE WAY   See TAOISM.

WEALTH   Among the many gods said to bring wealth or good fortune in ancient China were CAI SHEN, Lu Tou (also a god of crossroads), Wulu Cai Shen, Shen Wansan, Chao Gong Ming, HE-HE, the SAN XING, DUOWEN, the EARTH GOD, GUAN DI, and YUAN TAN.

WEAVER GIRL AND HEAVENLY OX   A Chinese variation of the story Westerners call Vega and Altair, which are the STARS that come together in the Milky Way once a year. The star Vega represents the weaver; Altair represents the heavenly OX (also known as the ox-driver, cowherd, and by similar names).

The weaver girl was the daughter of HEAVEN's god, known by various names, such as "August Sun." She was a diligent weaver of the fabric of the universe, which helped keep everything in its proper place.

But she fell in love with the heavenly ox across the river from her home. Her father saw how lovesick she was and allowed her to marry the ox.

After they were married, the girl neglected her work. Angry, her father sent her back across the river, saying that she could only cross once a year, on the seventh day of the seventh MOON of each year.

In some versions of the tale, the ox makes the crossing. Other variations have the weaver girl descending from heaven to help others by weaving large amounts of beautiful SILK.

While it refers to the stars, some scholars think that this myth may have also reflected the realities of ancient Chinese peasant life, in which husbands were obliged to travel far away from home for weeks at a time to work in the fields owned by their lords or CLANS.

WEISHUI RIVER   A river in China, considered a deity in ancient times.

WEN (WEN WANG, WEN-WANG, WEN-WANG)   The legendary father of the ZHOU DYNASTY, later called King Wen. Wen was duke or high official in the West for the last king of the SHANG DYNASTY, King Zhou. King Zhou and Wen had a falling out, and Wen went to war against the king and was killed. His son, WU, took up the cause, conquered the Shang rulers, and founded the Zhou.

Before his death and his son's victory, Wen was known as Chang, "Lord of the West," or Xi Bo, "King of the West." According to the myths, Wen met the Great Lord Jiang (also known as "Wang the Counselor") on a hunting trip and brought him home. Jiang provided counsel during the battles against King Chou.

Wen appears as a model or archetype of the concepts of culture WEN AND WU in Chinese lore.

WEN AND WU   Chinese words that mean, roughly, "written word" and "violent action," respectively, or "civilization" and "force." These basic meanings, however, were greatly expanded and applied to culture by ancient thinkers. Thus *wen* represented the forces necessary for culture, such as writing and education, and *wu* represented the forces necessary for creating and ruling an empire or government, such as military action and punishment of criminals. Chinese thinkers understood that both were necessary and that the relationship between the two was very complicated, like that between YIN AND YANG.

In history and legend, the words were sometimes used as part of a name to describe someone with those qualities. For example, Wen Wang, who was an early leader of the ZHOU DYNASTY, appears as a model or archetype of *wen* in the history of the times. His son, WU, showed how a person of action should behave.

WEN BU (WEN PU) The ministry of epidemics in Chinese mythology (see MINISTRIES OF GODS). The ministry was said to control the DEMONS that caused outbreaks of disease (see MEDICINE). Epidemics included the plague, for which there was no known cure. By appealing to the ministries, many thought they could prevent or stop epidemics.

WEN CHANG (WEN CH'ANG, WEN CH'ANG TI-CHÜN, WEN CHANG, WEN CHANG DIJUN) In Taoist and Chinese myth, the god of literature and a patron of all who take exams or tests. His name is also given to a constellation of six STARS.

Wen Chang was identified with several different figures. One, named Chang Ya, was said to have lived

Wen Chang, a patron of literature and scholars in Chinese myth (The Dragon, Image, and Demon, *1886*)

during the TANG DYNASTY. He was a great writer and died or disappeared in battle. Other legends identify him as a man named Zhang Yazi who lived during the QIN DYNASTY. According to other accounts, Wen Chang was a celestial god who decided to come down from his home in the stars in order to experience the adventures of being human. He had 17 different lifetimes, each filled with remarkable achievements. At the end of his 17th reincarnation, YU HUANG, the Jade Emperor, gave him the title of grand emperor of literature.

For much of Chinese history, examinations played an important role in filling government positions, much as the civil-service system does today in the United States. Thus Wen Chang was an important figure for many.

In a typical story, a student prayed to Wen Chang for help after he had taken an exam and done miserably. Wen Chang answered his prayer in a dream where he appeared in the examination office and threw several essays, including the student's, into a fire. The god then transformed the burnt papers into corrected papers and instructed the student to memorize the proper answers.

When the student woke up, he found out that there had been a fire in the examination hall where the essays were kept. Every student had to repeat the exam. Armed with Wen Chang's advice, the student passed.

In sculpture and paintings, Wen Chang is seated on the clouds or his steed and holds a scepter as a symbol of his official position. As a teacher, he is helped by his servant gods TIAN LONG and DIYA. His assistants are deaf and mute, and thus they cannot be bribed to tell the results of the tests or to give out answers.

WEN CHUNG See LEI ZU.

WEN DI (WEN TI, WEN-TI) The founder of the SUI DYNASTY, which reunited China after years of disruption. Born in A.D. 541, he ruled from 581 until 604. As EMPEROR, he strengthened and reorganized Chinese government bureaucracy. He brought the different legal systems of North and South China together and raised standards for government office. He also used BUDDHISM, CONFUCIANISM, and TAOISM to help unite the country. Because the words

Wen Di are a title (in English, we might say "wise divine emperor"), there are several emperors called Wen Di in Chinese history.

WENSHU   According to Chinese Buddhist tradition, Wenshu was a BODHISATTVA who lived as a holy man in China. Known as Mansjursi, he founded Nepal and lived on the mountain of five terraces (Wutaishan) in Shanxi. His birthday is celebrated on the fourth day of the fourth month.

A group of Chinese monks sailing to Japan in A.D. 736 was said to have realized that the Japanese monk Gyoki was actually the reincarnation of the bodhisattva, and he has been revered in Japan ever since (see REBIRTH AND REINCARNATION).

Scholars point out that Mansjursi is mentioned in early Indian texts, where he is known as a local king.

WEN TI   See WEN DI.

WEN ZHONG   See LEI ZU.

WHITE LOTUS REBELLION   A rebellion against tax collection that began in 1796 and continued to about 1804. It centered around followers of the White LOTUS sect, which believed that MILO FO, or Maitreya, a BODHISATTVA, would reappear on EARTH soon to end their suffering. The sect had many followers in the border areas of Hubei (Hupeh), Sichuan (Szechwan), and Shanxi (Shen-hsi), a mountainous region where agriculture was difficult and poverty reigned. Religious beliefs helped unite and inspire the rebels, but ultimately the central government put down the uprisings.

WHITE TIGER OF THE WEST   (BAI HU, PAI HU)   The White Tiger of the West, Bai Hu, was one of the guardians of Taoist temples, along with QING LUNG. It was also the name given to the western sector of the Chinese universe.

The title "White Tiger" was also applied to the name of a historical Chinese general, Yin Cheng-hsui, who served as the last EMPEROR of the Yin DYNASTY.

WILD BEASTS   One of the ancient legends about Huang Di, the YELLOW EMPEROR, claims that he organized an army of wild beasts that had suddenly invaded China and used them to conquer his enemies.

Wild animals and birds were often the subject of Chinese folktales or proverbs, which used animal habits to illustrate the ideals of proper human behavior.

WIND GOD   See FENG BO.

WOMAN CHOU   See NÜ CHOU.

WOMEN IN MYTH   In most cases, the roles of women in early myths and legends reflect their roles in society at the time the myths were written or created.

Women in ancient China were generally considered property, either of their fathers or husbands. Widows were discouraged from remarrying. They were not allowed to take the exams necessary to hold government jobs. In poor families, a woman's lot was even more restricted. A practice known as foot binding, which deformed feet in the name of beauty, literally hobbled many women, even those who had to work in the fields.

Among the few important historical women in Chinese history was the empress Wu or Wu Chao, who ruled during the TANG DYNASTY. This was also a period of more freedom and importance for Chinese women in general, but it was short-lived. The wives of the two Chinese EMPERORS who succeeded Wu were very influential, but there were few important or influential women in government afterward.

Since myths generally reflect society, there are relatively few important women in Chinese myth. There are, however, important exceptions to this rule:

NÜ GUA, along with her husband, FUXI, is mentioned as one of the earliest Chinese deities. She has many adventures on her own, including one where she reorders the universe after it is nearly destroyed.

The daughters of YAO, the XIANG QUEENS, are river goddesses. According to the myths, they were married to the emperor Shun; when he died, the women drowned themselves in the river. ZHANG E is the wife of YI, the divine archer. She is identified with the MOON.

Woman Zhou Corpse is a deity who overcomes drought. Another female rain goddess is DROUGHT FURY, the daughter of the RESPONDING DRAGON.

The SALT RIVER GODDESS, whose tales have been dated to about the late third or early second century B.C., is an opponent of the mythical LORD OF THE GRANARY.

XI WANG MU, the Queen Mother of the West, appears relatively late in Chinese mythology; her first surviving mention is from the fourth century B.C. The Queen Mother presides over WILD BEASTS in the wilds of the West.

Two of the BA XIAN, or Eight IMMORTALS, in TAOISM are women, including HE XIANGU, the patron of unmarried young woman, and LAN CAIHE, the patron of the poor. The LIGHTNING GODDESS was an early nature deity. The JASPER LADY is a Taoist figure with control over nature, including tornadoes.

A much later goddess is the QUEEN OF HEAVEN, whose position in the Chinese pantheon was enhanced by emperors trying to increase their popularity and power.

Perhaps the most popular Chinese goddess was SHENG MU, the mythological daughter of the powerful DONGYUE DADI, the god of one of the FIVE PEAKS, who supervised all areas of human life on EARTH. She looked after the welfare of women and children.

GUANYIN, considered the Buddhist goddess of mercy in China, was another popular and important mythological figure. Although he was male, artists often portrayed him as female.

WU (WU-WANG, WU DI, WU TI KING WU, WU WANG, WUWANG)
The founder of the ZHOU DYNASTY, who defeated the SHANG DYNASTY and its last ruler, King Chou.

While the stories about him have many fantastical elements, Wu was a historical figure, believed to have ruled from 1111 to 1104 B.C. King Wu was the son of WEN and continued the war with the Shang started by his father after his father died. He was helped by his brother, the DUKE OF ZHOU. Before he became king, he was known as Chi Fa.

According to the legends, Wu was afraid of nothing, not even the gods who ruled nature. When he was traveling across the river to fight King Zhou, the river god, Lord Yang, tried to make trouble. He raised the waves against the boats and brought a dark storm. Wu took his SWORD and threatened the god. The storm quickly cleared.

Before the battle, Wu's sword broke in three. The Duke of Zhou assured him that it was not an omen of bad luck, but an indication about how to fight the battle. They split the army into three for the attack.

Wu was joined by an assortment of gods, including the gods of the seas, the RAIN MASTER, and the god of the wind, FENG BO. The gods appeared at his palace in a raging snow storm. Though suspicious, he showed them hospitality and was rewarded with their allegiance.

Wu appears as a model or archetype of the man of action in Chinese myth (see WEN AND WU).

WU CHANG GUI (WU-CH'ANG KUEI)
Messengers from YANLOU WANG in Chinese mythology and folk belief. They are sent to take a soul to the AFTERLIFE. One is a man and another a woman; a horse-headed DEMON and an OX-headed demon accompany them. It is said that the local earth god escorts these messengers to the house of the dying person, where they are met by the kitchen god, ZAO JUN. The messengers are assisted by a walking Wu-chang, a special spirit of a living being.

The figures combine elements from different beliefs, especially BUDDHISM.

WU FU GUI   See WU CHANG GUI.

WU GUAN
In popular Chinese myth, Wu Guan is in charge of the fourth hell, known as the "Lake of Blood," where those who counterfeit money or papers or who cheat customers are punished.

WU-HSIANG   See LORD OF THE GRANARY.

WU HSING   See FIVE ELEMENTS.

WU KANG
In Chinese myth, an old man who lives on the MOON, sharing it with ZHANG E, the wife of YI, the divine archer, and a HARE. Wu Kang was forever trying to chop down the tree of longevity. One story about him said he was a musician who gave such a terrible performance that the gods banished him to the Moon, where he had to stay until he could chop down the cinnamon tree of immortality—an impossible task. Every time he chopped into the bark, the tree healed itself and closed the gash.

WU SHAMAN   A female SHAMAN.

WU XING   See FIVE ELEMENTS.

WU YUE   The ministry of the FIVE PEAKS (see MINISTRIES OF GODS). It was said to hold power over all humans. The head of the ministry—the spirit of the eastern peak, DONGYUE DADI—had authority over all life and death, as well as WEALTH and honors.

The ministry had a large number of bureaus and was said to handle affairs from birth to death. But some accounts hint that even in the spirit world, there were snafus and delays. A person who was murdered or committed suicide before the proper time was said to become a GUI, or GHOST DEMON, sentenced to wander the EARTH until it could rejoin the cycle of life.

The ministry developed from much more ancient Chinese beliefs about the Five Peaks, sacred mountains representing the FIVE DIRECTIONS of the Chinese kingdom.

Besides the spirits of the mountains, the members of the celestial ministry included generals and other government officials who had done service in the past.

XIA DYNASTY (HSIA DYNASTY) A mythical dynasty of prehistoric China. It was said to have lasted 471 years (or 600) and have 17 (in some texts, 16) kings. Traditionally, its founder was said to be YU. Its last king was KING CHIEH, an evil man overthrown by the founders of the SHANG DYNASTY. Many myths are set in this time, including the stories concerning YI and Yu.

The word *Xia* was used in some myths and popular accounts to describe the GOLDEN AGE and prehistoric China in general. Archaeologists now generally describe the periods of prehistoric China by names associated with archaeological digs.

Until recent discoveries, little was known about the Xia period. It is now believed to have existed at roughly the same time as the better-known SHANG DYNASTY, in the area to the north and west along the YELLOW RIVER. Some experts believe the two dynasties were in conflict.

XIAN See IMMORTALS.

XIANG (HSIANG) SHUN's half brother in Chinese myth.

XIANG CONG See CAI SHEN.

XIANG LIU (HSIANG LIU) One of the monsters killed by YU. He has nine heads.

XIANG QUEENS (HSIANG QUEENS) Two sisters in Chinese myth who were daughters of YAO and became wives of the mythical emperor SHUN. When the emperor died, they drowned themselves in the Xiang River and became spirits there.

The story, said to illustrate the true love and devotion desirable in a wife, was popular in ancient China. It was the subject of several romances and poems.

XIAN NONG See SHEN NONG.

XIAN REN (HSIEN JEN) The lowest class of IMMORTALS in Taoist belief. Xian Ren are humans who have achieved immortality, in one of several ways, often by preparing a special drug whose formula is learned after years of devotion and study (see ALCHEMY). Xian Ren include Taoist philosophers, mystics, alchemists, MAGICIANS, and many others.

XIAO GONG (HSIA KUNG) A deity who protected rivers in Chinese mythology.

The deity is identified with a man named Xiao Boxuan, who died in 1275. He was honored as the god of rivers and other water bodies by the emperor Yung Lo (1403–25) in 1419. Interestingly, scholars investigating his story have found that while he was well known as a sober and serious man, he seems to have had no particular connection with rivers during his life. There are no stories of him performing miracles or the like while alive. However, after his death, it was believed that he answered prayers and therefore deserved the honor of being named god of rivers.

XIE (HSIEH) The mythic founder of the SHANG DYNASTY. According to ancient Chinese myth, his mother, CHIEN DI, gave birth to him after touching the EGG of a bird sent by DI KU. His name is also given as Yin Xie, a reference to the last Shang capital of Yin. He is also called Qi.

XIE TIAN JUN (HSIEH T'IEN CHÜN) In Chinese mythology, the god of the planet Mars and the overseer of summer.

XIHE (HSI HO, HI-XIN, XI-HE) In Chinese myth, Xihe is generally said to be the wife of Taiyang Dijun and mother to the ten SUNS.

According to the stories, when her suns were young she would tenderly carry a different sun each day in her CHARIOT and would drive it to the edge of the sky to spend the day lighting up the world. When the suns became older, they rebelled against their mother's orders and appeared in the sky together, making the EARTH so hot and miserable that disaster loomed.

The people begged help from their ruler, YAO, who in turn prayed to Taiyang Dijun. When the suns would not obey their parents, Taiyang Dijun asked the divine archer YI to scare the suns into obedience. Yi decided that the only solution was to shoot them down. Just as Yi was about to shoot the 10th sun, it cried and begged for mercy. Yi spared its life after it promised to spend a portion of each day resting, thus creating night and day.

Alternate versions of the myth identify Xihe as simply the sun's female chariot driver. Another claims that Xi and He were ministers of the EMPEROR Yao, a legendary ruler. Still another identifies the god as male and as the master of the CALENDAR.

XING WENG (HSING T'IEN) According to Chinese myth, Xing Weng was a lesser god who fought Di, the great god, for the right to rule heaven. Di lopped off his head and buried it on Changyang Mountain. Xing Weng, however, made do by using his nipples as eyes and his navel as a mouth. Ancient Chinese writers saw him as a symbol of a spirit that could not be completely defeated.

XI SHEN (HSI SHEN) The god of joy in popular Chinese mythology. In art, Xi Shen is often shown carrying a basket with three arrows on it. This image was an important part of the ancient Chinese wedding ceremony; it was said to chase DEMONS from the bride's chair before she was carried to her groom's house.

Sometimes the god is seen riding on the shoulders of the god of wealth.

XI SHI A sweet-smelling royal concubine who became the patroness of those who sell women's beauty products.

XITIAN JIAOZHU See OMITU FO.

XI WANG MU (HSI WANG-MU) The "Queen Mother of the West" in Chinese mythology. Her oldest tales seem to date from the late ZHOU or HAN DYNASTIES, and her story and attributes underwent great changes as time went on and she grew more important as a Taoist figure.

The ancient goddess started out as the goddess of plagues. In early mythological tales, Xi Wang Mu was portrayed as a monster, with the head and face of a human being, the teeth of a TIGER, and the tail of a LEOPARD. She ruled over the DEMONS of plague and illness.

By the first century A.D., the monster had been transformed into a benevolent noblewoman who helped human beings become immortal. In late Taoist myth, she plays an important role in the many tales about the BA XIAN, or Eight IMMORTALS, helping them learn the secrets of immortality and inviting them to feast on the PEACHES of immortality from her garden orchard. She is also an important figure in the story of YI and his wife, ZHANG E, to whom she gives the ELIXIR OF ETERNAL LIFE.

Some later legends say she is the wife of DONG WANG GONG, the "Royal Lord of the East," who kept track of the Taoist Immortals. The royal couple had nine sons and 24 daughters and lived in KUN-LUN in a palace with buildings made of marble and jasper. A nine-story JADE tower rose to the sky, over-looking sparkling brooks and gorgeous gardens where magical peach trees grew. The fruit from these trees was said to blossom and ripen only once every 3,000 years. Eating it made a person immortal.

As the myths about her became more popular, she was further transformed into the wife of the Jade Emperor, YU HUANG, at the time the highest god in the pantheon of deities.

Various EMPERORS were said to have visited her mountain palace in order to legitimize their claims to rule. Taoist philosophers considered her to be YIN, the female element of the YIN AND YANG concept of harmony. Some mythologists have connected her to a deity mentioned as the "West Mother" in ORACLE BONES from the SHANG DYNASTY.

XIYOU JI (HSI-YU CHI) Known as *Journey to the West*, the classic Chinese epic celebrating the exploits of XUAN ZANG, a real-life monk who journeyed to India. Written in prose and first published in 1592, the story can be seen as one of the earliest novels. It uses a great deal of humor and satire.

According to legend, Xuan Zang was protected on his journey by a monkey, a PIG, and a dark spirit of the sands. In the *xiyou ji*, the monkey and pig journey together with him, taking part in many adventures. The monkey is a more noble, if at times mocking, guide; the pig is quite piggy (see MONKEY KING). Their interaction leads to much humor.

The work is rich with allegory and metaphor. There are many references to popular legends and myths, as well as to Buddhist theology.

XUAN DIAN SHANG DI (HSUAN-TIEN SHANG TI)

Called the "Lord of Black" in Chinese myth. He is said to have led the 12 legions of IMMORTALS that fought the DEMON kings (*gui wang*) during the SHANG DYNASTY. Xuan Dian Shang Di's forces had to contend with monsters, such as a huge serpent and a TORTOISE, manufactured from thin air. When his forces won, he returned triumphantly to HEAVEN and was named First Lord of the Highest Heaven.

XUAN ZANG (HSUAN TSANG)

A Buddhist monk (c. 596?–664) who traveled to India and returned with Buddhist scriptures, helping to lay the foundations of BUDDHISM in China.

The story of the historical monk's travels was woven into a rich legend. A narrative of these tales was published in 1592 as *XIYOU JI*, or *Journey to the West*, and the early novel remains popular to this day.

He is sometimes called "the traveling monk," and artists portray him with his aides, the MONKEY KING and PIG.

XUKONGZANG

The Chinese name for Akasagarbha, the BODHISATTVA of wisdom and compassion.

XU ZHENJUN (HSU CHEN-CHÜN)

A DRAGON slayer in Chinese myth. According to his basic tale, his mother conceived him after a dream that a PHOENIX had planted a pearl in her womb. As an adult, he became a devout Taoist.

According to the stories, Xu Zhenjun lived during turbulent times. After escaping a revolution, he found himself in the southern land of Lu Shan, where a dragon was causing many FLOODS. He chased the dragon until it turned itself into a yellow OX. Xu Zhenjun turned himself into a black ox. But the dragon jumped down a well and escaped. The dragon then took the shape of a human (see SHAPE SHIFTING). Xu Zhenjun once more tracked him down and shamed him into resuming his real shape so that he could be killed.

Y

YAMA   See YANLUO WANG.

YAN DI   The "Flame Emperor," an ancient fire god in Chinese mythology.

According to his tales, he rules half the EARTH; his brother Huang Di, the YELLOW EMPEROR, rules the other half. He is said to have been defeated by Huang Di after an epic battle.

Another account identifies this figure as one of the FOUR EMPERORS, where he is said to be the god of the South. He fights Huang Di in that account as well, and once more he loses.

Yan Di dates from before the HAN DYNASTY. He is sometimes confused with SHEN NONG. The name Yan Di is viewed by some mythologists as another name for Zao Ju, or for the original god from whose story the more popular story grew.

YANG   Part of the dual, interlocking concept of YIN AND YANG underlying all of the universe.

The yang concept represents the masculine ideals of activity, heat, dryness, and hardness—all that is opposite to but entwined with the female properties of YIN.

YANG CHENG (YANG CH'ENG)   A historical figure identified with FUXING, the god of happiness in Chinese mythology and one of the SAN XING, the three gods of good fortune.

Yang was court official during the reign of Emperor Wu Di (520–50). At the time, it was customary for dwarfs to be presented to the royal family as jesters. This was not a request one could refuse, and the number taken from Yang Cheng's home region made it hard for their families to survive. Yang is said to have told the emperor that dwarfs were not his slaves, and the practice stopped. Yang was then honored as the spirit of happiness.

YAN GONG (YEN KUNG)   A god of sailors in Chinese myth, identified with several different historic figures. According to lore, if a sailor prays to Yan Gong during a storm, the storm will die down.

YANGSHAO CULTURE   The name archaeologists use to refer to the prehistoric human inhabitants of China whose settlements have been found in the Huang He Valley.

These early Chinese used irrigation systems as they farmed and created elaborate pieces of ceramic. The culture and practices of these settlers are believed to be the foundations for those that are known to us from later periods (see LONG SHAN CULTURE).

YANG SSU CHIANG-CHUN   See YANSI QIANGZHUN.

YANG SSU LAO-YEH   See YANSI QIANGZHUN.

YANGTZE RIVER   Like all rivers in ancient China, this too was considered a deity.

YANLUO WANG (YENLO, YAMA, YANLUO, YEN-LO WANG)   In Buddhist myth, most sects consider Yanluo Wang the supreme king of the 10 courts of hell, or the underworld (see TEN KINGS OF HELL). In China DIZANG was usually called hell's ruler, and Yanluo was generally given lesser importance. Here he was most often the fifth king of the Buddhist court of hell and one of the PROTECTORS OF DHARMA.

Some say that this was because he was too easygoing, allowing souls to rush through to REBIRTH AND REINCARNATION without undergoing much penance.

Some sources, however, do refer to him as the "Lord of Death," the most important king of the underworld. He is usually shown with an OX head on a man's body. In TIBET the divinity is known as Chos-rgyal or Gshin-rje.

YANSI QIANGZHUN (YANG SSU CHIANG-CHUN, YANG SSU LAO-YEH) In Chinese myth, a protector of sailors. He carries an ax in his hand and also controls the DRAGON king, a god of the high seas. In ancient times, he was honored on the sixth day of the month.

YAO (T'ANG TI YAO) One of the three kings of the GOLDEN AGE whom legend says reigned during the prehistoric period of China. Yao comes before SHUN and YU. He was considered an ancestor by the HAN DYNASTY (see ANCESTORS AND ANCESTOR CULTS).

In the stories told about him, Emperor Yao's worst enemy was the black DRAGON KUNG KUNG, who was continually wreaking havoc (and, in one story, caused a FLOOD that wiped out the EARTH). Yao's reign was also connected with the legends about the divine archer, YI, who shot down nine of the 10 SUNS in the sky.

Yao chose his successor, Shun, to rule instead of his son, but then Yao subjected Shun to a series of tests before allowing him to take over the throne.

Yao was considered by followers of CONFUCIUS to be an example of an excellent ruler. Unlike many of the legendary rulers who spent their time warring against DEMONS, GODS, and other mythical enemies, Emperor Yao was described as a compassionate, humble, diligent, and wise ruler. He wore simple clothes, and stories about him show that he stood firmly with his suffering people during times of famine and flood.

Emperor Yao was also said to have invented the CALENDAR and created offices that were responsible for making sure that every season came and went in its proper order. Emperor Yao's ability to organize time and space was said to bring about an orderly balance of YIN AND YANG.

Among Yao's other names are Fang Hsun, Tao T'ang, and Tang (also a name for TANG THE CONQUEROR, a different mythic figure).

YAOSHI FO The Chinese name for Bhaisajyaguru, an important figure venerated by some Buddhist

sects. Yaoshi Fo, known in TIBET as Sangs-rgyas and Sman-bla, and in Mongolia as Otochi, was an early doctor and healer. Some Buddhist sects consider him an incarnation of the BUDDHA, administering to those who suffer in the present world. Images of him in Tibet generally show him in blue, sitting in a very similar pose to Buddha with a MEDICINE bowl.

According to some Chinese texts, Yaoshi Fo can take several forms as he heals. He is sometimes accompanied by two BODHISATTVAS, or Buddhas-to-be, who symbolize the SUN and MOON. TWELVE WARRIORS serve him; in some accounts of BUDDHIST MYTH, the warriors guard the different corners of the EARTH.

YAO WANG (SUN SIMIAO) The king of MEDICINE in Chinese myth and an important member of the celestial ministry of medicine, TIANYU YUAN-SHUAI (see MINISTRIES OF GODS).

Different traditions connect Yao Wang with historical people. He was said to be Sun Simiao, a Taoist HERMIT in the late ninth and eighth centuries B.C. According to myth, he cured a SNAKE, which turned out to be the son of LONG WANG, a dragon king. He was rewarded with a book of cures, to which he added his own great 30-volume book.

Yao Wang is also identified with Sun Simiao, a historical doctor in the court of Emperor Wen Di (r. 581–604) of the SUI DYNASTY. He is said to have refused the offer of being made the kingdom's doctor, explaining that he would become a saint in 50 years. It is said that when he died in 682, his body lay for a month without decomposing, a sign that he had been an IMMORTAL.

YARROW Also known as milfoil, the stalks of the plant were used by ancient Chinese seers to predict the future. The plant was believed to have magical powers, but the origin of its use in DIVINATION remains unclear.

The yarrow stalks were cast so that a reader could form lines, either broken or unbroken, from them. The lines were then used to form trigrams, or *ba gua* (*pa kua*), which consisted of three lines, broken or unbroken, arranged in any of eight possible combinations, known as the EIGHT DIAGRAMS. (For example, one trigram could have an unbroken line at the top, with broken lines in the middle and the bottom.)

The trigrams were then connected in pairs to form hexagrams of 64 different types, which could be read by the seer. The *I CHING* is believed to have been written as a guide to interpreting these hexagrams.

YELLOW DRAGON The DRAGON of the center, one of the FIVE DIRECTIONS in Chinese myth and lore.

YELLOW EMPEROR (HUANG DI, HUANG TI) An important mythological and legendary figure said to have lived in the prehistoric period. He appears in a variety of myths and legends. The later accounts often subtly include attempts by Taoist authors to show that he was inferior to Taoist figures.

The earliest stories portray Huang Di as a mythological ruler, a hero who fights other EMPERORS. He defeats YAN DI (the Flame Emperor), CHIYOU, the FOUR EMPERORS, and a variety of others.

The Yellow Emperor and the Flame Emperor were said to be brothers, each lord of half of the world. Their battles can be thought of as wars between the elements of water and fire. BEARS, wolves, and an assortment of other ferocious animals fought as part of the Huang Di's army. It took three years and much blood for Huang Di finally to defeat his brother.

Chiyou was a Chinese god of war and the inventor of metal weapons in Chinese mythology. In some legends he was with Huang Di; in others he was said to be defeated by him. Chiyou commanded the wind and rain, but Huang Di prevailed because he had power over YING LONG, the Responding DRAGON, and Ying's daughter, Drought Fury. He ordered them to prevent the rain from falling and gained the upper hand.

Huang Di also defeated the Four Emperors, though the legend that records this makes it clear that he went to war very reluctantly. In another tale, Huang Di captured a beast named KUI (a thunder beast or deity) and made a drum from its skin. The sound could be heard for 500 leagues.

A later story holds that the Yellow Emperor was helped in his battles by a Taoist goddess called the DARK LADY. The Dark Lady instructed him in the art of war and helped him win. Huang Di was also said to have learned alchemy from ZAO JUN, a god of the stove and kitchen in TAOISM.

The HAN DYNASTY considered Huang Di the third of the legendary emperors, after FUXI and Shen Nong. He was said to have lived from 2698 B.C. to 2598 B.C. Huang Di was credited with many inventions that made life better for his people, including writing, the pottery wheel, and a method of breeding SILK worms.

The Yellow Emperor is sometimes confused with Xian-yuan, an earlier primeval god.

YELLOW RIVER (HUANG HE) An important river in central China, called Huang He in Chinese. It runs to the Yellow Sea on the north Chinese coast. Early Chinese civilizations, including the SHANG, thrived in the valley along this river. The river was considered a deity by early Chinese peoples.

YELLOW SPRINGS A place mentioned in some Chinese myths as a spot where souls of the dead sank into the EARTH.

YEN See MASTER YEN.

YEN See KING YEN.

YEN KUNG See YAN GONG.

YENLO See YANLOU WANG.

YEN TI See YAN DI.

YI (YI YI, JEN I, HOU I, ARCHER LORD, DIVINE ARCHER, GOOD ARCHER) An important figure in ancient Chinese myth, Yi usually appears as a hero who saves the world, though in some tales he is a villain whose sins bring down the rule of the mythic XIA DYNASTY.

Yi was known as the "divine archer" for his skills in hunting with a bow and arrow. Earlier myths say he was a military chieftain in the service of Emperor Ku; later myths describe him as a descendant of Ku, who served Ku's successor, Emperor YAO.

The best-known story connected with Yi tells of how he shot nine of the 10 SUNS out of the sky. This caused him to be banished from HEAVEN and sent to EARTH, where he became a human being. The basic story was often modified and elaborated on, but the main details remained the same:

In the beginning of time, there were 10 suns, corresponding to the 10 days of the week in the early Chinese CALENDAR. These suns were the children of TIAYANG DIJUN and XIHE, the god of the eastern skies and goddess of the sun. The suns lived in a MULBERRY TREE named Fu Sang. To keep order on Earth, Xihe would drive just one of her suns to the edge of the sky each morning so that Earth would have light and warmth; she would then drive it back to the mulberry tree in her CHARIOT at the end of the day so that Earth could rest.

After many years, the 10 suns rebelled against their solo trips and decided all to go at the same time. They were so happy to be shining together that they decided to stay at the edge of the sky. The heat from their combined energy withered all the crops, dried

Yi, the divine archer, here protects a child from the Heavenly Dog. (The Dragon, Image, and Demon, *1886*)

up the soil, and even melted rocks. It was said that an EGG could be fried in someone's hand.

The drought began to dry up the forests and streams. Monsters and WILD BEASTS fled the forest in search of food and began to kill and eat people. The monsters included a CHA-YU (a dragon-headed beast), a huge SNAKE, and a bird so massive that its wings caused windstorms.

The people begged Emperor Yao to do something. He in turn prayed to Taiyang Dijun to take pity on Earth. The god ordered nine of the suns to return to the mulberry tree, but the suns would not leave the sky. So he asked the divine archer, Yi, to help him figure out a way to scare the suns back to the mulberry tree. He gave Yi a VERMILION (or bright RED) BOW and a quiver of white arrows, telling him to frighten the suns and kill the monsters or drive them back to the forests.

But Yi decided that the only way to stop the suns was to shoot them out of the sky. And so he did.

Some versions of the story say that Yi studied the situation and saw that each sun came up one by one, and so he shot them down as each appeared. Other versions have the suns lined up together, as Yi aims his arrows at each one. When he hit each sun, there was a huge ball of fire and a flaming explosion. The dead suns fell to Earth in the form of a three-legged raven.

Emperor Yao realized that if Yi killed all 10 of the suns, there would be no warmth or light left on Earth. According to one version, he told one of his soldiers to steal one of Yi's arrows so that Yi could not destroy all 10 suns. Another version has each of the suns begging for mercy. Only the last sun promised to come out faithfully each morning and go to sleep every night. Yi was so touched by its sincerity that he allowed the last sun to live. After shooting the suns, Yi went on to kill the monsters and drive the wild animals back into the forest.

Yao and the people of his empire praised Yi for saving them. But when the divine archer returned to heaven, Taiyang Dijun was furious that Yi had murdered nine of his suns. He ordered Yi and his wife to leave heaven and condemned them to live on Earth as human beings, with no divine powers. Yi didn't mind this too much, because he spent all his time hunting in the forests. But Yi's wife, ZHANG E, was miserable, since she knew that she would die one day.

Zhang E sent Yi to visit XI WANG MU, the Queen Mother of the West, at KUNLUN to beg her for the ELIXIR OF ETERNAL LIFE. The Queen Mother agreed to help. She gave the couple one vial of elixir. This was enough to allow two people to live forever on Earth or one person to gain complete immortality, which included supernatural powers.

Yi was perfectly willing to share the elixir with his wife. But Zhang E couldn't stand the thought of continuing to live on Earth. She wanted the elixir all to herself. An ASTROLOGER told her she could escape to the MOON where the gods couldn't reach her. And so she drank the elixir. But as she soared upwards, she changed into a striped toad, CHANCHU.

When Yi realized that his wife had taken the elixir, he knew that he would one day die. He decided that he should teach other humans his ARCHERY and hunting skills so that the knowledge would not be lost after his death. He took on a student named BENG MENG who soon became an expert archer. But Beng Meng was very competitive. Frustrated and jealous of Yi's superior abilities, Beng Meng killed his master with a club made from a PEACH tree.

Many other stories about Yi relate his bravery and incredible deeds. One myth tells of how he managed to control the winds that interfered with the Yellow Emperor's conquests.

But in a smaller group of stories that might be called the "bad Yi tales," the divine archer is also said to have neglected his duties overseeing the Xia empire. In these stories, Yi appears as an example of a bad king and is discredited. According to these stories, he spent his time hunting instead of governing. Finally, when he wouldn't mend his ways, his CLAN killed him. They cooked his body and served it to his sons. But his sons refused to eat him and were put to death.

YIN A capital during the SHANG DYNASTY. It has been excavated near modern-day Anyang in Henan Province, China.

YIN The female half of the YIN AND YANG, the creative part of energy and the universe. Part of the dual energy underlying everything in creation, according to common Chinese belief.

YIN A Chinese word for hand gestures known as *mudras* usually used for symbolic purposes on Buddhist statues. Rather than making the hands of their figures seem natural, Buddhist sculptors position the fingers in certain ritual ways to demonstrate a quality of the figure or to represent a certain idea. Sometimes the symbols are obvious: Hands clasped in prayer remind the viewer that offerings and prayers will be received. There are dozens of specific gestures, with some variations from sect to sect and region to region.

Some of the important gestures used in Chinese Buddhist art include the following:

Shiwuwei Yin, the symbol of protection and peace. The right hand is out and open, fingers together in a gesture that in the West might mean "stop"; the left hand is down at the side of the figure. (This is also known as *abhaya mudra*.)

Shiynan Yin, the symbol of charity and the wish to help humans achieve salvation. It appears as a similar gesture to Shiwuwei Yin, but it is made with the left hand. (It is also known as *varada mudra*.)

Anwei Yin, the symbol of the BUDDHA's teachings (see SUTRAS). In this gesture, the thumb and forefinger are held together; the fingers do not always touch. The circle they make symbolizes eternal perfection. The other three fingers are upright. (This is also known as *viarka mudra*.)

Din Yin, the symbol of meditation, has the two hands together and turned upright, thumbs touching. According to Buddhist traditions, the historical Buddha used this pose when meditating before enlightenment. (It is also known as *dhyana mudra*.)

YIN AND YANG According to ancient Chinese beliefs, there are two great opposing forces in the universe. These opposites form the basis for everything. YIN is the female, and YANG is the male. Yin is cold; yang is fire. Yin creates; yang illuminates.

The yin-yang concept underlies much Chinese thought, from folk belief to TAOISM. This powerful idea—that all nature has two essential and interrelated parts—remains an important concept throughout the world even today.

The concept of yin and yang is often symbolized by a circle divided into two opposing swirls, one black, one white.

The symbol for yin and yang

Some scholars say that yin and yang originally referred to the slopes of a mountain that faced away and toward the SUN. Others believe that yang was originally a SKY GOD and yin an EARTH god in very ancient China.

YING LONG (RESPONDING DRAGON, YING-LUNG)   A term used by mythologists to describe a mythological warrior said to live in the wilderness of the Northwest. He appears in Chinese mythology as a warrior fighting CHIYOU, a god of war and the creation of metal weapons. In one version, Ying Long and his daughter, DROUGHT FURY, fight at the command of Huang Di, the YELLOW EMPEROR. Ying Long absorbs the water that Chiyou has his minions release as a weapon, allowing Huang Di to defeat Chiyou.

In another version, Ying Long defeats Chiyou and KUAFU. But because of the ferociousness of the battle, he is wounded and cannot return to the sky. As a result, the land suffers frequent droughts.

YINGZHOU   See PENG LAI.

YI YIN   In Chinese myth, an adviser to TANG THE CONQUEROR, who defeated the XIA DYNASTY and founded the SHANG DYNASTY.

According to the story of his birth, Yi Yin's mother lived near the Yi River. When she became pregnant, a spirit came to her in a dream. The spirit warned that she must leave home if she found her

bowl leaking water. But as part of the warning, the spirit told her not to look back.

The frightened woman saw the sign and left. But when she was 10 leagues to the east of the city, she could not help herself and looked back. The city and all around it turned to water. Then the woman turned into a MULBERRY TREE.

A short time later, Yi Yin was found by a girl of the Yu Shen clan in the mulberry tree. The boy was raised by the lord's cook and grew to be quite a man. Tang the Conqueror wanted him to join his army, but the lord of Yu Shen did not want to let him go. So Tang asked for a bride from the family. Happily, the Yu Shen lord agreed, sending Yi Yen as a guarantee (or a guard).

Yi Yin was a great cook and won fame for this. He was also a very wise counselor. But his true value to Tang was as a spy, or double agent. Tang pretended to have an argument with Yi Yin and shot arrows at him. Yi Yin pretended that he barely escaped with his life. Hearing of this, the Xia rulers welcomed him to their kingdom. While there, Yi Yin gathered information from a former mistress of the king.

Yi Yin returned to Tang with his information after three years. Then he went back to Xia to gather more information. Finally, he helped Tang defeat the Xia in battle.

YOU CHUI (YU CH'UI)   According to ancient Chinese mythology, the gifted craftsman who helped DI KU fashion MUSICAL INSTRUMENTS.

YOU DI   See YU HUANG.

YU (YÜ, EMPEROR YÜ, EMPEROR YU)   One of the three kings of the GOLDEN AGE. He followed YAO and SHUN.

This mythological EMPEROR is the subject of a rich variety of stories. The most popular concern Yu's work rebuilding China after a great FLOOD wiped out most of the world. He is revered for his perseverance in the face of all obstacles. Here is the basic tale:

Before Yu was born, floods threatened EARTH. Yu's father, GUN, went to HEAVEN and took magic soil without the gods' permission as he tried to damn the rising waters.

ZHU RONG, an ancient fire god, executed Gun for this sin. Dead, Gun gave birth to Yu, who was born from his belly button. Zhu Rong, apparently taking pity on humankind and thinking that what Gun had done was not that bad, allowed Yu to take the soil and rebuild the Earth.

Yu drained the waters that had covered the plains of China and made islands of its nine provinces. On the western end of the country, he cut holes through the mountains and created rivers and streams to control and direct the floodwaters. On the eastern end of the country, he built an irrigation system to drain the water into the sea, reclaiming the land to grow crops (see AGRICULTURE). He also connected the roads of the provinces to one another. In his labors, he was helped by a YELLOW DRAGON, which dragged its tail before him to cut a path. Meanwhile, a dark tortoise carried the mud away.

At times, Yu was barely able to walk or work because of the thick calluses on his hands and feet. He was exhausted from his labors. Yet somehow he found enough strength to continue.

After Yu's work was done, the floodwaters were controlled. But there were still dangers. In one story, GONG GONG made the floodwaters rise, and Yu had to capture and exile him. In another, Gong Gong used a nine-headed dragon named XIANG LIU to harass the kingdom. Yu killed him, but nothing would grow in the area until Yu made a special terrace for the gods north of KUNLUN.

Yu also had special troubles with Wuzhiqi, the god of the Huai and Wo Rivers. Shaped like an ape, Wuzhiqi had a green chest and a white head. He could not be controlled by any of Yu's people until, at last, one was able to put a bell through his nose. From then on, the Huai River flowed peacefully.

According to the myths, Yu was so successful that the emperor Shun, one of the legendary FIVE EMPERORS, was grateful enough to retire and offer his throne to Yu. He accepted. According to this account, he became the first emperor of the mythic XIA DYNASTY, said to have come before the SHANG.

Among other things, Emperor Yu is said to have ordered that the Earth be measured. The stories give different figures for the result. One story from the second century B.C. declares the distance between the east and west pole of the Earth as 233,500 li and 75 paces, with the same measurement north to south. (A li was about a third of our mile.)

In some tales, Yu is credited with teaching people which spirits were evil and banishing these spirits with nine cauldrons, symbols of ritual and purity. In these stories, Yu is a metalworker as well as a hero.

Yu's adventures were said to have kept him from marrying until he was 30. At that point, a white FOX with nine tails appeared to him. He understood this as a sign that he should marry a woman from the Tushan CLAN, symbolized by the white fox. His wife's name was NÜ JIAO.

Yu was able to assume the shape of a BEAR and so find the strength to continue to work even when he was tired. Later he would change back to a man and beat his drum so that his wife would bring him his dinner (see SHAPE SHIFTING). One day, while Yu was breaking rocks, his pregnant wife mistakenly thought it was time to bring his dinner. Frightened by the bear, Nü Jiao ran away. Yu ran after her. She tripped and fell to the ground; she was so fearful that she turned to stone. Yu had to split the stone in order to allow his son, KAI, to be born. (In another variation of the story, he is said to dance at the prospect of his wedding and accidentally turn into a bear.)

Yu's stories continued to be told for centuries. As time went on, his mythic identity as a god was changed to something closer to a human hero. Writers often made changes in the story to suit different purposes. Taoist philosophers, for example, reworked the stories to show that members of the Taoist pantheon have more power than Yu did. In one late tale dating from the 10th century, Yu is helped by a goddess named the JASPER LADY, or Lady Yunhua.

YUANSHI TIANZONG (YÜAN-SHIH T'IEN-TSUN)

The "Celestial Venerable of the Primordial Beginning," or the principle or ideal of all beings. He began as an abstract principle but was personified as a powerful god in the Taoist pantheon. He was one of the SAN GUAN DADI. He is called by many names, such as "the first principle" and "the everlasting."

Yuanshi Tianzong came to be pictured literally as a god who set the universe in motion. He was said to live above the HEAVENS. The kitchen god, ZAO JUN, was seen as his lieutenant, as was LEI ZU, the thunder god.

Another tradition personified him as the incarnation of PANGU. In this story, he was born to a mother whom the spirit of Pangu impregnated. He was in the womb for 12 years, but, as soon as he was born, he walked and talked. A cloud of FIVE COLORS surrounded him.

YUAN TAN In Chinese mythology, a god of WEALTH. He was said to command a TIGER, which he could ride as a horse. Some scholars believe he was an early god of wealth, but was superseded by CAI SHEN.

YU CH'IANG See YU QIANG.

YÜ CH'ING See YU QING.

YU CH'UI See YOU CHUI.

YU DI See YU HUANG.

YUFUHUI April 8, the day traditionally believed to be the historical BUDDHA's birthday. Among the celebrations are the symbolic washing of Buddha's statues by the faithful.

YUGONG (YÜ-KUNG) The "Foolish old man" in Chinese folklore.

According to legend, Yugong was a 90-year-old man who was tired of having to walk around the mountains that lay in his way. So he got his son and grandson to help him cut a path through the mountains. A year passed without their getting far, but Yugong refused to give up. He predicted that eventually, the path would be used—if not by him, then by the son of his son of his son.

The god of HEAVEN took pity on the old man—or was perhaps he was impressed by Yugong's determination—and had the mountains separated.

YU HUANG (YU TI, YU DI, JADE EMPEROR, JADE AUGUST ONE) The "Jade Emperor," supreme ruler of HEAVEN, was an important figure in TAOISM and popular Chinese mythology. He determined everything in HEAVEN and EARTH and commanded hundreds of gods and spirits to carry out his orders.

The Jade Emperor is a comparatively late figure in Chinese mythology. An expression of Taoist philo-

Yu Huang, also known as Yu Di or the Jade Emperor, the highest god in the Chinese pantheon (The Dragon, Image, and Demon, *1886*)

sophical notions of the universe, he came to be personified as an all-powerful god. He was celebrated by the SONG DYNASTY and gained greatly in popularity after Emperor Hui Zong (1101–26) gave him the title of *Shang Di*, the highest god.

Myths and legends about Yu Huang developed to fill in details; they told of his beginnings as the son of an earthly king and made many references to other Taoist beliefs. It was said that before he was born, his mother dreamed that LAO-TZU, the founder of TAOISM, handed her a child; soon after, according to myth, Yu Huang was born. When he was still young, his father died. Yu Huang became king, but he had been interested in studying Taoism and allowed someone else to rule in his place so that he could continue learning the Tao. He lived in the mountains and attained perfection there. He devoted the rest of his life to helping the sick and the poor learn about Taoism. He became an IMMORTAL; after 1 million years, he attained the highest calling as the Jade Emperor.

Yu Huang's wife was said to be the Queen Mother of the West, XI WANG MU, who lived in the JADE palace in KUNLUN. Yu Huang's own palace, located in the highest level of heaven, was guarded by QING LONG PA JIANG JUN, the "Green DRAGON General."

Yu Huang's chief assistant was DONGYUE DADI, who was in charge of a spiritual organization that was similar to China's earthly system of government (see MINISTRIES OF GODS). Like the earthly officials, the gods and spiritual officials could be fired and assigned to lesser posts if their work was not up to the high standards of the Jade Emperor during his annual inspections.

Artists portrayed Yu Huang with a crown of gold and strings of pearls, holding a jade fan or tablet, and dressed in ceremonial robes embroidered with the pictures of dragons.

YÜ-KUNG See YUGONG.

YULAN HUI (YÜ-LAN HUI) The festival of the hungry GHOSTS, held in ancient China on the 15th day of the seventh month. Special offerings were made for PRETAS, who were said to leave the underworld at that time and roam the EARTH.

YU QIANG (YU CH'IANG) In Chinese myth, a god of wind and sea.

The lord of HEAVEN asked him to keep the floating ISLANDS OF THE IMMORTALS anchored in place, which Yu Qiang accomplished with the help of 15 giant TORTOISES, who were to take turns carrying an island on their backs for 60,000 years. A giant caught six of the tortoises, and two of the islands broke free and sank, leaving just three.

In art, Yu Qiang is seen riding two DRAGONS and having the body of a FISH to depict his role as god of the sea. Artists draw him as a bird with a human face for his role as a god of wind.

YU QING (YÜ CH'ING) One of three Taoist HEAVENS, or AZURES; a primeval god of the same name. Yu Qing is the Pearly Azure.

But the ordering of the heavens varies, with other sources listing Yu Qing as highest, though still others say SHANG QING had this distinction (see SAN GUAN DADI).

YÜ SHIH See RAIN MASTER.

YU TI See YU HUANG.

YU YU See SHUN.

Z

ZANG XIYONJI See XUAN ZANG.

ZANGWU (TSANG-WU) A mythological mountain where Emperor SHUN was buried. It is also called the "Nine Doubts."

ZAO JUN (ZAO SHEN, TSAO-CHÜN, TSAO-CHUN, TSAO CHÜN, SSÜ-MING FO-CHÜN, KITCHEN GOD) A Taoist figure who has been widely worshipped and revered since the second century B.C. His picture or likeness was often kept above the kitchen hearth or oven.

Zao Jun appears to have started as a god connected to ALCHEMY and the forge, the fiery furnace where metal is worked and changed into new shapes. Mythologists have traced his stories as a god of the furnace to the HAN DYNASTY. Later, Zao Jun was linked to the home fires and called Zao Shen, or God of the Hearth.

Zao Jun was said to report on a family's conduct to YU HUANG, the Jade Emperor, or the supreme being in HEAVEN. Some versions of the myth say that reports were given once or twice a month, but all agree that one was given at the end of the Chinese year. Families today still offer a meal of meat, fruit, and wine to his likeness at the New Year and smear his lips with honey, to keep him feeling sweet. Another custom is to burn the portrait afterward to let the smoke hasten Zao Jun's journey up to heaven. FIRECRACKERS are often set off in his honor during the New Year celebrations.

According to Taoist legend, Zao Jun granted a special boon to a priest named Li Shao jün. Zao Jun arranged for the priest never to grow old—and to live without having to eat. The priest then convinced EMPEROR Xiao Wu Di (140–86 B.C.) of the Han dynasty to honor the kitchen god and Taoism. Taoist myth also credits Zao Jun with teaching Huang Di, the YELLOW EMPEROR, alchemy. According to these myths, Huang Di is said to have been the first to worship him, though the god seems to have been invented long after the legendary emperor is said to have lived.

Zao Jun's popularity may account for the large number of stories concerning his origin. Some of these stories also explain how different hearth tools were invented. One tale speaks of a young man named Zhang Zao-wang (also known as Zhang Lang and written in pinyin as Chang Tsao-wang):

Zhang had the good fortune to marry a virtuous woman named Guo Ding Xiang. But he was foolish and soon fell in love with someone else. He sent away his first wife and so quickly fell on hard times, becoming both blind and penniless. Reduced to begging, he roamed the countryside.

One day he came to a strange house where a kind woman gave him a dish of noodles. The first bite was so wonderful that he cried out loud, "My wife cooked like this."

"Open your eyes," said the woman.

Zhang found that he could. Seeing that it was the wife whom he had wronged, Zhang was filled with guilt. He tried to hide—but instead fell into the hearth (stove), not realizing that it was lit. His wife tried to save him, grabbing his leg, but she was too late. The leg came off from his body; for this reason, the rake used to pull ashes from a stove fire is called Zhang Lang's leg.

Filled with sorrow, Guo Ding Xiang mourned her husband's death. She began then to honor and worship his memory. This worship, claims the story, led to his recognition as Kitchen God.

Some Buddhists claim that Zao Jun is the human reincarnation of a Buddhist divine spirit known as a JINNALALUO, a being who came to EARTH as a monk.

Zao Jun, the Kitchen God, one of the most popular figures in Chinese mythology (The Dragon, Image, and Demon, *1886*)

Because of his duty in reporting on the family, Zao Jun is also sometimes called the "Superintendent of Lives," or Siming Fo jun.

Yan Di is viewed by some mythologists as another name for Zao Jun or as the name of the original god from whose story the more popular one of Zao Jun grew.

ZEN BUDDHISM Known in China as Chan BUDDHISM, Zen Buddhism flourished in early China.

Zen can be viewed as a reaction to the complications of some Buddhist teachings (see SUTRAS and VEDAS). It stresses that ENLIGHTENMENT comes from looking within rather than studying complicated doctrine.

According to Buddhist tradition, Zen Buddhism was brought to China by BODHIDHARMA in the early sixth century.

ZENGZHANG The Chinese Buddhist GUARDIAN KING of the South. He presides over the summer. Taoists call him Moli Hong. In TIBET the Zengzhang is known as Hphags Skyese-po; he is Ulumchi Tereltü in MONGOLIA.

ZHANG DAOLING (CHANG TAO-LING) Historical person seen as an important early figure in TAOISM as it became a state religion. There is some question as to when he actually lived. His birth year is traditionally given as A.D. 34 or 35, but he is usually said to have died in A.D. 156.

Zhang Daoling lived in a mountainous area of Sichuan (Szechwan). He was said to have received a vision from LAO-TZU—the traditional founder of Taoism. According to Zhang, Lao told him that he must replace the present religious practices with new teachings. These teachings combined religion and government together in a form scholars call a Taocracy, or rule by Tao.

Under the system, China was divided into different parishes (*chih*), first 24, then later 36. Each was headed by a Taoist administrator. Every family was to pay a tax to the administrator of five measures, or pecks, of rice. Because of this tax, the movement itself became known as the "Way of the Five Pecks of Rice."

An important part of the administrator's duties involved cures for illness. Disease was seen as a punishment for sins, imposed by the SAN GUAN, or three judges of the dead. Ceremonies were needed to remove it. During the ceremonies, the Taoist priest made *zhang* (petitions or prayers), which were said to go to officials in one of three Taoist HEAVENS. These heavenly officials each had a responsibility for a specific ailment and its corresponding demon (see MEDICINE and MINISTRY OF GODS). There were many ways for this appeal to be made. One involved *FU*, or written talismans that were burned and then ingested with water by the sick patient.

Other important features of Taoism said to be influenced by Zhang were communal feasts, which were to be held during the first, seventh, and 10th months of the year. One rite practiced by followers was the Union of Breaths, which was supposed to be celebrated each new moon (He Qi). The rite was described by later Buddhists as a kind of sex orgy. The manuals describing it that have survived are fairly mysterious. Scholars believe that the ceremonies came from earlier times and were adopted by Taoism, rather than being invented by Zhang.

Under Cao Cao, the founder of the Wei dynasty in northern China, and Zhang Lu, Zhang Daoling's grandson, the Taoism practiced by Zhang was officially recognized in court. The sect then continued to grow in importance until, by the end of the third century, it was dominant in northern China.

A variety of legends were connected with Zhang Daoling. In one, he is said to have discovered the secret of creating a pill for immortality. Rather than eating it all, he cut it in half. In this way he was able to split himself into two people. One went and met visitors and did his work; the other spent his time sailing in a boat on a lake. Zhang Daoling's powers were said to include the ability to fly. Many stories of him tell how he taught his students the secrets of Taoism with the help of magic.

Descendants of Zhang in Taiwan have retained important positions in Taoism to the present day.

ZHANG E (CH'ANG O, CHANG O)   The wife of YI, the divine archer in Chinese myth. She is considered a goddess of the MOON and identified with a striped toad (CHANCHU).

Zhang E appears in the cycle of stories about Yi, the divine archer. After her husband shot down nine of the 10 SUNS, she and her husband were punished. The Lord of Heaven changed them into human beings and banished them to Earth. Zhang E was so angry she began to nag her husband to visit XI WANG MU, the QUEEN MOTHER OF THE WEST, and ask her help in obtaining the ELIXIR OF ETERNAL LIFE.

The queen gave Yi a small jar of elixir. There was just enough for either two people to live on Earth forever or for one person to become completely immortal, with all of a god's powers. Yi, a good and faithful husband, brought back the elixir to share with his wife and hid it in the rafters of their house.

The selfish Zhang E wanted the elixir all to herself, but she thought the gods might punish her for being so selfish. So she consulted an ASTROLOGER, who studied the movement of the stars and determined that the safest place to drink the elixir was on the Moon. The gods had no jurisdiction there, he told her, so they would not be able to punish her. He also told her that she would be miraculously transformed into a different creature on her way to the Moon.

Zhang E drank all of the elixir. She started to float up through the clouds to the Moon, but when she tried to call out, only a croak came from her mouth. She had been transformed, just as the astrologer said, but into the striped toad Chanchu.

There are several different versions of what happened when Zhang E finally reached the Moon. In one tale, she regained her human appearance as a woman and still lives there in a grand palace. In another, she found two other occupants on the Moon, a HARE and an old man, WU KANG, who keeps chopping away at a tree said to be a source of long life. The tree is impossible to cut down, though he keeps at it.

Zhang E is usually depicted as a beautiful, dark-haired woman wearing a golden crown and colorful, elaborately embroidered robes, holding the Moon in her right hand.

At one point in Chinese history, scribes were not allowed to write the word Zhang, because of a taboo on using the imperial name. Heng was substituted in its place, making Zhang into Heng. Additionally, an older writing style renders the name with an O, so it appears as Heng O. This still causes some confusion today when this popular story is translated from different sources into English.

There are several Chinese moon goddesses. See CHANGXI.

ZHANG FEI (CHANG FEI)   The god of butchers in ancient Chinese mythology. According to the tales told of him, he was eight feet tall, had a panther's head, and spoke with the voice of thunder. Zhang Fei was said to have been a real person, a pork seller in ancient China who traveled through the country selling his wares.

Zhang Fei is also associated in lore with the military hero Guan Gong. According to the tale, the two got into a fight, but Liu Bei stepped in to stop it. From that point on, the three friends were inseparable, like the Three Musketeers; the three became fast friends and military heroes who had many mythic adventures.

ZHANG GONGYI (CHANG KUNG-I)
Zhang Gongyi is more a role model than a deity in Chinese folklore. According to legend, Zhang had an unusually large family, with members of eight generations beneath the same roof. Yet it was always said that the many members lived in complete harmony, thanks to the efforts of the family head. The emperor Gaozong (650–684) of the TANG DYNASTY was impressed. He approached Zhang and asked how he managed it. Zhang Gongyi wrote a one-word (or symbol) answer: *patience*.

ZHANG GUOLAO (CHANG KUO-LAO)
According to Taoist legends, Zhang Guolao is one of the BA XIAN, or Eight IMMORTALS. He was said to have been a very old man who lived during the eighth century B.C. But he was also said to be an incarnation of the primeval CHAOS, which existed before the EARTH was made. He is considered the patron of childless couples and newlyweds.

In one of the stories about Zhang Guolao, an emperor was intrigued by him and asked a Taoist master who he was. The master had been warned that if he told the old man's true identity, he would immediately die. Finally, the master agreed to tell, but only on the condition that the EMPEROR humble himself by going barefoot and bareheaded to tell Zhang Guolao what had happened and to beg him to forgive the Taoist master for his betrayal. The emperor agreed. As soon as the master announced Zhang Guolao's true identity, he fell down dead. The emperor was so upset that he immediately removed his hat and his shoes and went to find Zhang Guolao, who kindly brought the master back to life.

Zhang Guolao is often portrayed in art as an elderly man with a long gray beard and a floppy cap, who rides his white mule facing backward. The mule could carry the old man thousands of miles at a time without stopping to rest. When Zhang Guolao had settled in one place for the night, he folded the ani-

Zhang Guolao, one of the Ba Xian, or Eight Immortals, in Taoist and popular Chinese myth (The Dragon, Image, and Demon, *1886*)

mal into a tiny scrap of paper and stored it in his wallet. When he wanted to ride the mule again, all he had to do was squirt a bit of water onto the wallet, and the mule would spring back to life.

Legends and stories noted many of Zhang Guolao's other powers: For example, he could make himself invisible, and he could endow childless couples and newlyweds with children.

ZHANG LU (CHANG LU)
The grandson of Zhang Daoling (fl. 142 A.D.), an important early Taoist teacher and leader, Zhang Lu lived in the second and third centuries A.D. He carried on his grandfather's teachings and expanded Taoist monasteries and schools, helping the poor and common people in north-central China. He eventually formed an army

and controlled most of modern Sichuan Province. However, in 215 A.D., he submitted to Cao Cao, a Han Dynasty general and the king of Wei in northern China. Cao Cao's son succeeded him and founded the Wei dynasty (220–265 A.D.). Cao Cao and his successors officially adopted the practices of Taoism, which helped spread the religion's influence throughout the land.

ZHANG XIAN (CHANG HSIEN) The god of childbearing in Chinese myth; the deity who helps women have children. Zhang Xian is male.

Numerous myths and stories are attached to the god. In one of them, he is said to keep the HEAVENLY DOG from eating the MOON and stealing children during an eclipse. Zhang is also said to preside over the heavenly kitchens.

Zhang Xian has a son, Jiantan, who brings male children; his daughter, Songzi Niangniang, brings girls.

ZHAO SAN-NIANG (CHAO SAN-NIANG) The goddess of wig sellers in Chinese mythology. Her story demonstrates perseverance despite poverty and other obstacles. It also illustrates the best qualities a Chinese wife could possess.

According to the basic tale, Zhao San-niang was the wife of a scholar. While her husband was away, she discovered that she was so poor she could only feed herself or her husband's parents, who lived with them. Zhao San-niang gave the food to her parents-in-law and ate only husks herself. They soon learned this and insisted on sharing this poor meal. When they died, Zhao San-niang had no money for coffins or a funeral. She managed to arrange a proper ceremony by selling her own hair. Then she sewed some hairs into a wig so that she would not be shamed when her husband arrived home.

ZHAO XUAN-TAN See CAI-SHEN.

ZHENG SANGONG (CHENG SAN-KUNG) A patron of fishermen in popular Chinese Buddhist myth. According to legend, Zheng Sangong and two friends were fishing one day in the CHIANG RIVER when they saw a yellow rock sticking up out of the water. They found that it was gold and wanted to take it away. When it stuck fast, they prayed to BUDDHA, vowing to build a temple to honor him if he helped them. The gold became light in weight, and they carried it away. The temple, called Hsüan-miao Kuan, was built near Suzhou.

ZHI NU See WEAVER AND HEAVENLY OX.

ZHONGGUEI A god of examinations and a protector of travelers in ancient Chinese myth.

It is said that while he was alive, Zhongguei was a great student and scholar. However, when it came time for him to take his examinations, he was unjustly denied first place on the tests. This distressed him terribly, and, in despair, he killed himself, becoming a GUI, or spirit.

Zhongguei was usually a good spirit, however, unlike many of the ghostly DEMONS. He was said to help dutiful and devoted students and to protect travelers from the evil demons who haunted roads.

In art, Zhongguei is usually shown in long RED robes with a scholar's cap and is often accompanied by a demon.

ZHONGLI QUAN (ZHONG-LI QUAN) One of the legendary BA XIAN, or Eight IMMORTALS.

The legends say he lived as a human being during the ZHOU DYNASTY around 1122 B.C. and studied the principles of TAOISM as a student of the first of the Eight Immortals, LI TIEGUAI. He was said to have found the instructions for gaining immortality hidden behind a wall of his house after it collapsed. Following these instructions, Zhongli Quan flew up to HEAVEN on a cloud.

One tale says that Zhongli Quan once had a beautiful young wife and lived in the countryside as a philosopher. One day he came across a woman sitting by a grave, fanning the freshly piled soil. She told him that just before her husband died, he made her promise to wait until the soil on his grave was dry before marrying again. But she had found a new husband, so she was trying to dry the gravesite faster by fanning it. Zhongli Quan offered to help her. He called on the spirits to help him and struck the tomb with her fan, and it immediately became dry. The widow was so happy that she thanked him and quickly ran away, leaving her fan behind. Back home, he told his own wife what had happened. She scolded him, calling the widow a monster for wanting to remarry so quickly. Zhongli Quan decided to test his wife's loyalty: He pretended to be dead, then used magic to turn himself into a young, handsome man. The wife quickly fell in love and agreed to marry the young man. Angry at his wife, the disguised Zhongli Quan asked her to steal the brain of her dead husband in order to make a powerful potion. The disloyal wife agreed. When she opened the coffin, Zhongli Quan appeared there—alive.

His wife was so shocked and ashamed that she killed herself. A heartbroken Zhongli Quan set their house on fire. When the house collapsed, he found a book with the secret of immortality. Taking only the fan and a sacred book with him, he left and wandered the world.

Zhongli Quan is usually shown as a fat, bearded, but bald man dressed in a sagging robe that shows his

Zhongli Quan carries his fan. He is one of the Ba Xian, or Eight Immortals, in Taoist and popular Chinese myth (The Dragon, Image, and Demon, *1886*)

bare belly. He is always holding a magic fan made of palm leaves that had the power to bring the souls of the dead back to life.

ZHOU (CHOU) Besides referring to the Zhou dynasty, the word Zhou is often used to refer to the region dominated by the Zhou clan and as a synonym for China. (Under the old writing system, Zhou is written as Chou.) The territory ruled by the clan centered around the YELLOW RIVER (see KING ZHOU).

ZHOU DYNASTY (CHOU DYNASTY) The Zhou dynasty succeeded the SHANG rulers in early China. The dynasty traced its ancestry back to JIANG YUAN, and from her to the ancient gods. WU was the first of the clan to be crowned king.

The dynasty's dates are generally given as between 1122 B.C. and 1027 B.C. Much of what is known of the period and dynasty comes from legendary accounts written following its reign. The legends are probably based on historical fact, though the precise details are a matter of debate and are still being studied.

According to these legends, the Zhou clan thrived in the area northwest of the region dominated by the Shang. Led by Ku-kung Tan-fu (or King Tai) and his brother Ji-li Chi-li, the Zhou moved to the area of the Ching and Wei Rivers (near Wei in modern China). Their descendants displaced the Shang and took over their kingdom.

According to the historical texts written long afterward, the final Shang ruler, Tsou-hsin, was a bad king. The leader of the Zhou clan was Wen, a duke or lord for the Shang. He extended their kingdom, ruling in the west with the title count of the west. A man of learning, he was also known as Chang (Ch'ang in the old style).

But then Wen fell from favor and began a rebellion against the Shan finished by his son, Wu, who led an army and overthrew the Shang ruler. Wu's brother Zhou Kung (or duke of Zhou) was an adviser to Wu and later a regent for Wu's son, Wu Wang. He extended Wu Wang's victories and established the ancient state of Lu.

Scholars studying the texts where this history is recorded point out that parts of the story may have been enhanced or improved by writers wanting to show how a good king should rule. CONFUCIUS himself used

Lu many years later to explain how rulers and people should live. Wu and Wen are names used to describe important qualities needed by kings and society.

Hao, near modern Sian, was the dynasty's capital. There was also an eastern capital called Lo-yi (near Loyang), which the Zhou used to rule the eastern portion of the kingdom, once dominated by the Shang.

The Zhou dynasty period is broken into two parts by scholars. The first, from the 11th century B.C. until 771 B.C., is the Western Zhou. This was a time of feudalism, with lesser lords owing allegiance to greater lords. It appears to have been very much like the Shang dynasty, with fortune-telling, or DIVINATION, an important part of the king's rule.

In 771 a fight developed between two princes over the throne. The Zhou Empire had already been under turmoil from rebellions and outside attacks. The conflict led to a split in the kingdom. Ping Wang (also known as Yi Jiu, his name as prince) ruled the east, and Yuchen ruled the west as king of Hui. Yuchen was succeeded by his son, Huan, who eventually lost the conflict. Dukes who controlled large estates and armies had more power than the Zhou rulers in most cases. However, the rulers remained important, partly because of their connection to religious rites and divination.

The Eastern Zhou period is usually broken into several large subperiods. One is the Spring and Autumn period, or Chunqiu, the title of a history of Lu covering 722–481 B.C. The second is the Warring States period, whose dates are usually given from 453 B.C. or 403 B.C. to 221 B.C. During the period of the Warring States, the kingdom was split into different states: Zhou, Qin, Wei, Han, Chao, Chu, Yen, and Qi. The states were reunified by the Qin rulers in 256 B.C., with the last Zhou king stripped of his title and the remains of his authority in 249 B.C. However, the date 221 B.C. is usually used by historians as the end of the Warring States, because this year was when Qin Shihuangdi established himself as emperor over the reunited land.

The Eastern Zhou is an important time in the history of China. It was during this time that Confucius lived and TAOISM took on much of its form.

ZHUANGZI (CHUANG-TZU) Taoist writer and philosopher (c. 368 B.C.–286 B.C.) who greatly influenced TAOISM and Chinese thought in general.

Zhuangzi is considered the second most important figure in early Taoism after LAO-TZU. His influence extended beyond philosophy and religion to poetry and painting, and it was even said that he influenced the development of BUDDHISM as well.

His book is usually titled *Zhuangzi* (or *Chuang-tzu* in Wade-Giles), after its author, though it is also called *Nan-hua Chen Ching,* or the Pure classic of Nan-hua. Over time the original shape and content of the work may have been altered as it was copied, edited, and interpreted. However, of the 33 chapters that survive (there is evidence that there may have been as many as 53 at one point), the first seven, or the "inner books," are believed to be his. The authorship of the rest is doubtful, though it may include passages by Zhuangzi.

At the heart of Zhuangzi's beliefs was the idea that the Tao, or "Way of the Universe," could not be known. Scholars often quote the following passage, here loosely translated, to show the essence of Zhuangzi's ideas:

> Once Chuang dreamed he was a BUTTERFLY. The butterfly did not know it was Zhuang. It was joyful and carefree. Then it awoke and was truly Zhuang again. But was it Zhuang, dreaming he was a butterfly? Or is it now a butterfly, dreaming about Zhuang?

Though he was a real person, not much is known about Zhuangzi's life. He was a minor official in Qiyuan, or Ch'i-yüan, and lived during the reign of Prince Wei (d. 327 B.C.).

ZHU BAJIE (CHU PA-CHIEH) A Chinese god said to be half PIG and half man.

According to his myth, Zhu Bajie had been serving in HEAVEN as "Overseer-General for Navigation on the Milky Way." The Milky Way galaxy was said to be a road of stars that the gods used to visit each other in heaven. Zhu Bajie took care of the road. But he got in trouble for attacking YU HUANG's daughter. Exiled to Earth, he entered through the womb of a pig instead of a human mother.

ZHU JUAN SHEN (CHU CHÜA SHEN) The Chinese god of pigsties.

ZHU LONG See TORCH DRAGON.

ZHU RONG (CHU JONG, CHU YUNG) The divine lord of fire in Chinese myth. An important member of the ministry of fire, Huo Bu, in Chinese myth (see MINISTRIES OF GODS). He was also known as regent of the southern quadrant of HEAVEN. He helped to divide heaven and EARTH from each other. Zhu Rong executed KUN after he stole heavenly soil and tried to stop a great flood.

One story tells how Zhu Rong and GONG GONG were jealous and began to wrestle and fight with each other in heaven, to determine who was the more powerful. Falling out of heaven, Zhu Rong managed to defeat Gong Gong, who was so ashamed that he tried to kill himself by running into a mountain, BUZHOU, but he only managed to cause a massive FLOOD.

Zhu Rong is identified with several legendary and historic figures. The most common is a legendary emperor from the prehistoric period. It is said that the emperor (or Zhu Rong) taught people how to set small fires to drive off beasts.

Zhu Rong is often depicted in art as riding on a TIGER. He presided over the South and helped break the link between HEAVEN and EARTH. After that, his job was to keep men in their appointed positions in the universal order.

ZHU TIAN (CHU T'IEN) Three princes of storms and hurricanes in Chinese myth. These fearsome gods command fear and respect.

Yu Shih, the RAIN MASTER, is sometimes called Zhu Tian.

ZHU XI (ZHUZI) An important Chinese philosopher (1130–1200) whose ideas on CONFUCIANISM combined some Buddhist influences. Sometimes called NEO-CONFUCIANISM, Zhu Xi's teaching emphasized that CONFUCIUS's morality was meant to help a person understand the constant, unchanging Way, or life force. The Way lies beyond the YIN AND YANG of the spirit and material being that give shape to the familiar world. Zhu Xi emphasized the FOUR BOOKS as the basis of learning: the *Analects*, *Ta hsüeh* (Great learning), *Chung Yung* (also written as *Chung-yung*, [The Great mean]), and *Meng-tzu* (a work by early Confucian teacher Master Meng, or Mencius).

ZHUZI ZHEN (CHU TZU CHEN) The Chinese god of PIGS, or the perfect pig.

IMPORTANT GODS AND MYTHIC FIGURES

A
Achu
Amoghasiddhi
Ānanda
Ao Bing

B
Ba
Bai Zhong
Baosheng Fo
Ba Xian
Ba Zha
Bei Dou
Beng Meng
Bian Qiao
Bodhidharma

C
Cai Shen
Can Cong
Can Nü
Cao Guojiu
Chanchu
Chang Liang
Changxi
Cha Yu
Cheng Huang
Chien Di
Chien-mu
Chi-jia Xian
Chi Jingzi
Chi Songzi
Chiyou

Chong and Li
Chou Hua
Chu Xie Yuan

D
Dabiancaitian Nu
Danzhu
Di Guan
Di Ku
Diya
Dizang
Dongyue Dadi
Dong Wang Gong
door gods
Dou Mu
Dou Shen
Drought Fury
Duke of Zhou
Duowen
Du Yu

E
Earth God
Empress Wu
Erlang

F
Fang-feng
Fan Wang
Fei Lian
Feng Du Dadi
Feng Bo

Feng Po Po
Fire Driller
Five Great Kings
Fukurokujo
Fuxi
Fuxing
Fu Yueh

G
Gan Jiang and Mo Ye
Gao Yao
Gong Gong
Guan Di
Guangmu
Guan Yu
Guanyin
Guardian Kings
gui
Gun
Gunsho Mingwang

H
Han Ping and his wife
Han Xiang
He He
He Xiangu
Ho-po
Hou Ji
Hou Tu
Hua Fu
Hua-kuang Fo
hun
Hun Dun

Huo Bu
Hu Shen

I
Immortals

J
Jigong Laofo Pusa
jinnalaluo
ju-i
Ju Ling

K
Kai
kaiguang
King Chieh
King Miao Zhong
King Yen
Kongiue Dongnan Fei
Kong Jia
Kuafu
Kui
Kui Xing

L
Lai Cho
Lan Caihe
Lao Jun
Lei Bu
Lei Gong
Lei Zhe Zi
Lei Zu
Liang Wu Di
Lightning Goddess

Li Tian
Li Tieguai
Liuhai Xian
Liu Meng Jiang Zhun
Lobin
Long Shan
Long Wang
Lord of the Granary
Lu Ban
Lu Dongbin
luohan
Luohuluo
Lu Shang
Luxing

M

Ma Gu
Mang Shen
Mara
Ma Shihuang
Master Yen
Ma Wang
Ma Yuan-shai
Meng Po
Miao
Milo Fo
Molizhi
Monkey King
Mo Xi
Moyo
Muclinda
Mulian

N

naga
Nazha
Niu Wang
Nü Gua
Nü Jiao
Nü Wa

O

Omitu Fo

P

Palushena
Pangu
Pan Guan
Pan Hu
Pearly Emperor
Pengzu
Po Yi
Po Yi and Shu Chi

Q

qi
Qian Fo
Qi Guzi
Qing Long
Qing Long Pa Jiang Jun
Qin Guang Wang
Qing Wa Shen
Queen of Heaven

R

Rain God
Rain Master
raksas

S

Salt River Goddess
San Bao
San Guan Dadi
San Xing
Sa Zhenren
Sen Shin
Shang Di
Shao Hao
Sheji
Sheng gu
Sheng Mu
Shen Nong
shen tu
She Wang
Shi Huang Di
Shouxing
Shubojia
Shui Fang
Shui Guan
Shui Yong

Shun
Sunbi

T

Tai Hao
Taiyang Dijun
Tang the Conqueror
Taodie
Tao Wu
Tian Di
Tian Fei
Tian Long
Tian Yiyuan
Tianyu Yuanshuai
Tien Guan
Torch Dragon
touziguei
Twelve Warriors

V

Vidyarajas

W

Weaver Girl and
   Heavenly Ox
Wen
Wenshu
White Tiger of the West
Wu
Wu Chang Gui
Wu Guan
Wu Kang

X

Xiang
Xiang Liu
Xian Ren
Xiao Gong
Xie
Xie Tian Jun
Xihe
Xing Weng
Xi Shen
Xi Shi
Xi Wang Mu

Xuan Zang
Xukongzang
Xu Zhenjun

Y

Yan Di
Yang Cheng
Yan Gong
Yanlou Wang
Yansi Qiangzhun
Yao
Yaoshi fo
Yellow Emperor
Yi
Ying Long
Yi Yin
You Chui
Yu
Yuanshi Tianzong
Yuan Tan
Yugong
Yu Huang
Yu Qiang
Yu Qing

Z

Zangwu
Zao Jun
Zengzhang
Zhang Daoling
Zhang E
Zhang Fei
Zhang Gongyi
Zhang Guolao
Zhang Lu
Zhang Xian
Zhao San-niang
Zheng Sangong
Zhongguei
Zhongli Quan
Zhu Bajie
Zhu Juan Shen
Zhu Rong
Zhu Tian
Zhuzi Zhen

SELECTED BIBLIOGRAPHY

Birrell, Anne. *Chinese Mythology*. Baltimore, Md.: Johns Hopkins University Press, 1993.

Christie, Anthony. *Chinese Mythology*. New York: Peter Bedrick Books, 1985.

Fairbank, John King. *China: A New History*. Cambridge, Mass.: Belknap Press of Harvard University Press, 1992.

Frédéric, Louis. *Buddhism*. Paris, France: Flammarion, 1995.

Getty, Alice. *The Gods of Northern Buddhism*. Mineola, N.Y.: Dover Publications, 1988.

Gordon, Antoinette K. *Tibetan Religious Art*. Mineola, N.Y.: Dover Publications, 2002.

Hook, Brian. *Cambridge Encyclopedia of China*. Cambridge, England: Cambridge University Press, 1982.

Humphreys, Christmas. *A Popular Dictionary of Buddhism*. Lincolnwood, Illinois: NTC Publishing Group, 1997.

The Internet Sacred Text Archive. Available on-line. URL: http://www.sacred-texts.com. Accessed December 2003.

Jagendorf, M.A., and Virginia Weng. *The Magic Boat and Other Chinese Folk Stories*. New York: Vanguard Press, 1980.

Lao-tzu. *Tao Te Ching*. Translated by D. C. Lau. New York: Penguin, 1963.

Leeming, David. *A Dictionary of Asian Mythology*. New York: Oxford University Press, 2001.

Mackenzie, Donald A. *Myths of China and Japan*. London: Gresham Publishing Company Ltd., n.d.

Storm, Rachel. *Asian Mythology*. New York: Lorenz Books, 2000.

Werner, E.T.C. *A Dictionary of Chinese Mythology*. New York: Julian Press, 1961.

Williams, C.A.S. *Outlines of Chinese Symbolism & Art Motives*. Mineola, N.Y.: Dover Publications, 1976.

Yu, Anthony C., trans. *Journey to the West*. Chicago: University of Chicago Press, 1978.

INDEX

Note: **Boldface** page numbers indicate main entries. *Italic* page numbers indicate illustrations.

Sheng Gu (Sheng-ku) **107**
Sheng Jen 59–60, **107**
Sheng-ku. *See* Sheng Gu
Sheng Mu (Bixia Shengmu, Pi-hsia
    Yüan-chün) *107*, **107**, 126
Shen Gongbao 77
Shen I. *See* Yi
Shen Nong (Shen Nung)
    107–108
Sheno Wang **108**
Shen Tu **108**
She Wang **108**
Shi Gan Dang **108**
Shih-jou. *See* Shirou
Shi Huang Di **108**
Shi Ji (Shih-chi) **108**
*Shijing (Shih-ching, Mao Chih, Mao
    Shih)* **108–109**
Shirou (Shih-jou) **109**
Shiwuwei Yin 137
Shiynan Yin 137
shoe makers 112
Shouxing (Shou Hsing, Shou-
    hsing Lao T'ou-tzu) **109**
Shu 32, **109**
Shuboijia (Subhuti) **109**
Shu-ching. See Shujing
Shui Fang **109**
Shui Fu **109**
Shui Guan (Shui Kuan) 104, **109**
Shui Yong (Shui Yung) **109**
Shujing (Shu-ching) **110**
Shun (Ch'ung Hua, Yu Ti Shun,
    Yu Yu) 49, 55, 84, **110**
Siddhartha Gautama. *See* Buddha
silk 12–13, 84, **110**, 123
Sima Qian (Ssu-ma Ch'ien) 108,
    110
Sku-inga **110**
Sky God. *See* Tian Di
Sky River **110**
snakes (serpents) 84, 108, **110**
Song dynasty (Sung Dynasty)
    110–111
Songs of Chu 99, **111**
soul *(shen)* 48, 107
south 3, 41, 144
spring
    beating the spring ox 90
    Chiguo 16
    Four Flowers 44
    Green Dragon of the East 49
    Mang Shen 80
    Nü Chou 86
Spring and Autumn (Chun-qiu)
    111
Ssu-ma Ch'ien. *See* Sima Qian
Ssu-ming-fo-chun. *See* Zao Jun
stars **111**
    Bei Dou 7
    Feng Bo 39
    Molizhi 82
    San Xing 104–105, 109
    Sky River **110**
    Ti-sha 118
    Weaver Girl and Heavenly Ox
        123
    Wen Chang 124
    Zhu Bajie 149
storms. *See also* thunder
    Jasper Lady 61
    Kui 67
    Lei Bu 70

Lei Zu 71
Lightning Goddess 72
Rain God 101
Yan Gong 133
Zhu Tian 150
strength 6–7, 29, 36
Sui dynasty **111**, 124–125
Sui-jen. *See* Fire Driller
summer 10, 44, 101, 129, 144
Sun **112**
    creation myths 22
    crows 23
    Mount Yen 84
    Taiyang Dijun 113
    Xihe 130
    Yi 135–137
Sun Bi (Sun-pi) **112**
Sung dynasty. *See* Song dynasty
Sun Hou Tzu. *See* Monkey King
Sun Ssu-miao. *See* Yao Wang
Sun Wukong. *See* Monkey King
Superintendent of Lives. *See* Zao
    Jun
Sutizi 12
sutras 27, 76, **112**, 121
swords 47, 62–63, 76, **112**, 126
Szechwan. *See* Shu

T
Tabun Qaghar 113
T'ai Ch'ing. *See* Tai Qing
Tai Hao (T'ai Hao) **113**
Tai Qing (T'ai Ch'ing) **113**
Tai Shan (T'ai Shan) 28, 42,
    113
Tai Sui (T'ai Sui) **113**
Taiyang Dijun (Ti Chün) 112,
    113
Tan Chu. *See* Danzhu
Tang dynasty 18, 52, 105, **114**
Tang the Conqueror **114**, 138
Tantric Buddhism 96
Taodie (T'ao-t'ieh) **114**
Taoism (Daoism) viii, **114–115**
    afterlife 2
    alchemy 2, 115
    animism 3
    Azure **4**, 103, 113, 141
    Ba Xian. *See* Ba Xian
    Beast of the White Marsh 7
    butterflies 10
    Chang Liang 14
    Chi-jia Xian 17
    Chin Kuang Hsien 17
    Chu 18
    cinnabar 19
    cosmology 22
    creation myths 23
    Dark Lady 25
    Dou Mu 29
    Elixir of Eternal Life 36
    exorcism 19
    Feng Du Dadi 39
    Five Peaks 42
    folk beliefs 116
    fu 44
    Han dynasty 53
    Heaven 54
    He Qi 54
    hell x
    He Qi 54
    hermits 44
    Immortals. *See* Immortals
    Jasper Lady 61

Ju Ling 63
Kunlun 67
Lao-tzu 70, 114
magicians 79
Ma Yuan-shai 80–81
medicine 81
Molishou 32
numbers 87
paradise 93
peaches 93
Pearly Emperor 93
priests 114–115, *115*
Purple Palace 95
Qing Long 98
Qin Guang Wang 98
Queen of Heaven 98–99
reincarnation. *See* rebirth and
    reincarnation
San Guan Dadi. *See* San Guan
    Dadi
Sa Zhenren 105
Sen Shin 105
Shang Qing 106
shape shifting 106
Sheng Gu 107
Tai Qing 113
Tao-te Ching 114, 116
Ten Thousand 117
Tian Shi Dao 117–118
White Tiger of the West
    125
Yin and Yan 114
Yuanshi Tianzong 139
Yu Huang 140–141
Yu Qing 141
Zao Jun 143
Zhang Daoling 144–145
Zhang Lu 146–147
Zhuangzi 114, 149
Taoist folk beliefs 116
Tao T'ang. *See* Yao
Tao-te Ching (Daodejing) 70, 114,
    116
T'ao T'ieh. *See* Taodie
Tao Wu (T'ao Wu) 47, 116
tea 116
Ten Celestial Stems (Shih T'ien
    Kan) 116
Ten Great Disciples of Buddha.
    See Buddha's disciples
Ten Kings of Hell **116–117**,
    133–134
Ten Suns. *See* Yi
Ten Thousand **117**
Thao Wu. *See* Tao Wu
theater 14, 20
Theravada Buddhism 9, **117**
Three Eras **117**
Three Kings of the Golden Era.
    See Golden Age
Three Officials. *See* San Guan
    Dadi
Three Stars of Good Luck. *See* San
    Xing
Thu (She) **117**
thunder 70–71
Thunder God. *See* Lei Gong
Ti. *See* Di
tian (t'ien) **117**
Tian Di (T'ien Ti, Tiandi) **117**
Tian Fei (T'ien Fei) **117**
Tian Hou. *See* Queen of Heaven
Tian Long (Tian-long) 27, **117**

Tianong Dijun. *See* Taiyang Dijun
Tian Shi Dao (Tien Shih Tao)
    117–118
Tian Yiyuan (T'ien I-yuan) **118**
Tianyu Yuanshuai (T'ien-yu Yuan-
    shuai) **118**
Tiayang Dijun 130, 136
Tibet **118**
    Dalai Lama **25**, 118
    Five Great Kings 42
    klu 66
    lamas 69
Ti Chün. *See* Taiyang Dijun
T'ien. See Tian
Tien Fei. *See* Tian Fei
Tien Guan 104, 118
T'ien I-yüan. *See* Tian Yiyuan
T'ien Kuan. *See* Tien Guan
Tien Shih Tao. *See* Tian Shi Dao
T'ien-yü Yüan-shuai. *See* Tianyu
    Yuanshuai
tigers *118*, **118–119**, 125
Ti K'u. *See* Di Ku
Ti Kuan. *See* Di Guan
time
    calendars 11
    Tai Sui 113
    Ten Celestial Stems 116
    Twelve Terrestrial Branches
        120
    Yao 134
Ting-jian. *See* Gao Yao
Ting Ling-wei 22
Ti-sha 118
Ti-tsang Wang. *See* Dizang
Ti Yu **119**
Torch Dragon (Chu Lung) **119**
tortoises **119**, 141
Tou Mu. *See* Dou Mu
Tou Shen. *See* Dou Shen
touziguie **119**
tricksters 82–83, **119**
Ts'ai Shen. *See* Cai Shen
Ts'ang-wu. *See* Zangwu
Ts'an Nü. *See* Can Nü
Ts'an Tsung. *See* Can Cong
Tsao Chün. *See* Zao Jun
Ts'ao Kuo-chiu. *See* Cao Guojiu
Tsao Shen. *See* Zao Jun
Tung Wang Kung. *See* Dong Wang
    Gong
Tung-yueh Ta-ti. *See* Dongyue
    Dadi
turtles. *See* tortoises
Tu-shan Girl. *See* Nüjiao
Tu Yu. *See* Du Yu
Twelve Terrestrial Branches 110,
    120
Twelve Warriors **120**
Tz'u-hua. *See* Cihua

U
umbrella (emblem) 35
unicorns. *See qilin*
Union of Breaths 54, 145
Upali **121**

V
Vairocana. *See* Palushena
vase (emblem) 35
vedas 121
Vermilion Bow **121**
Vidyarajas **121**